PRASHĀD

Cooking with Indian Masters

PRASHĀD

Cooking with Indian Masters

J. Inder Singh Kalra

Photographs: **Pradeep Das Gupta**

ALLIED PUBLISHERS PVT. LTD.
New Delhi • Mumbai • Kolkata • Chennai • Bangalore • Hyderabad

ALLIED PUBLISHERS PRIVATE LIMITED

D-5, Sector-2, **Noida**–201 301
Ph. Nos.: 0120-4320295/2542557/4352866
E-mail: delhi.books@alliedpublishers.com

17 Chittaranjan Avenue, **Kolkata**–700072
Ph.: 033-22129618 • E-mail: cal.books@alliedpublishers.com

15 J.N. Heredia Marg, Ballard Estate, **Mumbai**–400001
Ph.: 022-42126969 • E-mail: mumbai.books@alliedpublishers.com

No. 25/10, Commander-in-Chief Road, Ethiraj Lane (Next to Post Office)
Egmore, **Chennai**–600008
Ph.: 044-28223938 • E-mail: chennai.books@alliedpublishers.com

P.B. No. 9932, No. 15, 3rd Floor (Next to Vijaya Bank), 5th Cross, Gandhinagar,
Karnataka, **Bangalore**–560009,
Ph.: 080-41530285 / 22386239
E-mail: bngl.journals@alliedpublishers.com / apsabng@airtelmail.in

Sri Jayalakshmi Nilayam, No. 3-4-510, 3rd Floor (Above More Super Market)
Barkatpura, **Hyderabad**–500027
Ph.: 040-27551811, 040-27551812 • E-mail: hyd.books@alliedpublishers.com

Website: www.alliedpublishers.com

First Published, 1986
First Indian Reprint, 1987
Fortieth Reprint, 2020
Thoroughly Revised Edition, 2022
Forty-First Reprint, 2023
Forty-Second Reprint, 2025

ISBN: 978-93-90951-17-8

Published by Sunil Sachdev and printed by Ravi Sachdev at
Allied Publishers Pvt. Ltd., D-5, Sector-2, Noida–201 301

Preface to the First Edition

This book is a celebration of the best in Indian cooking. It is my intention to introduce the foods of India through the culinary genius of some of the finest Chefs in the Nation. Over the past 16 years it has been my privilege—and pleasure—to work with some of the best known names in Indian cooking. When I discussed this project with them, they were enthusiastic. The reason for such enthusiasm was very simple: even today many Indians regard these artistes—no less—of the kitchen as nothing more than *bawarchis,* a term that rudely reduces Chefs to the level of menials. The truth is that most of them are well-educated and command salaries which are the envy of senior executives in other industries and businesses. And this is an indication of their true worth.

There was another reason: while it was true that until a few years ago the best Indian food was cooked in the homes, not any more.

Stung by constant criticism and the unchanging attitude of the multitudes toward their profession—the Chefs decided to refurbish their image. The fact that every other book on Indian cookery was written by a housewife rankled. While some of the books were excellent, most were of a poor quality, inaccurate, incomplete and shoddy. Most important, they did not reflect the changes that were taking place in the eateries around the country. They did not take into account the fact that more and more Indians were dining out—a tribute to the quality of food being prepared by the Chefs. They became my 'co-authors' and this book became the perfect 'vehicle' for them to put forth their own ideas on how Indian food should be prepared.

It is no secret that Indian cuisine is 'in' and the time ripe to introduce the 'Grand Ol' Men' and the 'Whiz Kids' of the Indian kitchen: the present day Chefs, who are inventive and daring—ready to tryout anything new and different. The result has been a wonderful collection of recipes—old and new—from their respective repertoires. My only regret has been my inability to incorporate a chapter on "Game Cooking". Maharaj Kumar Arvind Singh Mewar, my 'co-author' for the section, and I were working on the recipes when his father, Maharana Bhagwat Singhji of Udaipur, unexpectedly passed away. ASM and I are now planning to do a book on Indian Game Cooking—in tribute to the late Maharana Sahib.

To be sure, the recipes penned are not the usual restaurant fayre, where it is not unusual to sacrifice the palate to please the eye. The delicacies, though exotic, are easy-to-make and a veritable housewife's delight. We spent 14 months perfecting each and every recipe to make sure that 'exotic' was not misconstrued as 'expensive'. It must be remembered that Indian exotica is available outside India—in abundance and much cheaper than at home.

It is our hope that this quest for perfect—and standardized—recipes would clear any lingering doubts about Indian cuisine. It is unfortunate that the excessive use of *desi ghee* (clarified butter) or vegetable fat and *masalas* (spices) by a handful of half-baked Chefs made ours an unsaleable food. It was 'rich'—read that as 'fatty'—and 'spicy'—to be read 'chilli hot'.

Our food is 'rich', but not 'fatty'. It is true that we sometimes cook in excess fat, but the amazing thing about our cuisine is that the cooking is deemed complete when the fat leaves the sides (of the utensil in which the food is being cooked or comes to the surface. In other words, the ingredient 'expels' all fat when fully cooked. The excess fat merely eases the cooking process and is supposed to be drained off before service. In fact, the drained fat or *rogan* can be re-used and inevitably makes a better fat medium because of the flavour and aroma of spices it has acquired during the cooking of the first delicacy. Which is not to say that it can be used again and again, but just once again.

Similarly, our food is 'spicy', not 'chilli hot'. We make use of our exotic spices for their special flavour and aroma. The use of red chillies is at one's own discretion. The recipes in the book are 'light' and 'spicy'. The reader is at liberty to increase or decrease the chillies, according to her/his taste.

Every recipe in this book has been tried and tested over and over again until we felt it was perfect. It was penned when we were convinced that a housewife or an amateur Chef would be able to reproduce it almost exactly. This exercise would not have been possible without Arvind Saraswat and Richard Graham. Saraswat, a friend of nearly two decades, helped me with practically half the book. Graham, who has become one in the short time I have known him, went to bat for me in a moment of crisis.

It was a rewarding experience to work with Manjit S. Gill, Manu Mehta, N.P. Singh and S.P.S. Chaudhury. These young Chefs patiently worked on each and every recipe with me until we were fully satisfied. They practically made a Chef out of me—a 'theoretical' one anyway.

What can I say about my team-mate, Pradeep Das Gupta, except that it was a pleasure to work with him and that his superb lenswork has added another dimension to this book.

My thanks to Camellia Punjabi, Divyabhanu S. Chawda, Biri Parmar, Subhir Bhowmik, Anil Channa, Ravi Dubey, Sunil Chandra and Dinesh Khanna. They provided encouragement and support in more ways than one. I can hardly afford to forget my *guru* Khushwant Singh, and my only other editor, Manohar Shyam Joshi—both gave me the opportunity to indulge in my love for writing on good food.

Thanks are also due to Abhimanyu Singh for his valuable suggestions and help in editing the manuscript. I must mention Manu Mehta once again for helping with the proofs. But for him there would have been some glaring—and terribly embarrassing—errors in this book.

Finally, my eternal gratitude to my family who accepted my odd hours without a fuss and took my tantrums in their stride. To Lovjeet and Rominder for the long hours in the kitchen helping my mother try out innumerable recipes. To Manvinder, who along with my father, took care of my young sons, spending his entire vacation with our children.

New Delhi
August 15, 1986

(J. Inder Singh Kalra)

Dedicated to

My Mother
Pritpal Kalra, Super Cook
&
My Father
Brigadier Joginder Singh Kalra,
whose discerning taste has made ours
a Family of Gourmets.

Introduction

with Arvind Saraswat

Like the inevitable flashback in the Hindi potboiler, a part of every Indian's memory is dedicated to a delicacy-by-delicacy, bite-by-bite, munch-by-munch recall of a lifetime of meals. Food is an integral part of every Indian's conversation. Get into one or eavesdrop on almost any, and soon you will be treated to a graphic description of a meal eaten or served anywhere from the night before to several years ago. Today, fortunately, there is much more to talk about.

Ours is a land of traditions. Despite the drawbacks that stem from them, great changes are taking place in the Nation's culinary life—changes evolutionary as well as revolutionary. One of the more important recent 'discoveries' is its own wealth of culinary styles and regional foods. Whereas once restaurants here took pride—misplaced, to be sure—in the 'international' cuisine they could serve, they are now going into specialisation. To cater to changing tastes, many Chefs are reviving styles like *Handi, Dum Pukht, Kadhai* and *Tawa* cooking. Others are specialising in regional—*Marwari, Goan, Hyderabadi, Parsee*—foods. The effort is being duly lauded: the success of the spate of festivals being hosted in almost every city within—and many cities without—the country is eloquent testimony to this fact.

To the uninitiated, Indian cooking seems like a jigsaw puzzle incapable of solution. It seems like a complex problem, difficult to solve. The reason is simple: there is no recorded text for Indian cuisine. Every genre of cooking has innumerable schools, each school more than one style, each style its own *Guru.*

Recipes are handed down from generation to generation, but never put on record—only memorized. As a consequence, every recipe is open to interpretation and there is no standard recipe at all. Every great artiste of the kitchen—and there are quite a few—believes that the method he adopts to make a delicacy is the correct one. Innovation is often mistaken for originality.

The recipes were never recorded because most of the Master *Bawarchis,* if we may coin the designation, were and still are paranoid—fearful that someone will 'pinch' their recipes. This is the only reason why India's culinary art, despite thousands of years of refinement, is not as well known as that of France or China.

Moreover, Indian cuisine varies from region to region. The taste, colour, texture, appearance and aroma of the same delicacy changes every few kilometers. The resultant mayhem has only led to confusion—especially for the serious student of Indian cooking.

After nearly two decadess of watching and working with Master Chefs, after having spent thousands of hours on experimentation and after careful evaluation, we have concluded that Indian cooking is based on three major factors: the choice of ingredients, their proportions and quantities, and the sequence of cooking.

Choice of Ingredients

For better cooking, it is imperative to use fresh and seasonal ingredients. Before that, however, it is important to understand each and every ingredient individually—its salient qualities, nourishment value, calorie count, shelf life, changes in its characteristics with temperature variations etc. Without this knowledge, it would be practically impossible to buy the correct ingredients in the market. It is obvious, therefore, that buying right is half the battle.

For example, when buying leafy vegetables (spinach, coriander, mint) the leaves should be crisp (and not withered), green (and not brownish) in colour, and 'young' (not overgrown, which would make the stem thick and hard).

When buying meat (goat or lamb), to cite another example, it goes without saying that you will need specific cuts for different dishes. However, the meat for every cut must be firm, lean and not excessively fatty, 'pinkish' in colour, odourfree, of a fine texture and the bones must be porous and of a pink hue. Weight of chicken acquires special importance for different delicacies.

Proportions and Quantities

The bane of Indian cooking has been the use of *andaaza* (literally, approximation from experience) rather than exact proportions and quantities. Such approximation leads to inconsistency. It is for this reason that each ingredient should be used in the exact proportion and quantity.

For example, excessive use of yoghurt in a dish will make it sour and unappetizing. Similarly, the excessive use of chillies will 'kill' almost any curry.

To give you another example, in the making of *Pulao,* the proportion is two parts of boiling water for every part of rice. Any deviation from this cardinal principle would either make the rice sticky (excess water) or leave the cereal raw (less water).

Sequence of Cooking

To give a preparation the right colour, texture, aroma and taste, the sequence of cooking plays a significant role. Do not cut corners and take the easy way out. Very often, cooks tend to put all the ingredients in cold fat simultaneously. The resultant disaster is a tasteless mess without any colour or flavor.

If the recipe demands that the onions be fried until golden brown, it would be absurd to introduce the whole garam masala or fresh ground masala before the onions have achieved the requisite colour. This would, doubtless, destroy the dish, and, there will be the taste of raw onions in the mouth.

Again, let's take the example of *Sambhar,* the Southern lentil delicacy, where tamarind pulp is added *after* the *dal is* cooked and never before. If the sequence is not followed it is likely to end up a bitter witches' brew. The *dal* will also stay undercooked.

Basic Kitchen Equipment

Indian cooking demands a range of pots and pans which is unthinkable in any other genre of cooking. Regional cuisines require distinctive utensils which often cannot be used for cooking foods from other areas. Consequently, the Indian kitchen is forced to keep a large inventory of equipment. The most commonly used are:

- *Degchi/Pateela/Handi/Deg*—which all belong to the same family of pots and are traditionally made of brass or copper. Now-a-days, the use of stainless steel and aluminium has also come into vogue. The shape of the vessel may vary. The *pateela* has straight sides and a horizontal rim. The bottom is slightly rounded. The *handi,* on the other hand, has a neck that is narrower than the base. A *deg* is a bigger version of the *handi.*
- *Kadhai* is a deep frying pan akin to the Chinese *wok.* It is made from various metals and alloys, the most common being iron and stainless steel.
- *Pauni* is a perforated frying spoon.
- *Karhchchi* is a ladle used for stirring.
- *Chimta* is a tong.
- *Tawa* or griddle is slightly concave and is used for making *chappati, paratha,* etc. It is made of iron.
- *Parat* is a utensil in which dough is kneaded.
- *Chakla-Belan: Chakla* is a small marble or wood platform, *belan* the rolling pin, usually made of wood. They are used for rolling dough to make various Indian breads.
- *Sil-Batta*—which is two pieces of stone, one a flat platform or *sil,* and the other—*batta*—which is much smaller and is akin to a rolling pin without the handles. The *sil-batta* is used to grind fresh masala and other pastes.
- *Hamam-Dasta*—or mortar-pestle—is used to pound dry masala.
- *Masala Dani*—or spice box—contains the commonly used dry spices and is always kept by the side of the stove or cooking range.
- *Plus* the usual graters, sieves, strainers, knives, *dattri* (to chop leafy vegetables) and lemon squeezer.

Culinary Terms

Spices may be the *basis,* blending the spices the *essence,* but by themselves the do not go to make a complete dish. The *heart* and *soul* of India's culinary art is to be able to combine the two with the nitty-gritty of Indian cooking—*dum, bhunao, talna, baghar, dhuanaar* and *bhunnana*. Each one of these 'methods' or a combination of two or three or even all may be necessary to prepare a delicacy. It is important, therefore, to be able to understand the basic principles of each.

Dum, literally steam, has been described as the 'maturing of a prepared dish'. *Dum,* is the forerunner of the modern day slow cooking. In the good old days, when *handi* cooking was the vogue, the utensil was sealed with *atta* (whole-wheat flour) dough, to ensure that the moisture stayed within, and put on smouldering coal. At the same time, some of the coal was placed on the lid. This ensured even heat—from top and below. Today, the oven is used to perform the function of providing even heat.

In this process, the main ingredient is cooked partially with all the accompaniments (in some cases, some of the accompaniments are added only at the time of sealing) and then the utensil is covered with a lid, sealed with *atta* dough and then placed in the oven.

The food continues to cook in its own steam, so to speak. The advantage of giving *dum* is that since the vapour cannot escape, the delicacy retains all the flavour and aroma.

Dum is usually given when, say, the meat has become sufficiently tender and the curry is nearly ready. The fact that *dum* also brings the ghee or oil to the top helps to improve the appearance of the dish.

Bhunao is a combination, of light stewing, sauntering and stir frying. It is the process of cooking over *medium to high* heat, adding small quantities of liquid—water or yoghurt—to prevent the ingredients from sticking, which also makes it necessary to stir constantly. Almost every recipe needs *bhunao* at some stage, very often at more than one stage.

At the outset it may be the spices and/or ingredients like onions, ginger, garlic, tomatoes, etc., which require *bhunao.* The process would not only extract the flavour of each of the spices and/or ingredients, but also ensure that they do not get burnt or remain raw. In fact, the masala must be fully cooked.

Subsequently, the main ingredient may also require *bhunao.* This ensures that the initial cooking is done in the ingredients' own juices. The process is complete only when the fat leaves the masala or the sides.

Bhunao is not a complete process in itself but a part of the process that helps to prepare a dish. It usually requires the addition of substantial quantities of liquid to complete the cooking process.

Talna or Frying: In Indian cooking, frying is done in a *kadhai* and not a deep fat fryer. Not that there is anything wrong in using a deep fat fryer. It is just that a *kadhai* has some advantages:

- The quantity of ghee or oil required is less, which makes it possible for the oil to be changed regularly. Needless to say, any food fried in clean fat will look good in every way—colour, appearance, flavour etc. Moreover, it would be free from the odour of oil that has been repeatedly heated and used.
- The shape of the *kadhai* not only allows larger quantities of food to be fried but also results in even frying.

Baghar, Tarhka, Chhonkna or Tempering: Hot oil has an extraordinary ability to extract and retain the essence, aroma and flavour of spices and herbs. This process is performed either at the beginning of cooking a dish (the whole garam masala is tempered before the rice is fried, when making a *Pulao)* or after (cumin and asafoetida are tempered and then added to the lentil, when making *dal).* The salient features of *baghar* are:

- The ghee or the oil is brought to smoking point and then the heat is reduced.
- No water is ever added.
- The ingredients are usually added in rapid succession, rarely together.
- The crackling of the spice or spices or a change in their colour indicates that the process is complete, unless fresh herbs and vegetables are also being used.
- The prepared tempering is poured sizzling hot over the cooked dish, except when a dish requires pre-tempering.

Dhuanaar or Smoking: *Dhuan* is smoke and to smoke dry meat delicacies is a simple, but effective, process. It is usually done at the end of cooking. It requires charcoal, ghee and a dry spice, usually cloves. The procedure is:

- Put glowing charcoal in a *katori* (small metal bowl) and place the *katori* in the centre of a *handi* or casserole, and arrange the cooked meat around it.
- Drop the dry spice over the charcoal and pour a little clarified butter on top.
- Quickly cover the *handi* or casserole with a lid to enable the smoke to permeate the meat.

Bhunnana or Roasting: In Indian cooking, roasting is usually done in a *tandoor,* fired by charcoal, which acts as a catalyst to impart a flavour that is unique in the world of cuisine. What happens is that the juices of the meats drip on the charcoal which sizzles and sends up billows of smoke, giving the *tandoor* a smoking chamber effect. It is this smoke that gives *tandoori cooking—kebab,* breads vegetables and *paneer* (Indian cottage cheese) a special aroma.

Kebab, paneer and vegetables, but not breads, can also be roasted on a *sigri* which is an open iron grill. However, the flavour would be much milder.

The only imperative in roasting Indian style is that all foods, except breads, have to be marinated.

Spices

It is no secret that, spices, freshly ground each day, are the basis of Indian cooking. The fact that a *masalchi* (spice grinder) spends most of his day grinding or pounding herbs and exotic spices and his Chef might then take the rest of the day to get a dish pluperfect is what Indian cooking is all about. All spices have their own characteristics and they are used in varying proportions to make the correct combination for a particular delicacy. If you can perfect the art of blending, individual spices and herbs, it is possible to create a plethora of dishes, each distinctive and different.

On the other hand, using the same combination or the pre-packaged garam masala or curry powder can restrict your cooking because just about everything—vegetables, meats, lentils—would taste the same. There is absolutely no concept—or place—for curry powder in Indian cooking.

The magic of Indian cooking is in the blending of spices. It is important, therefore, to know which spice is ideally suited to a particular food. For example, *kalonji* or black onion seeds is a must with *Naan,* mace goes well with lamb, and seafood cannot be prepared without *ajwain.* Curry leaves are an essential ingredient in Southern cooking and pickles are not pickles without *rai* (mustard seeds). Also, certain herbs and spices can only be used during a particular season. For example, mace is taboo in summer (it can lead to a nose bleed) whereas poppy seeds can really cool things during the same months.

If you can grasp this aspect of Indian cooking, you can perform miracles with something as mundane as the potato. You could make dishes—ranging from the simple to the exotic—depending on how simple or exotic the masala you blend.

There are two types of masalas: dry masalas in powder form and wet masalas in the form of a paste—ground with water, vinegar or oil.

Spices and Dry Herbs

English Terms	*Hindi Terms*	*English Terms*	*Hindi Terms*
Carom Seeds	*Ajwain*	Black Onion seeds	*Kalonji*
Alum	*Fitkari*	Black Peppercorns	*Kali Mirch*
Aromatic Ginger	*Saunth*	Cinnamon	*Dalchini*
Asafoetida	*Hing*	Cloves	*Laung*
Bay Leaves	*Tejpatta*	Coriander	*Dhania*
Black Cardamom	*Motti Elaichi*	Curry Leaves	*Karipatta*
Black Cumin	*Shahi Jeera* or *Kala Jeera*	Dessicated Coconut	*Sukha Narial*
		Fennel	*Saunf*

Spices and Dry Herbs

English Terms	*Hindi Terms*	*English Terms*	*Hindi Terms*
Fenugreek	*Kasoori Methi*	Rock Salt	*Kala Namak*
Fenugreek seeds	*Methi Dana*	Saffron	*Kesar*
Green Cardamom	*Chhoti Elaichi*	Saltpetre	*Kalmi Shora*
–	*Kokum*	Sesame seeds (Beige and White)	*Kale Til, Safed Til*
Mace	*Javitri*		
Mango powder	*Amchur*	Star Anise	*Chakriphool*
Mustard seeds	*Rai*	Tamarind	*Imli*
Nutmeg	*Jaiphal*	Turmeric	*Haldi*
–	*Phoolpatri*	White Cardamom	*Safed Elaichi*
Pomegranate seeds	*Anardana*	White Cumin	*Jeera*
Poppy seeds	*Khus Khus*	White Peppercorns	*Safed Mirch*
Red Chillies	*Lal Mirch*	Yellow Chillies	*Peeli Mirch*

Nuts and Dry Fruits

English Terms	*Hindi Terms*	*English Terms*	*Hindi Terms*
Almond	*Badaam*	Peanut	*Moongphali*
Cashewnut	*Kaju*	Pine Nut	*Chilgoza*
Date	*Khajur*	Pistachio	*Pista*
Dry Date	*Chhuara*	Raisin	*Kishmish*
Dry Plum	*Jardaloo*	Sultana	*Munakka*
Glazed Cherry	–	Sunflower seeds	*Chironji*
Melon Seeds	*Magaz*	Walnut	*Akhrot*

Essences / Special Garnishes

English Terms	*Hindi Terms*	*English Terms*	*Hindi Terms*
Rose Water	*Gulab Jal*	Gold Leaves	*Sone ka varq*
Vetiver	*Kewda, Ittar*	Silver Leaves	*Chandi ka varq*

A Word about the Recipes

For this book, the Chefs and I conducted trials for over a year. Every recipe had to be gram perfect and so every dish was tried out at least twice, usually more often. No recipe was committed to paper until the Chefs were convinced that I could reproduce their 'creation' to perfection without any help from them. While everything has been done to ensure that the recipes are perfect, there is every chance of the timing—and timing alone—going awry. The quality of ingredients has a considerable bearing on this aspect of cooking. Consequently, the quantity of liquid used to cook a dish will vary. The recipes in this book were perfected with Indian ingredients. To overcome the problem, we have provided the requisite indication of a process being completed by the colour or consistency achieved.

To make cooking simple, the ingredients in this book have been listed in the order in which they will be used, the exception being the main ingredient(s). For example, in any lamb delicacy, the lamb itself would be used after most of the other ingredients have been cooked to make the masala. However, since it is a lamb dish, it is listed as the first ingredient.

If the recipe, for example, says, 'add onions, ginger and green chillies', then these ingredients must be added as suggested without any deviation in the order. Also, before adding each spice or herb, stir the masala.

All weights are *nett,* not *gross.* If the recipe says 1 kg/2¼ lb of lamb, weigh the ingredient after cleaning and, if necessary, deboning. Similarly, if 15 g/¼ cup of fresh coriander is required, it should be weighed only after cleaning (removing the stalks), washing and chopping. In other words, complete the PREPARATION and then weigh the ingredient, unless the preparation includes cooking. In which case, weigh prior to cooking but after the initial preparation.

Whenever PREPARATION TIME exceeds two hours, it is likely to cause consternation. Rest assured. Your individual attention is not required whilst a meat is kept in a marinade for 6 or 8 or 10 hours or even overnight as the case may be. Read the recipe at least twice before you start cooking. This will enable you to decide which ingredient must be prepared first. Remember, it is only the *ingredients* that are listed in the order of use, not their preparation.

PREPARATION is as important as COOKING the delicacy. It is imperative that all the ingredients, duly weighed, are placed in separate containers and in neat little rows—again in order of use—before you start cooking. A split second's delay in hunting for a spice could ruin the dish.

Almost every recipe calls for some paste or the other. It is best to make substantial quantities in advance and refrigerate them *(see section on Pastes).*

The distinction between fresh and dry ingredients is very clear. 'Coriander' implies 'fresh coriander', not 'coriander powder' or 'coriander seeds'. *'Kasoori Methi'* is 'dried fenugreek leaves'. *'Kashmiri Deghi Mitch'* is a 'red chilli powder'—the difference, is that it is milder than the common 'red chilli powder' and—like paprika—provides excellent coloration. 'Cream' should always be 'fresh single cream' unless otherwise specified and 'yoghurt' is always 'full fat yoghurt'. 'Hung Yoghurt' is curd without whey. It is hung in muslin to allow the whey to ooze out.

The 'oil' and 'ghee' are refined fats, not raw. 'Corn oil' or any other refined fat medium will make a suitable alternative.

Each recipe yields four (4) full portions (unless otherwise specified) and, if served as the main—and only—course, the meal requires no additional dishes besides accompaniments like salad, *Raita,* rice or Indian bread, *papad* and pickle or chutney. If the meal is more elaborate—two, three or even four dishes—then prepare half the portions or invite more people. The full portions can easily be shared by more people.

When preparing a menu, never take two dishes from the same style of cooking. For example, two dishes from the *Kadhai* or *Tawa* sections may end up tasting almost the same. You could, however, take any number of dishes from the *Handi* and *Dum Pukht* sections or for that matter the regional cuisines, but it is not advisable. The only exception is the *Kebab* section and that too if you have planned a barbeque in your backyard.

An ideal Indian menu should start with *kebab* or one of the *garde manger* delicacies, followed by a *fish* or *chicken* dish, a *lamb* dish, a *vegetable,* and a *lentil* along with the usual accompaniments. Be sure to draw a balance between the gravy and the dry dishes, as also the colour of the dishes.

Weights and Measures

The recipes in this book were perfected in the metric measures. The quantities, however, are given in both metric and American measures. As it is difficult to exactly convert from one to the other, adjustments have been made ensuring that the taste would not vary in the slightest.

Fortunately, in Indian cooking a few extra grams of onions or ginger or tomatoes will not make much of a difference. Nor would a few extra millilitres of water. Nevertheless, whenever the recipe has demanded exactness, it has been provided. For example, the reader will occasionally come across something like 3 cups + 4 tsp.

The following chart should help with the conversions:

1 Gram = 0.035 ounces

10 Grams = 0.35 ounces

100 Grams = 3.5 ounces

200 Grams = 7.0 ounces

To convert grams into ounces, multiply the grams by 0.035.

To give convenient working equivalents, the metric measures have been rounded off into units of 5 or 25 (see the following chart):

Ounces	*Grams*	*Nearest Equivalent*	*Conversion*
1	28.35	28	20/30
2	56.70	57	50/60
3	85.05	85	75/90
4	113.40	113	100/120
5	141.75	142	150
6	170.10	170	175
7	198.45	198	200
8	226.80	227	225
9	255.15	255	250
10	283.50	284	275/290
11	311.85	312	300/325
12	340.20	340	350
13	368.55	369	375
14	396.90	397	400
15	425.25	425	425
16 or 1 lb	453.60	454	450

For more convenient conversions, the following chart will be useful:

1 Tsp (teaspoon)	=	5 g
2 Tsp	=	10 g
3 Tsp	=	15 g
1 Tbs (tablespoon)	=	15 g
1 Tbs	=	3 Tsp or ½ oz
¼ cup	=	4 Tbs or 2 oz
⅓ cup	=	5 Tbs + 1 Tsp
½ cup	=	8 Tbs or 4 Oz
⅔ cup	=	10 Tbs + 2 Tsp
¾ cup	=	12 Tbs or 6 oz
1 cup	=	16 Tbs or 8 oz
1 cup (liquid measure)	=	237 ml
1 oz (dry measure)	=	28.35 g
16 oz (dry measure)	=	1 lb
16 oz (liquid measure)	=	2 cups or 1 pint
2 pints (liquid measure)		4 cups or 1 quart

To convert the commonly used ingredients in this book, the following chart will be a convenient guide:

Vegetables

Coriander (chopped)	1 cup	60 g
	1 Tbs	4 g
Green Peas (shelled)	1 cup	160 g
Mint (chopped)	1 cup	60 g
	1 Tbs	4 g
Mushrooms	1 cup	70 g
Onions (chopped, diced)	1 cup	170 g
Potatoes (diced, cubes)	1 cup	150 g
Tomatoes (chopped)	1 cup	225 g

Lentils

All *dals*	1 cup	200 g
All dry beans	1 cup	200 g
All gram (White, Bengal, etc.)	1 cup	200 g

Cereals

Rice	1 cup	200 g
Semolina	1 cup	200 g

Flour

Atta (whole-wheat flour)	1 cup	120 g
Cornflour	1 cup	80 g
Gramflour	1 cup	150 g
Flour of roasted *Channa dal*	1 cup	150 g
Flour (all purpose)	1 cup	125 g
Breadcrumbs	1 cup	100 g

Dairy

Cheddar Cheese (grated)	1 cup	110 g
Cream	1 cup	240 ml
Milk	1 cup	240 ml
Yoghurt	1 cup	225 g
Hung Yoghurt	1 cup	260 g

Fats and Oils

Desi Ghee or Clarified Butter	1 cup	225 g
	1 Tbs	15 g
Ghee or Vegetable Fat	1 cup	200 g
	1 Tbs	12½ g
White Butter	1 cup	225 g
	1 Tbs	15 g
Groundnut Oil	1 cup	220 ml
	1 Tbs	15 ml
Mustard Oil	1 cup	220 ml
	1 Tbs	15 ml

Sugar and Spice

Castor (confectioner's) Sugar	1 cup	120 g
	1 Tbs	8 g
Granulated Sugar	1 cup	200 g
	1 Tbs	12 g
Ajwain	1 Tsp	2.5 g
	1 Tbs	7.5 g
Black Onion seeds (*Kalonji*)	1 Tsp	3.3 g
	1 Tbs	10.0 g
Black Peppercorns	1 Tsp	3.3 g
	1 Tbs	10.0 g
Coriander seeds	1 Tsp	2.0 g
	1 Tbs	6.0 g
Cumin seeds	1 Tsp	3.0 g
	1 Tbs	9.0 g

Sugar and Spice

Fennel seeds	1 Tsp	2.5 g
	1 Tbs	7.5 g
Fenugreek seeds	1 Tsp	4.5 g
Kasoori Methi (Dry Fenugreek Leaves, broiled and powdered)	1 Tbs	13.5 g
	1 Tbs	12.0 g
Melon seeds	1 Tsp	3.3 g
	1 Tbs	10.0 g
Pomegranate seeds	1 Tsp	3.3 g
	1 Tbs	10.0 g
Poppy seeds	1 Tsp	3.0 g
	1 Tbs	9.0 g
Sesame seeds	1 Tsp	3.5 g
	1 Tbs	10.5 g
Sunflower seeds	1 Tsp	3.3 g
	1 Tbs	10.0 g
All powdered spices	1 Tsp	5 g

Dry Fruits and Nuts

Almonds (blanched, peeled)	1 cup	140 g
Cashewnuts (peeled)	1 cup	140 g
Coconut (grated)	1 cup	80 g
Coconut (dessicated)	1 cup	60 g
Peanuts (shelled, peeled)	1 cup	140 g
Pistachio (blanched, peeled)	1 cup	140 g
Raisins	1 cup	145 g
Walnuts (chopped)	1 cup	120 g

Pastes

Boiled Onion paste	1 cup	240 g
Cashewnut paste	1 cup	250 g
Coconut paste	1 cup	260 g
Fried Onion paste	1 cup	265 g
Garlic paste/Ginger paste	1¾ Tsp	10 g
	2½ Tsp	15 g
	4 Tsp	25 g
	5 Tsp	30 g
	3 Tbs	50 g

Liquids

Lemon juice	1 cup	240 ml
Water	1 cup	240 ml

Glossary

Atta	:	Whole-wheat flour.
Besan	:	*Channa dal* flour or gramflour.
Bharwaan	:	Stuffed.
Biryani	:	Rice dish cooked with spiced lamb or chicken—usually on festive occasions.
Boti	:	Boneless cubes of meat.
Falooda	:	A transparent vermicelli, used as a garnish with *Kulfi,* the creamy Indian ice-cream *(see recipe in the Dessert section).*
Kari	:	Tamil word for sauce and, probably, the origin for the word 'curry'.
Katori	:	Small metal (silver, brass, stainless steel) bowl.
Kebab	:	Meats (fish, chicken and lamb), usually skewered (whole, cubed or minced) and grilled in a *tandoor* or over an open iron grill. Also, shallow fried (minced) on a griddle (e.g. *Shammi Kebab, Galouti, Rakhand-e-Kebabi.*
Kheema	:	Minced lamb, raw or cooked.
Khansamah	:	A cook. The term came into vogue in the days of the Raj.
Khichri	:	A delicately spiced rice and *dal* preparation, popular as an infant feed and as an easily digested meal when suffering from a stomach disorder.
Kofta	:	Meat balls or vegetable balls.
Masalchi	:	A grinder of masalas—dry and wet.
Paan	:	Betel leaf eaten with a stuffing of *supari* (betel nut), quicklime paste, katechu paste, *gulukand* (rose-petal preserve), fennel, grated coconut, occasionally. *Zarda* (tobacco), and garnished with silver *varq*—digestive to some, aphrodisiac to others.
Papad	:	Wafer-thin discs prepared from lentils, spiced with black peppercorns and asafoetida.
Pulao	:	Rice, gently simmered with fat and vegetables or lamb or, occasionally, a spice like cumin.
Raita	:	Yoghurt whisked and garnished with vegetables or deep-fried corn-niblet size *besan* (gramflour) dumplings.
Shikora	:	Small unglazed earthenware bowl.
Tikka	:	Shashlik-sized chunks of meat, usually chicken, which can be skewered before roasting in the *tandoor.*

Contents

Milk Products

Salads and Cold Food

With JEROME GOMES

There are many things that a number of Indians are loath to accept. The concept of cold food, for example, is still anathema. The reason has everything to do with the fact that until recently refrigerators were not considered a necessity. Our climate leads to instant degeneration of food. Besides, habits formed over the centuries are hard to change and an indication of this is our continuing mistrust of frozen foods.

What surprised the author was that many chefs were reluctant to even discuss the subject of Indian *garde manger*. Why, many laughed—to my face—when I proposed that they at least try out some of the salads and cold cuts I had in mind. The more they rejected the idea, the more determined I became to see it succeed. After innumerable rejections, the concept of the Indian 'cold kitchen' became a fixation. The result is this humble contribution to Indian cuisine—with a lot of help from my 'co-authors' for this section.

Jerome Gomes: Enthusiastic and brimming with ideas, the versatile Gomes is Senior Chef at *The Oberoi**, New Delhi. Not only is he a skilled *Garde Manger* man—he added his own highly inventive touches to the recipes in this section—but is also a fine exponent of the art of French cooking.

*Designation subject to change.

Salads presented few problems. We wanted to be different from the usual French and Italian dressings. We did not want our dressings to be mayonnaise-based. It is an old adage that the soul of a salad is a good oil. Westerners generally use olive oil. What a pity! They haven't reckoned with mustard oil, coconut oil or groundnut oil.

For *Jhinga Aehaar Salaad,* we chose mustard oil, which is most commonly used to make pickles. When we realised that it would take many days to pickle prawns, we decided to use the oil and masala of the commercially packed mango or mixed pickle (which is available in every grocery store) in combination with groundnut oil and lemon juice. We used coconut oil, with *Sambhar Masala* and lemon juice to prepare the dressing for *Dakshini Salaad,* which owes its origin to the traditional Southern staples: *Sambhar Rice* and *Lemon Rice.*

The major problem we faced in our endeavour to create cold cuts was how to blend Indian exotica with an hitherto Occidental concept. In the case of the *Raan-e-Gulmarg,* the problem was not so much the spicing as the fact that it had to be moist—not dry—when served cold and that too without losing its shape. So, instead of cooking it in the *tandoor* over charcoal, the leg was roasted in the oven. Remember, in the *tandoor,* the fat just drips off and the *jus* dries up.

There was one other problem we perceived: presentation. We wondered how to present the cold cuts. That was before we commenced our 'experiment'. We are happy to report that we decided to forego decoration (a major aspect of Western *garde manger)* and, instead, to emphasise the ingredients used, their colours and their flavours and aromas.

Assisted by Mohan Lal Thakur and Bijoy K. Joseph

Jhinga Achaar Salaad

A piquant salad that can be used as a cocktail snack as well.

Preparation

Prawns: Shell, devein, wash and pat dry.

Vegetables: Remove stems, wash, cut capsicum into halves, deseed and make ½-inch dices. Peel, wash and cut onions into ½-inch dices.

Dressing: Mix lemon juice and mustard oil with *achaar masala.* Adjust the seasoning.

Garnish: Wash and cut lemons and tomatoes into wedges. Remove stems, wash, slit and deseed green chillies. Clean, wash and chop coriander.

Cooking

Heat oil in a *kadhai,* add prawns and saute over medium heat for 3–4 minutes. Add tomato puree and stir for a minute. Remove and cool. Then add the diced vegetables, toss and refrigerate.

To Serve

Transfer prawns to a salad bowl, pour on the dressing and mix gently with a wooden fork. Garnish with lemons, tomatoes and green chillies. Sprinkle coriander on top. Serve chilled.

INGREDIENTS

400 g/14 oz Prawns (medium size)

30 g/2 Tbs Groundnut Oil

25 g/1 oz Tomato Puree

100 g/⅔ cup Capsicum

100 g/⅔ cup Onions

Dressing

75 ml/5 Tbs Lemon juice

50 ml/3 Tbs Mustard Oil*

45 g/3 Tbs Achaar Masala**

Seasoning

Garnish

1 Lemon

2 Tomatoes (medium size)

2 Green Chillies

10 g/2 Tbs Coriander

*Use oil in which mango pickle is preserved.

**The masala, too, must come from the mango pickle jar. A bit of chopped mango pickle itself could make the salad a little sharper.

Serves 4

Preparation time: 45 minutes

Cooking time: 8–9 minutes

Murgh Salaad

INGREDIENTS

600 g/1⅓ lb Murgh Tandoori*
250 g/1 cup Tomatoes
125 g/¾ cup Onions
2 Green Chillies
10 g/2 Tbs Coriander

Dressing
45 ml/3 Tbs Lemon juice
3 g/½ Tsp Mace and Green Cardamom powder
10 g/2 Tsp Chaat Masala**
90 ml/6 Tbs Groundnut Oil
Seasoning

Garnish
2 Tomatoes (medium size)
1 Lemon
20 g/2 Tbs Ginger
30 ml/2 Tbs Lemon juice

*See Section on Kebab.
**See Section on Masalas.

Serves 4
Preparation time: 30 minutes (Plus time taken to roast and cool Murgh Tandoori)

There is a common fallacy that *Tandoori Chicken* cannot be eaten cold. On the contrary, it is the basis for this magnificent salad.

Preparation

Chicken: Debone and cut into ¾-inch dices. Refrigerate.

Vegetables: Wash and cut tomatoes into quarters, deseed and make ½-inch dices. Peel, wash and cut onions into ½-inch dices. Remove stems, wash, slit, deseed and chop green chillies. Clean, wash and chop coriander.

Dressing: Mix lemon juice, mace and cardamom powder and *chaat masala* with groundnut oil in a bowl. Adjust the seasoning.

Garnish: Wash and cut tomatoes into quarters. Wash and cut lemon into wedges. Scrape, wash and cut ginger into juliennes, soak in the lemon juice.

To Serve

Mix vegetables with chicken in a salad bowl, pour on the dressing and toss. Garnish with tomato quarters, lemon wedges and sprinkle ginger juliennes on top. Serve chilled.

Boti ka Salaad

Yet another *Tandoori* salad, done in a clove-flavoured mint and yoghurt dressing.

INGREDIENTS

400 g/14 oz Boti Kebab*
100 g/3½ oz Button Onions
100 g/3½ oz Tomatoes
2 Green Chillies

Dressing
225 g/1 cup Yoghurt
20 g/⅓ cup Mint
30 ml/2 Tbs Lemon juice
3 g/½ Tsp Clove powder
Seasoning

*See section on Kebab (Gosht Pasanda).

Serves 4
Preparation time: 30 minutes (Plus time taken to roast and cool Boti Kebab)

Preparation

Boti: Cut into ¾-inch dices and refrigerate.

Vegetables: Peel, wash and cut onions into roundels to make rings. Wash and cut tomatoes into quarters, deseed and make dices. Remove stems, wash, slit, deseed and chop green chillies.

Dressing: Hang yoghurt in muslin for 1 hour to remove the whey, then whisk in a bowl. Clean, wash, finely chop mint and mix with the yoghurt. Add lemon juice and clove powder, mix well. Adjust the seasoning.

To Serve

Mix the vegetables with the *Boti* in a salad bowl, pour on the dressing and toss well. Serve chilled.

Veg

Dakshini Salaad

INGREDIENTS

100 g/½ cup Rice

100 g/¼ cup Coconut

Dressing

90 ml/6 Tbs Coconut Oil

8 Curry leaves

10 g/2 Tsp Sambhar Masala*

3 g/½ Tsp Turmeric

45 ml/3 Tbs Lemon juice

Seasoning

Garnish

2 Tomatoes (medium size)

50 g/⅓ cup Roasted Peanuts

10 g/4 Tsp Dessicated Coconut

*See section on Masalas.

Serves 4

Preparation time: 55 minutes

A Sambhar-flavoured coconut-and-rice salad, can be served as an appetizer or as an accompaniment. If ever you have some left over boiled rice, don't throw it away—use it to make the *Dakshini.*

Preparation

Rice: Pick, wash in running water, soak for 30 minutes, drain, replenish with fresh water and boil until cooked. Drain and cool.

Coconut: Remove the brown skin and cut into fine juliennes.

Dressing: Wash curry leaves. Heat oil in a *kadhai,* remove from heat, add curry leaves, stir, add *Sambhar masala* and turmeric, stir. Transfer to a bowl, cool and add lemon juice, whisk. Adjust the seasoning.

Garnish: Wash and cut tomatoes into roundels.

To Serve

Mix rice and coconut in a salad bowl, pour on the dressing and toss. Garnish with tomatoes on the sides and sprinkle roasted peanuts and dessicated coconut on top. Serve chilled.

Aloo-Salaad Anarkali

Veg

A tartly spiced potato salad garnished with fresh pomegranate.

Preparation

Potatoes: Boil, cool, peel and cut into ¾-inch cubes.

Gram: Soak overnight in a *handi*, drain, replenish with fresh water, add soda bi-carb and salt, boil until tender.

Pomegranate: Shell and reserve half of the fruit for garnish.

Dressing: Mix lemon juice, cumin powder and *chaat masala* with groundnut oil. Adjust the seasoning.

Garnish: Wash mint leaves. Peel, wash and cut onions into roundels to make rings. Wash and cut tomatoes into roundels.

To Serve

Mix potatoes, gram and pomegranate in a glass bowl, pour on the dressing and toss gently. Arrange onions and tomatoes on the sides, sprinkle the reserved pomegranate and mint leaves on top. Serve chilled.

INGREDIENTS

600 g/1⅓ lb Potatoes
150 g/¾ cup Bengal Gram
A pinch Soda bi-carb
Salt
50 g/⅓ cup Pomegranate

Dressing
75 ml/5 Tbs Lemon juice
10 g/2 Tsp Cumin powder
10 g/2 Tsp Chaat Masala*
75 ml/5 Tbs Groundnut Oil
Seasoning

Garnish
20 g/⅓ cup Mint Leaves
2 Onions (small size)
2 Tomatoes (medium size)

*See section on Masalas.

Serves 4
Preparation time: 50 minutes

Kachumbar

Veg

The common Indian tossed salad, served with the main meal or as a garnish with innumerable delicacies.

Preparation

Vegetables: Peel, wash and roughly chop onions. Wash, cut tomatoes into quarters, deseed and roughly chop. Peel and cut cucumber into quarters, deseed and roughly chop. Remove stems, wash, slit, deseed and chop green chillies. Clean, wash and chop mint and coriander. Wash and cut lemon into wedges.

To Serve

Mix all the vegetables in a salad bowl and pour on the lemon juice. Adjust the seasoning. Serve chilled with lemon wedges.

INGREDIENTS

300 g/11 oz Onions
200 g/7 oz Tomatoes
150 g/5 oz Cucumber
4 Green Chillies
5 g/1 Tbs Mint
10 g/2 Tbs Coriander
60 ml/4 Tbs Lemon juice
Seasoning
1 Lemon

Serves 4
Preparation time: 20 minutes

Thandi Ajwaini Machchli

INGREDIENTS

2 kg/4½ lb Fish fillet
225 g/½ lb Prawns (large size)
15 g/2 Tbs Ajwain
10 g/2 Tsp Kashmiri Deghi Mirch powder
50 g/3 Tbs Garlic paste
160 g/1 cup Onions
Groundnut Oil to saute prawns and onions
6 Eggs
20 g/⅓ cup Coriander
Seasoning
160 ml/⅔ cup Cream

Garnish

200 g/7 oz Carrots
3 Lemons

Note: Thandi Ajwaini Machchli can also be prepared en croute: use the Khasta Kheema dough replacing cumin seeds with ajwain seeds.

Serves

10 (2 moulds of 1 kg/2¼ lb each)

Preparation time: 1 hour

Cooking time: 45–50 minutes

The inspiration for this cold fish delicacy came from *Amritsari Machchli (see Punjab Section)*—hence the exclusive use of *ajwain.*

Preparation

Fish: Clean, wash, pat dry and cut into small chunks. Mix *ajwain* and *Deghi Mirch* with garlic paste and rub the chunks with this mixture.

Prawns: Shell, devein and cut into ½-inch cubes. Heat oil in a *kadhai,* saute over medium heat for 5 minutes, remove, discard the fat, cool and refrigerate.

Onions: Peel, wash and finely chop. Heat oil in a *kadhai,* saute over medium heat until transparent, remove, discard the fat and cool.

Mince: Mince the marinated fish and sauteed onions twice or thrice in a mincer.

Eggs: Separate the whites and discard the yolks. Beat the whites (use eggs out of the refrigerator).

Coriander: Clean, wash, chop, put in a napkin and squeeze dry. Ensure it is completely devoid of moisture.

Cream: Whip in a blender.

Mousse: Put the mince in a blender, add the beaten egg whites in a steady trickle and make a mousse. Transfer the mousse to a bowl, add the sauteed prawns, coriander and seasoning, mix well. Fold in whipped cream. Divide into 2 equal portions.

Garnish: Peel, wash and cut carrots into fine juliennes. Wash and cut lemons into wedges.

Oven: Pre-heat to 230°F.

Cooking

Grease two moulds, fill each with a portion of the mousse, compress, cover, place in a water bath and bake in the pre-heated oven for 45–50 minutes. Remove, cool and refrigerate overnight.

Finishing

Demould, slice (¼-inch thick), arrange on a silver platter and refrigerate for 30 minutes.

To Serve

Remove the platter from the refrigerator, garnish and serve cold.

Murgh Reshmi

A saffron-flavoured chicken roll, spiced with pepper and nutmeg.

INGREDIENTS

1.2 kg/2⅔ lb Chicken
6 Chicken Fillet
3 Eggs
15 g/4½ Tsp Black Peppercorns
2 g/4 Tsp Saffron
15 ml/1 Tbs Milk
8 g/1½ Tsp Nutmeg powder
5 g/1 Tsp Garam Masala
Salt
150 ml/⅔ cup Cream
5 litres/5 qrt Clear Chicken Stock
4 Black cardamom
2 Bay Leaves

Garnish
4 Tomatoes (medium size)
Eggs

Serves 10
(1 mould of 1 kg/2¼ lb)
Preparation time: 1:45 hours
Cooking time: 50 minutes

Preparation

Chicken: Clean, remove the skin, debone and cut into small chunks. Mince the chunks twice or thrice in a mincer, spread the fine mince on a flat tray and put it in the freezer for an hour.

Chicken Fillet: Remove sinews and cut into strips. Season and refrigerate.

Pepper: Pound with a pestle.

Saffron: Dissolve half the flakes in warm milk.

Cream: Whip in a blender.

Mousse: Put the frozen mince in a blender, add eggs (one at a time) and make a mousse. Transfer the mousse to a bowl, add pepper, the dissolved saffron, nutmeg, garam masala and salt, mix well. Fold in the whipped cream.

Garnish: Wash and cut tomatoes into wedges. Hard boil eggs, cool, shell and quarter.

Assembling

Place a wet napkin on the table, cover with silver foil cut to the same size, spread the mousse on the foil, arrange the chicken strips in three rows, sprinkle the remaining saffron flakes and make a roll (approx 3-inch diameter). Wrap the foil and the napkin tightly around the roll. Firmly tie the ends with a string.

Cooking

Heat stock in a large *handi,* add cardamom and bay leaves, bring to a boil, reduce to low heat, immerse the wrapped roll in the stock and simmer for 45 minutes. Remove, untie and unwrap the napkin and the foil, retie firmly and cool in the stock. Remove, transfer to a tray and refrigerate overnight.

Finishing

Untie and unwrap the napkin and the foil, slice the roll (as thin as possible), arrange on a silver platter and refrigerate for 30 minutes.

To Serve

Remove the platter from the refrigerator, garnish and serve cold.

Murgh Lajawab

INGREDIENTS

12 Chicken Breasts (with bone)
60 g/¼ cup Yoghurt
3 g/½ Tsp Garam Masala
3 g/½ Tsp Yellow Chilli powder
3 g/½ Tsp Turmeric
Salt
10 Green Cardamom
5 Cloves
1 Bay Leaf

Sauce

35 g/7 Tsp Butter
25 g/3 Tbs Gramflour
20 g/7½ Tsp Flour
3 g/½ Tsp Garam Masala
3 g/½ Tsp Yellow Chilli powder
3 g/½ Tsp Turmeric
400 ml/1⅔ cups Clear Chicken Stock
Salt
3 g/½ Tsp Mace and Green Cardamom powder
80 g/3 oz Gelatin powder
100 ml/7 Tbs Cream

Serves 6

Preparation time: 2:15 hours

Cold breasts of chicken dressed in a creamy mace 'n' cardamom-flavoured sauce.

Preparation

Chicken Breasts: Clean, but retain the skin. Whisk yoghurt in a bowl, add garam masala, yellow chillies, turmeric and salt, mix well. Rub the breasts with this marinade and keep aside for 45 minutes.

Put stock in a large, flat-bottomed *handi* or pan, add cardamom, cloves and bay leaf, bring to a boil and then simmer until there is just enough to cover the chicken. Arrange the marinated breasts, side-by-side, in the stock and simmer until tender (approx 10–15 minutes). Remove, cool, remove the skin and the bone carefully, ensuring that the surface remains smooth. Trim the edges, transfer to a wire-rack and refrigerate.

Sauce: Melt butter in a *kadhai,* add gramflour and flour and *bhunno* over low heat until light brown. Add garam masala, yellow chillies and turmeric, stir. Whisk in stock and simmer for 15 minutes. Adjust the seasoning. Then add mace and cardamom powder, stir and remove. Strain into a saucepan and cool.

Soak gelatin in tap water (approx 240 ml/1 cup) for 10 minutes and then stir over a double boiler until it melts and a clear solution is obtained. Strain through fine muslin and add to the sauce, stir. Put some ice in a large pan and cool the sauce until it shows signs of sticking to the sides of the sauce pan. Whip cream and fold into the sauce.

Assembling

Keep the breasts on the wire-rack, place a tray below to collect the excess sauce and pour on the requisite quantity of the sauce over each breast in one go to get a smooth coat (Coat only on one side). Refrigerate for 30 minutes.

To Serve

Remove the rack from the refrigerator, carefully transfer the breasts to a silver platter and serve cold with a garnish of your choice.

Raan-e-Gulmarg

Nutmeg-flavoured, cold leg of lamb, spiced with *Shahi Jeera* and coriander, and garnished with cashewnuts.

INGREDIENTS

2 legs of Lamb (1 kg/$2\frac{1}{4}$ lb each)

1 Egg (for eggwash)

Groundnut oil to baste Raan and grease roasting tray

Clear Lamb Stock to partially immerse lamb legs while roasting

The Marination

225 g/1 cup Yoghurt

50 g/3 Tbs Garlic paste

50 g/3 Tbs Ginger paste

10 g/1 Tbs Black Peppercorns

5 g/1 Tsp Black Cumin powder

3 g/$\frac{1}{2}$ Tsp Clove powder

10 g/2 Tsp Coriander powder

5 g/1 Tsp Garam Masala

Salt

Preparation

Lamb Legs: Clean, remove the thigh and blade bones carefully by scraping along them, without cutting from the side, to make a pocket for stuffing (*see photographs*).

Marination: Whisk yoghurt in a bowl. Pound pepper with a pestle. Mix pepper and the remaining ingredients with the yoghurt and rub the lamb legs with this mixture. Refrigerate for 3 hours.

Filling: Clean, debone and cut lamb into small chunks. Scrape, wash and roughly chop ginger. Mince the lamb and ginger twice or thrice in a mincer, spread the fine mince on a flat tray and put it in the freezer for an hour. Clean, wash and chop mint. Remove stems, wash, slit, deseed and chop green chillies. Soak cashewnuts in water, drain. Put the frozen mince in a blender, add eggs (one-at-a-time) and salt, make a mousse. Transfer the mousse to a bowl, add the remaining ingredients and mix well. Divide into 2 equal portions.

Stuffing: Beat the egg and give an egg wash inside the pocket of each leg. Stuff a portion of the filling in each of the lamb legs and with a trussing needle and string, stitch the open end and knot the ends of the string securely. Bind each stuffed leg with string to retain the shape whilst cooking. Baste the legs and prick with a needle.

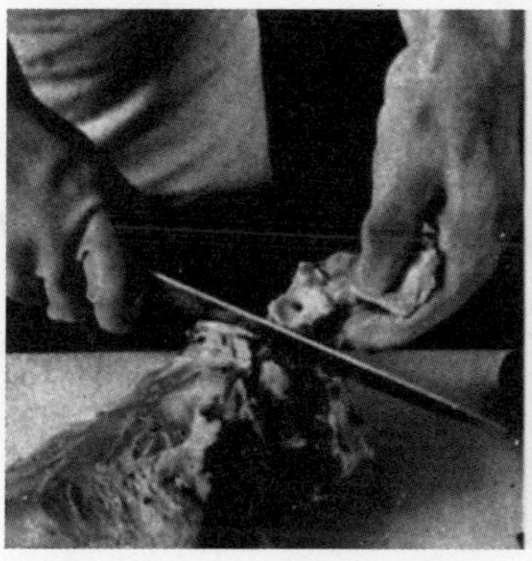

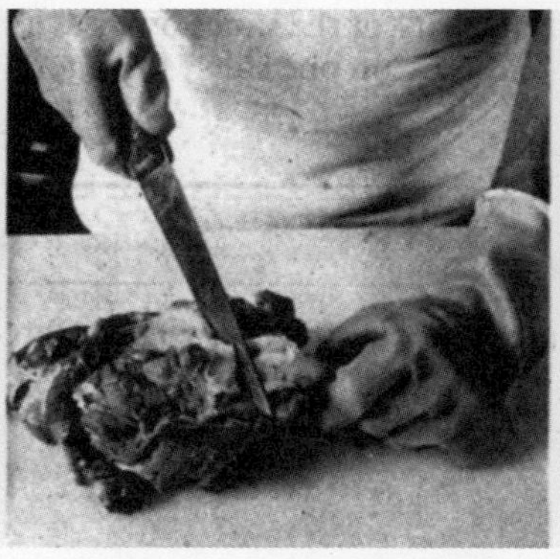

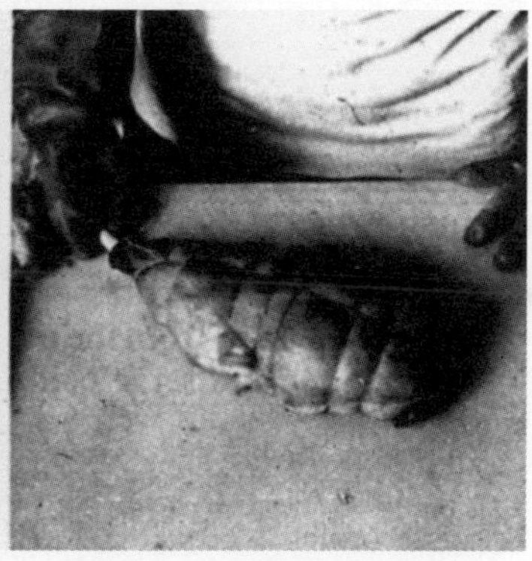

The Filling

450 g/1 lb Lamb

20 g/2 Tbs Ginger

3 Eggs

Salt

5 g/1 Tsp Garam Masala

2 g/⅓ Tsp Nutmeg powder

8 g/2 Tbs Mint

2 Green Chillies

25 g/1 oz Cashewnuts (split)

Garnish

4 Onions (medium size)

3 Lemons

Serves 10

Preparation time: 3:25 hours

Cooking time: 1:30 hours

Garnish: Peel, wash and cut onions into roundels to make rings. Wash and cut lemons into wedges.

Oven: Pre-heat to 250°F.

Cooking

Grease a baking tray, arrange the legs in it, add enough stock to immerse one-third of the legs and roast in the pre-heated oven for 90 minutes. Baste at regular intervals, using the stock, and turn occasionally for even colouring. Remove, untie the binding string, snip off the stitching and cool the legs in the stock. When cool, remove from the stock, transfer to a tray and refrigerate overnight.

Assembling

Slice the lamb (¼-inch thick), arrange on a silver platter and refrigerate for 30 minutes.

To Serve

Remove the platter from the refrigerator, garnish and serve cold.

Khasta Kheema

A cardamom-flavoured lamb pate, spiced with cumin and garnished with almonds.

Preparation

Lamb: Clean, debone and cut into small chunks.

Vegetables: Scrape, wash and roughly chop ginger. Peel, wash and roughly chop garlic. Clean, wash and finely chop mint. Remove stems, wash, slit, deseed and finely chop green chillies.

Mince: Coarsely mince the lamb chunks in a mincer, reserve one-third and refrigerate. Add the chopped ginger and garlic with the remaining *kheema* and mince twice again. Spread the fine mince on a flat tray and put it in the freezer for an hour.

Almonds: Blanch, cool, remove the skin and split. Soak in water, drain.

Mousse: Put the frozen mince in a blender, add the eggs (one-at-a-time) and salt, make a mousse. Transfer the mousse to a bowl, add the remaining ingredients, except gelatin, and mix well. Fold in the reserved coarse mince.

Dough: Sieve flour and salt together into a *paraat.* Put butter in a frying pan, add water (approx 140 ml/5 oz) and heat until the butter melts. Beat one egg. Make a bay in the sieved flour, pour the butter-water mixture and the beaten egg in it, add cumin and start mixing gradually. When fully mixed, knead to make a semi-hard dough, cover with a moist cloth and keep aside for 15 minutes. Beat the remaining egg for egg wash. Divide the dough into two equal portions. Place on a lightly floured surface and flatten with a rolling pin into two 1/8-inch thick rectangular shapes.

Garnish: Wash and cut tomatoes into roundels. Peel and cut cucumbers into roundels.

Gelatin: Soak in tap water (approx 135 ml/5 oz) for 10 minutes and then stir over a double boiler until it melts and a clear solution is obtained. Strain through fine muslin

INGREDIENTS

1.6 kg/3½ lb Lamb (lean)
15 g/4½ Tsp Ginger
15 g/4½ Tsp Garlic
6 Eggs
Salt
6 g/2 Tsp Cumin seeds
5 g/1 Tsp Cumin Powder
10 g/2 Tsp Green Cardamom powder
5 g/1½ Tsp Black Peppercorns
5 g/1 Tsp Yellow Chilli powder
3 g/½ Tsp Nutmeg and Mace powder
20 g/⅓ cup Mint
4 Green Chillies
35 g/¼ cup Almonds
45 g/1½ oz Gelatin powder

Dough

450 g/1 lb Flour
Salt
115 g/4 oz Butter
2 Eggs
10 g/1 Tbs Cumin seeds

Garnish

4 Tomatoes (medium size)
2 Cucumber

Serves

10 (2 moulds of 1 kg/2¼ lb each)

Preparation time: 1:30 hours

Cooking time: 1:30 hours

into a clean bowl. Place the bowl in lukewarm water so that the jelly does not set before use.

Oven: Pre-heat to 240°F.

Assembling

Grease two moulds, line each with the flattened dough, with enough overlapping to seal. Tightly pack the lined mould with the mousse, cover with overlapping dough and crimp the edges. Pierce the dough to make two small openings a few inches from each end and place a nozzle in each—to allow the steam to escape whilst cooking and subsequently to facilitate the pouring in of the gelatin. Give an egg wash.

Cooking

Bake in the pre-heated oven for 90 minutes. Remove, pour the warm gelatin through the cones ensuring it does not overflow. Cool and refrigerate overnight.

Finishing

Demould, slice (¼-inch thick), arrange on a silver platter and refrigerate for 30 minutes.

To Serve

Remove the platter from the refrigerator, garnish and serve cold with mint chutney.

Tandoori and Other Kebab

With MADAN LAL JAISWAL AND TODAR MAL

North India's traditional clay oven is probably the most versatile kitchen equipment in the world. One cannot make a decent bread without one, nor can one savour the popular *kebab.* Gravies and *dals* made in them acquire a unique taste, vastly different from the stuff cooked on the open fire. It would be no exaggeration to say that it is the *tandoor* which has helped popularise Indian cuisine around the globe.

The traditional *tandoor* is a clay oven, fired by charcoal. Until recently, the only variation was an iron *tandoor,* used largely for making *kebab.* During the last decade, we

Madan Lal Jaiswal: By giving a gastronomic accent to the rustic and simple kebab, Jaiswal has helped make *Bukhara,* Welcomgroup's Frontier restaurant at the *Maurya Sheraton,* quite simply the finest Indian restaurant—anywhere. He is presently busy recreating the culinary magic of his New Delhi eatery in New York—at the *Bukhara** in the Big Apple.

Todar Mal: The one-time *Bukhara* partner and *Gurubhai* (which means that they were trained by the same *Guru)* of Madan Lal Jaiswal, Todar Mal now practises his wonderful skills in the kitchen of the *Mughal Room* at *The Oberoi*,* New Delhi.

*Designation subject to change.

have seen the advent of the gas and electric *tandoor.* It goes without saying that neither of the innovations is capable of matching the versatility of the clay oven. It is well nigh impossible to achieve the flavour or the aroma in these contraptions.

Should you choose to acquire a clay *tandoor,* it will have to be seasoned. As a first step, ensure that the inner surface is smooth and without any cracks. Next, take spinach or any other leafy vegetable and make a paste. Rub this paste evenly on the inside and leave it to dry. Then make an emulsion of mustard oil, buttermilk, jaggery and salt, apply it over the spinach paste with the help of a cloth. Start the *tandoor* by lighting a small fire and allowing the temperature to rise gradually. The prepared emulsion will peel off. Replace it with another application of the emulsion. Repeat the process three or four times to 'season' the *tandoor.* Finally, sprinkle brine on the sides and leave it to dry (this facilitates the sticking of breads to the sides).

Remember, temperature plays an important part in *Tandoori* cooking. Thus, a small fire is lit and the temperature is allowed to rise gradually. This is done to prevent any cracks from developing in the *tandoor.* If you light a big fire, the sudden variation in temperature would leave cracks in the clay and the oven will become ineffective. Nor, for that matter, would you be able to stick the *Naan* or *Roti* to the sides.

In the conventional ovens (gas and electric) different ingredients cook at various temperatures. Similarly, in the *tandoor* too different foods require specific temperatures to cook. Of course, one cannot get it correct to the degree but, from experience, one can get it almost right. To control the temperature one needs a convex lid for the top and an iron disc for the little opening at the bottom.

If the temperature is too high, the charcoal is moved to one side with the help of a skewer. If the temperature is low, then both the openings are shut off. For the novice, the only way to find out if the temperature is right is to try and stick a *Naan* or a *Roti* to the side. If it falls off, it means the temperature is low.

To maintain an even temperature in the *tandoor,* it is important that the charcoal be evenly spread at the bottom.

It is commonly believed that the only way to cook *kebab* is in a *tandoor* or an open iron grill. Nothing could be farther from the truth. For this section, we have included several *non-tandoori* delicacies. Shallow fried or deep fried, these *kebab* are as popular as the *tandoori* variety. What both types of *kebab* share in common is the need for marination. The success of a *kebab* depends entirely on the exact time for which the meat is kept in marination.

For *tandoori kebab,* basting acquires special significance. It is the application of butter or oil which seals in the juices and makes *kebab* succulent.

Tandoori Lobster

There could hardly be a better way to treat Newfoundland's off-shore bounty—it's succulent and flavoured with India's unique spice—*ajwain.*

Preparation

Lobster: Boil, cool, shell and devein (if you wish to serve the lobster in the shell, cut into half and then shell; wash the shell and reserve).

Marination: Scrape, wash and finely chop ginger. Break the egg in a bowl, add the chopped ginger and the remaining ingredients, whisk and rub lobster with this mixture. Keep aside for 2 hours.

Oven: Pre-heat to 350°F.

Skewering: Skewer the lobster an inch apart. Keep a tray underneath to collect the drippings.

Cooking

Roast in a moderately hot *tandoor,* charcoal grill or pre-heated oven for 3–4 minutes. Remove and hang the skewers to allow the excess moisture to drip off (approx 2 minutes), baste with butter and roast again for 2 minutes.

Note: If you wish to make the lobster without boiling, which is always tastier, marinate for 3½ hours and roast for 12 minutes instead of 8 minutes.

INGREDIENTS

4 Lobster (large size)
Butter for basting

Marinade

20 g/2 Tbs Ginger
1 Egg
150 ml/⅔ cup Cream
12 g/5 Tsp Ajwain
50 g/3 Tbs Ginger paste
50 g/3 Tbs Garlic paste
30 ml/2 Tbs Lemon juice
50 g/⅓ cup Gramflour
10 g/2 Tsp Garam Masala
3 g/½ Tsp White Pepper powder
Salt

Serves 4

Preparation time: 45 minutes
Cooking time: 8–9 minutes

Tandoori Pomfret

INGREDIENTS

4 Pomfret (450 g/1 lb each)
Butter for basting

Marinade

60 g/¼ cup Yoghurt
2 Eggs
45 ml/3 Tbs Cream
20 g/3½ Tsp Ginger paste
20 g/3½ Tsp Garlic paste
10 g/4 Tsp Ajwain
20 g/2 Tbs Gramflour
3 g/½ Tsp White Pepper powder
Salt
10 g/2 Tsp Red Chilli powder
30 ml/2 Tbs Lemon juice
5 g/1 Tsp Turmeric
10 g/2 Tsp Cumin powder

Serves 4

Preparation time: 3:30 hours
Cooking time: 12–15 minutes

An eloquent tribute to India's most popular sea-fish—this delicacy is a mouth-watering sight to behold.

Preparation

Fish: Clean, wash and make 3 deep incisions across each side.

Marination: Hang the yohurt in muslin for 15 minutes to remove the whey. Separate 'the egg yolks, discard the whites. Transfer yoghurt and yolks to a large bowl, add the remaining ingredients, whisk and rub the fish with this mixture. Keep aside for 3 hours.

Oven: Pre-heat to 350°F.

Skewering: Skewer the fish, from mouth to tail, two inches apart. Keep a tray underneath to collect the drippings.

Cooking

Roast in a moderately hot *tandoor* for 8 minutes. In a charcoal grill for the same time. In a pre-heated oven for 12 minutes. Remove and hang the skewers to allow the excess moisture to drip off (approx 3 minutes), baste with butter and roast again for 3 minutes.

Jhinga Achaar Salaad

Khasta Kheema
Murgh
Reshmi
Thandi Ajwaini Machchli

Tandoori Lobster

Tandoori Pomfret

Shaan-e-Murgh

Tandoori Murgh

The 'King of Kebab', *Tandoori Murgh* is the best known Indian delicacy and the tastiest way to barbecue chicken.

INGREDIENTS

2 Chicken (600 g/1 1/3 lb each)
Salt
5 g/1 Tsp Red Chilli powder
60 ml/4 Tbs Lemon juice
Butter for basting

Marinade

100 g/6 Tbs Yoghurt
100 g/7 Tbs Cream
15 g/2½ Tsp Ginger paste
15 g/2½ Tsp Garlic paste
5 g/1 Tsp Cumin powder
3 g/½ Tsp Garam Masala
½/1 Tsp Saffron
1 drop Orange Colour

Serves 4

Preparation time: 4:30 hours
Cooking time: 15 minutes

Preparation

Chicken: Clean, remove the skin, make deep incisions—3 on each breast, 3 on each thigh, 2 on each drumstick. Make a paste of salt, red chillies and lemon juice and rub over the chicken evenly. Keep aside for 15 minutes.

Marination: Whisk yoghurt in a large bowl, add the remaining ingredients and mix well. Rub the chicken with this mixture. Keep aside for 4 hours.

Oven: Pre-heat to 350°F.

Skewering: Skewer the chicken, from tail to head, leaving a gap of at least 2 inches between the birds. Keep a tray underneath to collect the drippings.

Cooking

Roast in a moderately hot tandoor for approx 8 minutes. In a charcoal grill for about the same time. In a pre-heated oven for 10 minutes. Remove and hang the skewers to let the excess moisture drip off (approx 4–5 minutes), baste with butter and roast again for 3–4 minutes.

Murgh Tikka

INGREDIENTS

800 g/1¾ lb Chicken (legs)
Butter for basting

Marinade

50 g/¼ cup Yoghurt
40 g/6¾ Tsp Ginger paste
40 g/6¾ Tsp Garlic paste
3 g/½ Tsp White Pepper powder
3 g/½ Tsp Cumin powder
5 g/1 Tsp Mace-Nutmeg-Green Cardamom powder
3 g/½ Tsp Red Chilli powder
3 g/½ Tsp Turmeric
60 ml/4 Tbs Lemon juice
20 g/2 Tbs Gramflour
Salt
75 ml/5 Tbs Groundnut Oil

Serves 4

Preparation time: 4 hours
Cooking time: 10 minutes

A succulent and boneless *kebab*—possibly the most popular after the incomparable *Tandoori Murgh*—makes a great cocktail snack.

Preparation

Chicken: Clean, remove the skin and debone. Cut each leg into 4 pieces—24 *tikka* in all.

Marination: Whisk yoghurt in a large bowl, add the remaining ingredients and mix well. Rub the chicken pieces with this mixture. Keep aside for 3½ hours.

Oven: Pre-heat to 350°F.

Skewering: Skewer the marinated *tikka* at least an inch apart. Keep a tray underneath to collect the drippings.

Cooking

Roast in a moderately hot *tandoor* for about 6–7 minutes, basting at least once. In a charcoal grill, for about the same time, basting once. In a pre-heated oven, roast the *tikka* for 8–10 minutes, basting at least twice. Make sure that the chicken does not touch the sides or the bottom of the oven.

Note: A tasty variation of the *Murgh Tikka* is the *Tikka Harra Bharra,* made with the addition of mint and coriander paste (50 g/3 Tbs) to the marinade.

Murgh Nawabi

A creamy, gently spiced chicken *kebab,* flavoured with mace.

INGREDIENTS

2 Chicken (700 g/1½ lb each)
60 ml/4 Tbs Malt Vinegar
8 Green Chillies
10 g/2 Tsp White Pepper powder
3 g/½ Tsp Mace powder
Salt
25 g/4 Tsp Ginger paste
25 g/4 Tsp Garlic paste
450 g/2 cups Yoghurt
100 ml/7 Tbs Cream
Butter for basting

Serves 4

Preparation time: 7:45 hours

Cooking time: 15 minutes

Preparation

Chicken: Clean, remove the skin and cut each into 8 pieces.

First Marination: Remove stems, wash, slit, deseed and finely chop green chillies. Mix the chillies, pepper, mace, salt and the ginger and garlic pastes with vinegar in a large bowl and rub the chicken pieces with this mixture. Keep aside for 15 minutes.

Second Marination: Hang yoghurt in muslin for 4 hours to remove the whey. Mix with cream in a large bowl, transfer the chicken to this marinade. Keep aside for 3 hours.

Oven: Pre-heat to 350°F.

Skewering: Skewer the chicken pieces an inch apart. Keep a tray underneath to collect the drippings.

Cooking

Roast in a moderately hot *tandoor* for 10 minutes. In a charcoal grill for the same time. In a pre-heated oven for 12 minutes. Remove and hang the skewers to allow the excess moisture to drip off (approx 2 minutes), baste with butter and roast again for 3 minutes.

Shaan-e-Murgh

INGREDIENTS

8 Breasts of Chicken

Ghee to deep fry stuffed breasts of chicken

Marinade

20 g/3½ Tsp Ginger paste

20 g/3½ Tsp Garlic paste

3 g/3½ Tsp Yellow Chilli powder

Salt

60 ml/4 Tbs Lemon juice

Filling

300 g/11 oz Paneer*

8 Green Chillies

20 g/⅓ cup Coriander

2 Pineapple rings

40 g/⅓ cup Cashewnuts

3 g/1 Tsp Black Cumin seeds

3 g/½ Tsp Yellow Chilli powder

Salt

Batter

3 Eggs

150 g/5 oz Cornflour

50 g/6 Tbs Flour

Salt

*See Section on Milk.

Serves 4

Preparation time: 1:15 hours

This is a magnificent *kebab* of tender chicken breasts stuffed with black cumin-flavoured *paneer.*

Preparation

Chicken: Clean, remove the skin and debone, keeping the winglet bone intact. With a knife-tip make a deep slit along the thick edge of the breast, taking care not to penetrate the opposite side *(see photographs).* Open out the flaps thus formed and flatten with a bat.

Marination: Mix yellow chillies, salt and lemon juice with the ginger and garlic pastes and apply this mixture on the flattened chicken breasts. Keep aside for at least 30 minutes.

Filling: Mash the *paneer* in a bowl. Remove stems, wash, slit, deseed and finely chop green chillies. Clean, wash and chop coriander. Finely chop the pineapple rings. Roughly chop cashewnuts. Add these chopped ingredients, cumin, yellow chillies and salt with the mashed *paneer* and mix well.

Stuffing: Place a portion of the filling in the middle of the marinated chicken breasts and fold to make round balls, with the bone sticking out. Refrigerate for 15 minutes.

Batter: Break eggs in a bowl, add cornflour, flour, salt and water (approx 100 ml) and whisk to make a batter.

Oven: Pre-heat to 275°F.

Cooking

Heat ghee in a *kadhai,* dip the stuffed chicken breasts in the batter and deep fry over medium heat until light golden.

Finishing

Grease a roasting tray with a little ghee, arrange the fried chicken breasts on it and roast in a pre-heated oven for 10–12 minutes.

Murgh Malai

A creamy *kebab* made from the breasts of chicken the *Murgh Malai* combines the joys of the traditional *kebabi* herbs and spices with cheddar.

Preparation

Chicken: Clean, remove the skin, debone and cut each breast into two. Add ginger and garlic pastes to the seasoning and rub the chicken pieces with this mixture. Keep aside for 15 minutes.

Marination: Break egg in a bowl. Grate cheese and mash. Remove stems, wash, slit, deseed and finely chop green chillies. Clean, wash and finely chop coriander. Mix cheese, green chillies, coriander and the remaining ingredients with egg, whisk and rub the chicken pieces with this mixture. Keep aside for 3 hours.

Oven: Pre-heat to 275°F.

Skewering: Skewer the chicken pieces an inch apart. Keep a tray underneath to collect the drippings.

Cooking

Roast in a moderately hot *tandoor* for approximately 5 minutes. In a charcoal grill for about the same time. In a pre-heated oven for 6 minutes. Remove and hang the skewers to let the excess moisture drip off (approx 2–3 minutes), baste with butter and roast again for 3 minutes.

INGREDIENTS

12 Breasts of Chicken

40 g/6¾ Tsp Ginger paste

35 g/6 Tsp Garlic paste

5 g/1 Tsp White Pepper powder

Salt

Butter for basting

Marinade

1 Egg

60 g/½ cup Cheddar Cheese (semi-hard)

8 Green Chillies

20 g/⅓ cup Coriander

160 ml/⅔ cup Cream

3 g/½ Tsp Mace and Nutmeg powder

15 g/3 Tbs Cornflour

Serves 4

Preparation time: 3:45 hours

Cooking time: 12 minutes

Kastoori Kebab

INGREDIENTS

12 Breasts of Chicken
40 g/6 Tsp Ginger paste
40 g/6¾ Tsp Garlic paste
45 ml/3 Tbs Lemon juice
5 g/1 Tsp White Pepper powder
Salt
60 g/4 Tbs Butter
10 ml/2 Tsp Groundnut Oil
100 g/⅔ cup Gramflour
80 g/¾ cup Breadcrumbs
20 g/2 Tbs Ginger
20 g/⅓ cup Coriander
2 g/⅓ Tsp Green Cardamom powder

Batter

3 Eggs
3 g/1 Tsp Black Cumin seeds
½ g/1 Tsp Saffron

Serves 4

Preparation time: 2:30 hours
Cooking time: 10 minutes

An egg-coated variation of the *Murgh Tikka,* spiced, with cumin and flavoured with cardamom.

Preparation

Chicken: Clean, remove the skin, debone and cut each breast into two. Mix ginger paste, garlic paste and lemon juice with the seasoning and rub the chicken pieces with this mixture. Keep aside for 1 hour.

Vegetables: Scrape, wash and finely chop ginger. Clean, wash and chop coriander.

Gramflour: Heat butter and oil in a *kadhai,* add gramflour and saute over medium heat until golden brown. Remove 20 g/4 Tsp and keep aside. Add breadcrumbs, chopped ginger, coriander and the marinated chicken, saute for 3–4 minutes.

Batter: Separate the egg yolks, discard the whites, transfer to a bowl, add cumin, saffron and the reserved gramflour, whisk.

Oven: Pre-heat to 300°F.

Skewering: Skewer 6 chicken pieces together and overlapping. Leave a gap of 2 inches and then skewer the next lot. Coat each set with the batter.

Cooking

Roast in a moderately hot *tandoor* for 5–6 minutes. In a charcoal grill for 6–7 minutes. In a pre-heated oven for 8–10 minutes. Remove and sprinkle cardamom powder.

Reshmi Kebab

A tender *kebab* made from chicken mince and cashewnut paste.

INGREDIENTS
1 kg/2¼ lb Chicken Mince
2 Eggs
15 g/1 Tbs Cumin powder
5 g/1 Tsp Yellow Chilli powder
5 g/1 Tsp White Pepper powder
Salt
20 ml/4 Tsp Groundnut Oil
50 g/⅓ cup Cashewnuts
30 g/3 Tbs Ginger
20 g/2 Tbs Onions
20 g/⅓ cup Coriander
5 g/1 Tsp Garam Masala
Butter for basting

Serves 4

Preparation time: 30 minutes

Cooking time: 5–6 minutes

Preparation

Eggs: Break in a bowl and whisk.

Cashewnuts: Pound with a pestle.

Vegetables: Scrape, wash and finely chop ginger. Peel, wash and finely chop onions. Clean, wash and chop coriander.

Mince: Add the whisked eggs, cumin, yellow chillies, white pepper, salt and oil to the mince and mix well. Keep aside for 15 minutes. Then add cashewnuts, chopped vegetables and garam masala, mix well. Divide into 8 equal portions and make balls.

Oven: Pre-heat to 300°F.

Skewering: Using a wet hand, spread the balls by pressing each along the length of the skewers two inches apart and making each *kebab* 5 inches long *(see photographs).*

Cooking

Roast in a moderately hot *tandoor* for 6 minutes, basting once, until they are light golden. In a charcoal grill, for about the same time, basting once. In a pre-heated oven, roast for 8 minutes, basting once.

Galouti Kebab

INGREDIENTS

1 kg/2¼ lb Leg of Spring Lamb

50 g/3 Tbs Ginger paste

50 g/3 Tbs Garlic paste

75 g/2½ oz Raw Papaya

50 g/3 Tbs Butter

5 g/1 Tsp Red Chilli powder

Salt

3 g/½ Tsp Mace powder

5 g/1 Tsp Green Cardamom powder

40 g/4 Tbs Flour of Roasted Channa dal

Ghee to shallow fry

Serves 4

Preparation time: 1:10 hours

Cooking time: 15 minutes for each set

The remarkable thing about the ace and cardamom flavoured Galouti is that it melts in the mouth. It is the 'royal kebab'.

Preparation

Lamb: Clean, debone, mince and refrigerate for 15 minutes.

Papaya: Peel, deseed, put in a blender and make a fine paste.

Patties: Mix all the ingredients, except ghee, with the refrigerated mince and mince the mixture. Divide into 32 equal portions and make balls. Apply a little melted ghee on the palms and flatten the mince balls into round patties (approx 2-inch diameter).

Cooking

Heat ghee on a *tawa* and shallow fry over low heat until both sides are evenly brown.

Malai Seekh

Herbs and cashewnuts combine to make this succulent *kebab* of lamb mince an extraordinary cocktail snack.

INGREDIENTS

900 g/2 lb Lamb Mince
150 g/5 oz Lamb Fat
40 g/¼ cup Onions
40 g/¼ cup Ginger
8 Green Chillies
20 g/⅓ cup Coriander
75 g/⅔ cup Cashewnuts
2 Eggs
50 ml/3 Tbs Groundnut Oil
3 g/½ Tsp White Pepper powder
Salt
10 g/2 Tsp Garam Masala
Butter for basting

Serves 4

Preparation time: 40 minutes
Cooking time: 14 minutes

Preparation

Fat: Mince.

Vegetables: Peel, wash and finely chop onions. Scrape, wash and finely chop ginger. Remove stems, wash, slit, deseed and finely chop green chillies. Clean, wash and chop coriander.

Cashewnuts: Pound with a pestle.

Eggs: Whisk in a bowl.

Mince: Add all the ingredients, except butter, to lamb mince in a large bowl and mix well. Keep aside for 15 minutes. Divide into 12 equal portions and make balls.

Oven: Pre-heat to 325°F.

Skewering: Using a wet hand, spread the balls by pressing each along the length of the skewers, two inches apart, and making each *kebab* 4-inches long *(see photographs on p. 25)*.

Cooking

Roast in a moderately hot *tandoor* for 8 minutes. In a charcoal grill for about the same time. In a pre-heated oven for 8–10 minutes. Remove and hang the skewers to let the excess moisture drip off (approx 2 minutes), baste with butter and roast again for 2 minutes.

Dum ke Kebab

INGREDIENTS

500 g/18 oz Lamb Mince
75 g/½ cup Cashewnuts
30 g/¼ cup Almonds
50 g/⅔ cup Coconut
10 g/2 Tsp Coriander powder
3 Cloves
2 Sticks Cinnamon (1-inch)
6 Green Cardamom
3 g/1 Tsp Black Cumin seeds
20 g/2 Tbs Onions
Groundnut Oil to fry Onions
5 g/1 Tsp Red Chilli powder
3 g/½ Tsp Turmeric
Salt
50 ml/3 Tbs Groundnut Oil for smoking
10 g/2 Tbs Mint
10 g/2 Tbs Coriander
4 Green Chillies

Serves 4

Preparation time: 45 minutes

Cooking time: 7 minutes

For this delicacy the mince is smoked before the *kebab* is cooked.

Preparation

Almonds: Blanch, cool and peel.

Coconut: Remove the brown skin and grate.

Onions: Peel, wash and slice. Heat oil in a frying pan and fry until golden brown. Remove and keep aside.

Remaining Vegetables: Clean, wash and chop mint and coriander. Remove stems, wash, slit, deseed and chop green chillies.

Paste: Put cashewnuts, almonds, coconut, coriander powder and the whole spices in a blender, add water (approx 120 ml/½ cup) and make a fine paste.

Mince: Mix fried onions, red chillies, turmeric and salt with the mince in a *handi,* add the paste and mix well. Keep aside for at least 30 minutes.

Smoking: Spread the mince on a tray, make a well (an area of 6-inch diameter). Place glowing charcoals in the well, pour oil on the charcoals and cover the tray with a dome for 10 minutes. Uncover and transfer the mince back to the *handi.* Add mint, coriander and green chillies, mix well.

Cooking

Ideally, *Dum ke Kebab* should be skewered and cooked in a moderately hot *tandoor* or over a charcoal grill. Alternatively, make round patties, heat enough oil on a *tawa* and shallow fry until the *kebab* are cooked.

Shikampuri Kebab

The common *Shammi* pales in comparison with this superlative *kebab* from *Shikampur,* a hamlet near Hyderabad. Kakori, a few miles from Lucknow, was put on the Nation's culinary map by a *kebab* named after the city. The *Shikampuri* is sure to do the same for the place of its origin.

INGREDIENTS

500 g/18 oz Lamb Mince
50 g/¼ cup Channa dal
10 cloves Garlic
3 g/1 Tsp Black Cumin seeds
5 Green Cardamom
2 sticks Cinnamon (1-inch)
5 Cloves
30 ml/2 Tbs Groundnut Oil
30 g/¼ cup Almonds
50 g/⅔ cup Coconut
30 ml/2 Tbs Lemon juice
3 g/½ Tsp Turmeric
5 g/1 Tsp Red Chilli powder
2 Eggs
Salt
Groundnut Oil to deep fry

Filling

2 Eggs
30 g/3 Tbs Onions
10 g/2 Tbs Mint
10 g/2 Tbs Coriander
4 Green Chillies
Salt

Serves 4

Preparation time: 25 minutes

Cooking time: 2–3 minutes for each set

Preparation

Lentil: Pick and wash in running water.

Garlic: Peel.

Almonds: Blanch, cool and peel.

Mince: Mix *channa dal,* garlic, black cumin, cardamom, cinnamon, cloves and oil with the mince in a *handi,* add water (approx 180 ml/¾ cup), bring to a boil, reduce to medium heat and cook until the mince is completely dry. Then add almonds and coconut, fry over medium heat for 2–3 minutes. Remove, cool, put in a blender and make a fine paste. Transfer the paste to the *handi,* add lemon juice, turmeric, red chillies, eggs and salt, mix well. Divide the mixture into 8 equal portions and make balls.

Filling: Hard boil the eggs, cool, shell, cut into halves and discard the yolks. Roughly chop the whites. Peel, wash and finely chop onions. Clean, wash and chop mint and coriander. Remove stems, wash, slit, deseed and finely chop green chillies. Mix these ingredients with salt in a bowl and divide into 8 equal portions.

Stuffing: Flatten each ball against a wet palm, place a portion of the filling in the middle, seal and flatten again into round patties.

Cooking

Heat oil in *kadhai* and deep fry the patties over medium heat until dark brown.

Adraki Chaamp

INGREDIENTS

12 Lamb chops (3-rib)

50 g/2 oz Raw Papaya

75 g/¼ cup Ginger paste

20 g/3½ Tsp Garlic paste

3 g/½ Tsp Black Pepper powder

Salt

Butter for basting

Marinade

50 ml/3 Tbs Cream

15 g/1 Tbs Cumin powder

10 g/2 Tsp Red Chilli powder

10 g/2 Tsp Garam Masala

45 ml/3 Tbs Lemon juice

Serves 4

Preparation time: 4:30 hours

Cooking time: 20 minutes

Ginger-flavoured, juicy lamb chops done to perfection in a creamy cumin-based marinade *sans* yoghurt.

Preparation

Lamb Chops: Clean, remove the two side bones and flatten with a bat. Peel and mash papaya, add the ginger paste, garlic paste and seasoning, rub the chops with this mixture. Keep aside for 3 hours.

Marination: Mix all the ingredients with cream in a large bowl and rub the chops with this mixture. Keep aside for 1 hour.

Oven: Pre-heat to 350°F.

Skewering: Skewer the chops an inch apart. Keep a tray underneath to collect the drippings.

Cooking

Roast in a moderately hot *tandoor* for 9–10 minutes. In a charcoal grill for about the same time. In a pre-heated oven for 10–12 minutes. Remove and hang the skewers to allow the moisture to drip off (approx 4–5 minutes), baste with butter and roast again for 3 minutes.

Gosht Elaichi Pasanda

A cardamom-flavoured *kebab* made from *picatta* of lamb.

Preparation

Lamb: Clean, debone, cut into 1½-inch chunks and flatten with a bat to make *picatta* of ⅛-inch thickness. Peel and mash the papaya, add ginger paste, garlic paste and seasoning, rub the *picatta* with this mixture. Keep aside for 1½ hours,

Marination: Hang yoghurt in muslin for 4 hours to remove the whey. Transfer to a large bowl, add the remaining ingredients, whisk and rub the *picatta* with this mixture. Keep aside for 1 hour.

Oven: Pre-heat to 350°F.

Skewering: Skewer the *picatta*—by piercing at both ends—an inch apart. Keep a tray underneath to collect the drippings.

Cooking

Roast in a moderately hot *tandoor* for 9–10 minutes. In a charcoal grill for about the same time. In a pre-heated oven for 10–12 minutes. Remove and hang the skewers to allow the moisture to drip off (approx 4–5 minutes), baste with butter and roast again for 3 minutes.

Note: To make *Boti Kebab,* debone lamb and cut into ¾-inch cubes, do not flatten. For the marinade, use 100 g/½ cup yoghurt (instead of 80 g), 5 g/1 Tsp cumin powder (instead of green cardamom powder) and 5 ml/1 Tsp orange colour. The rest of the procedure is the same.

INGREDIENTS

1 kg/2¼ lb Lamb

75 g/2½ oz Raw Papaya

50 g/3 Tbs Ginger paste

50 g/3 Tbs Garlic paste

3 g/½ Tsp Black Pepper powder

Salt

Butter for basting

Marinade

80 g/⅓ cup Yoghurt

10 g/2 Tsp Red Chilli powder

10 g/2 Tsp Green Cardamom powder

20 ml/4 Tsp Lemon juice

20 g/4 Tsp Garam Masala

Serves 4

Preparation time: 7 hours

Cooking time: 20 minutes

Paneer ka Tikka

INGREDIENTS

800 g/1¾ lb Paneer*
3 g/1 Tsp Black Cumin seeds
5 g/2 Tsp Ajwain
10 g/2 Tsp Garam Masala
3 g/½ Tsp White Pepper powder
3 g/½ Tsp Turmeric
Salt
3 g/1½ Tsp Fenugreek (Kasoori Methi)

Batter

1 Egg
30 g/3 Tbs Gramflour
120 ml/½ cup Cream
Salt

*See section on Milk.

Serves 4

Preparation time: 1:30 hours
Cooking time: 13 minutes

In a largely vegetarian country, it is improbable that there would be nothing for the vegetarians in *tandoori* cooking. This is an exotic *kebab* of Indian cottage cheese.

Preparation

Paneer: Cut into 16 equal-sized *tikka* (2″ × 2″ × 1″). Evenly sprinkle black cumin, *ajwain,* 7 g/1½ Tsp of garam masala, white pepper, turmeric and salt, keep aside.

Batter: Whisk egg in a bowl, add the remaining ingredients, mix well, and leave the *paneer* in this batter for 45 minutes.

Oven: Pre-heat to 275°F.

Skewering: Skewer the *tikka,* one inch apart, then skewer a raw onion to prevent the paneer from sliding down. Keep a tray underneath to collect the drippings.

Cooking

Roast in a moderately hot *tandoor* for 10–12 minutes. In a charcoal grill for about the same time. In a pre-heated oven for 12–14 minutes. Remove and sprinkle *Kasoori Methi* and the remaining garam masala.

Handi, Kadhai and Tawa

With ARVIND SARASWAT

Until recently—and this is most unfortunate—Indian food was synonymous with either the 'rich' food of the Maharajas or the 'chilli-hot' fare served in the run-of-the-mill restaurant. Neither is truly representative of the real Indian cuisine—one with thousands of years of refinement behind it. There is no denying that Indian cuisine can be elaborate and Indian hospitality overwhelming. However, as in other parts of the world, food habits here are changing.

To cater to changing tastes, many chefs started to look for alternatives. My 'co-author' for this and the following two chapters chose to experiment with delicacies that can be prepared in/on the most commonly used utensils in Indian cooking—*handi, kadhai* and *tawa.*

Though *Handi* cooking is prevalent in most of India, it has carved a permanent niche in the Northern states. *Handi* comes in different shapes and sizes, but there are features common to all: a thick bottom to ensure that the food does not stick and, consequently, burn; tinning on the inside to prevent any chemical reaction; and, a lid to help retain the aroma and flavour.

The most important aspects of *Handi* cooking are *bhunao* and *dum,* both described in detail in the Introduction.

Arvind Saraswat: A methodical man, Saraswat is Director of Kitchen Planning and Food Production, Taj Group of Hotels, has spent many years researching the history of cooking with different utensils. Many of his exquisitely wrought dishes have set new standards of excellence and made his kitchens the envy of other leading hotel chains in the country. An alumnus of the Culinary Institute of America, the Hilton-trained Saraswat is also a member of the Sicilian Chefs' Association. At present he is presiding the Delhi Chapter of the *Les Toques Blanche,* the Paris-based International Chefs Club*.

*Designation subject to change.

Originally, there were only two *Kadhai* delicacies—*Kadhai Murgh* (chicken) and *Kadhai Gosht* (goat or lamb)—popular in Peshawar and West Punjab, both now provinces of Pakistan. Traditional *Kadhai* shops, which still exist and serve the two dishes, have an in-house butchery. Diners select a chicken (or chickens) or cut of meat, which is weighed in *pao* (½ lb. approx.) and *seer* (2 lb. approx.), the old Indian weights, and then cut into small pieces or chunks. A facile *Kadhai* chef can handle anything up to 16 *Kadhai* simultaneously, ensuring each is taken off the fire at exactly the right moment and reaches the right table. The diners are at liberty to watch the 'performance' or sit at their respective tables. The *kadhai,* in which the food is prepared, is placed in the centre of the table and everyone eats out of it, breaking pieces from a large, family-size *Naan*-like *Roti* to go with it.

Based on the originals, we have created a whole section of *Kadhai* delicacies—dry, cooked in a thick tomato-based masala and finished with *Kasoori Methi* and garam masala. Except for the lamb dishes, *Kadhai* cooking is quick. Lamb has to be three-fourths cooked before being finished in the *kadhai.* The reason: there is no water used in *Kadhai* cooking. The main ingredient is cooked in the 'juice' of tomatoes and the meat itself. Because lamb takes longer to cook, the 'juice' would evaporate long before it is tender.

When the cooking process is about to be completed, the food is stirred constantly and the sides scraped vigorously to prevent sticking. The scraped masala adds to the flavour.

There is a certain fresh and light quality about *Kadhai* cuisine. To enjoy it to the fullest, the dish must be consumed immediately. Unlike *Handi* cooking, where many dishes can be prepared in advance, *Kadhai* cooking has to be done 'on site'. In the main, it is a chilli-hot food. However, one is at liberty to reduce the chillies.

Pao-Bhaji and *Tak-a-Tak!* One a simple potato 'n' tomato dish served with miniature bread loaves, *pao,* which found everlasting fame in Bombay's Dhobi Talao, once the city's washermen's pond. The second, originally a dish of chopped offals made famous in the back alleys of Karachi—the other great metropolis on the West coast of the Subcontinent, derives its unique name from the sound of metal spatulae striking the *tawa* or griddle. These two simple dishes provided the inspiration for this section.

The *tawa* on which these delicacies are cooked is not the conventional household griddle—it is thicker and larger (at least 15-inch diameter). The thickness prevents sticking to a large extent, but does not eradicate the danger altogether. The larger surface allows the food to be moved to the periphery—away from the heat of the flame or hot plate. In case of a small delay, the use of the periphery also helps to keep the food warm. Besides, the *tawa* offers one great advantage over the other utensils: the cooking process takes the least time. However, during that short time, it *demands* constant attention—stirring, chopping and/or folding.

When it comes to *masala,* use only pounded or powdered, never whole spices. The spices are usually added last to ensure that they do not get burnt and that the flavour is enhanced.

Tawa cooking, like *Kadhai* cooking, has to be done 'on site' and the delicacies consumed immediately.

Handi

Gosht aur Vadi Biryani

Lamb and *urad dal* dumpling, simmered in an exotic gravy, go to make this Chef's original rice delicacy a magnificent meal.

INGREDIENTS

250 g/1¼ cups Basmati Rice
800 ml/3⅓ cups Milk
Whole Garam Masala
- 5 Green Cardamom
- 1 Black Cardamom
- 5 Cloves
- 1 stick Cinnamon (1-inch)
- 1 Bay Leaf
- A pinch Mace

Salt

Lamb

450 g/1 lb Leg of Spring Lamb
200 g/¾ cup Yoghurt
5 g/1 Tsp Red Chilli powder
3 g/½ Tsp Coriander powder
Salt
5 g/1 Tsp Ginger paste
5 g/1 Tsp Garlic paste
100 g/½ cup Ghee
125 g/¾ cup Onions
Whole Garam Masala
- 5 Green Cardamom
- 1 Black Cardamom
- 5 Cloves
- 1 stick Cinnamon (1-inch)
- 1 Bay Leaf
- A pinch Mace

10 g/1 Tbs Ginger
4 Green Chillies

Preparation

Rice: Pick, wash in running water and soak for 30 minutes. Drain.

Lamb: Clean and cut into 1½-inch chunks.

Marination: Whisk yoghurt in a bowl, reserve half. In the remaining yoghurt, add red chillies, coriander powder, salt and the ginger and garlic pastes. Leave the lamb chunks in this marinade for at least 30 minutes.

Gravy: Peel, wash and slice onions. Scrape, wash and cut ginger into juliennes. Remove stems, wash, slit, deseed and chop green chillies.

***Vadi*:** Heat oil in a *kadhai* and deep fry until golden brown. Cool and break into pieces.

Garnish: Clean, wash and chop mint and coriander. Wash and cut tomatoes into quarters. Scrape, wash and cut ginger into juliennes. Dissolve asafoetida in 30 ml/2 Tbs of water. Dissolve saffron in warm milk.

Oven: Pre-heat to 350°F.

Cooking

To prepare rice, boil water (approx 1 litre/4 cups) and milk together in a *handi*, add whole garam masala, salt and rice, cook until almost done (7–8 minutes).

To prepare lamb, heat ghee in a *handi*, add onions and saute over medium heat until light brown. Add whole garam masala, ginger juliennes and green chillies, saute until onions are brown. Then add the marinated lamb and cook over low heat until tender. Use as much water as is required to make the meat tender.

Vadi

50 g/2 oz Vadi (Urad dal dumplings)*
Groundnut Oil to fry

Garnish

20 g/⅓ cup Mint
15 g/¼ cup Coriander
100 g/½ cup Tomatoes
10 g/1 Tbs Ginger
25 g/4 Tbs Onions
A pinch Asafoetida
1 g/2 Tsp Saffron
60 ml/¼ cup Milk

Serves 4

Preparation time: 45 minutes
Cooking time: 1:25 hours

*See recipe for Mongodi ki Subzi in the Rajasthan section. Substitute urad dal for moong dal. Vadi are available in most Indian stores.

Assembling

In the *handi* with the cooked lamb, sprinkle *vadi* and the garnish of mint, coriander, tomatoes, ginger juliennes, golden brown onions, the remaining yoghurt and asafoetida. Spread rice over the garnished lamb. Sprinkle saffron, place a moist cloth on top, cover with a lid and seal with *atta*-dough.

Finishing

Put the sealed *handi* on *dum* in the pre-heated oven for 15–20 minutes.

To Serve

Break the seal, remove the moist cloth and shift the rice from one side (just enough to remove the cooked lamb and *vadi*). Make a bed of lamb and *vadi* on the serving dish, spread rice on top and serve.

Murgh Navrattan

INGREDIENTS

1.2 kg/2⅔ lb Chicken (2 birds)
350 g/1½ cups Yoghurt
Salt
150 g/¾ cup Ghee
Whole Garam Masala
- 5 Green Cardamom
- 1 Black Cardamom
- 5 Cloves
- 1 stick Cinnamon (1-inch)
- 1 Bay Leaf
- A pinch Mace

200 g/1¼ cup Onions
10 g/1 Tbs Ginger

A delicacy for rare occasions, *Murgh Navrattan* is mild—but 'heavy'. It has a thick, creamy gravy flavoured with mace and cardamom. The original *navrattan*—nine jewels—were the incomparable courtiers of the Great Mughal, Akbar. This dish, named after them, is an eloquent tribute to the Emperor's nobles.

Preparation

Chicken: Clean, remove the skin and cut each into 8 pieces.

Marination: Whisk yoghurt in a large bowl, add salt and leave the chicken pieces in this marinade for at least 30 minutes.

Vegetables: Peel, wash and slice onions. Scrape, wash and chop ginger. Remove stems, wash, slit, deseed and chop green chillies.

***Shahi* Paste:** Soak poppy seeds for 30 minutes. Blanch almonds, remove the skin, put in a blender, along with poppy seeds, cashewnuts, melon seeds and water (approx 120 ml/ ½ cup) and make a fine paste.

Garnish: Blanch pistachio and almonds, remove the skin. Soak in lukewarm water with the remaining ingredients for 15 minutes.

Cooking

Heat ghee in a *handi*, add whole garam masala and saute over medium heat until it begins to crackle. Add onions and saute until golden brown. Then add ginger and green chillies, stir for a minute, add turmeric and red chillies—dissolved in 30 ml/2 Tbs of water (this is done to ensure that turmeric and chillies do not burn, and ruin the masala)—*bhunno* for 2 minutes, add the marinated chicken, alongwith the marinade, add water (approx 100 ml/7 Tbs), bring to a boil, cover and simmer until chicken is tender. Now add *Shahi* paste, bring to a boil, then simmer until the fat comes to the surface, add cream and stir. Sprinkle mace and cardamom powder and half the garnish, stir. Adjust the seasoning.

To Serve

Remove to a dish, garnish with the remaining *Navrattan* and serve with *Pulao* or an Indian bread of your choice.

4 Green Chillies
2 g/⅓ Tsp Turmeric
10 g/2 Tsp Red Chilli powder
120 ml/½ cup Cream
3 g/½ Tsp Mace and Green Cardamom powder

Shahi Paste

20 g/2 Tbs Poppy seeds
40 g/¼ cup Almonds
40 g/¼ cup Cashewnuts
20 g/2 Tbs Melon seeds

Garnish

15 Pistachio
10 Almonds
10 Cashewnuts
10 Walnut halves
10 Pine Nuts
10 g/1 Tbs Raisins
10 g/1 Tbs Watermelon seeds
10 g/1 Tbs Melon seeds
10 g/1Tbs Sunflower seeds

Serves 4

Preparation time: 1:05 hours
Cooking time: 30 minutes

Kachchi Mirch ka Gosht

INGREDIENTS

1 kg/2¼ lb Leg of Spring Lamb

225 g/1 cup Yoghurt

10 g/4 Tsp Coriander seeds

10 g/1 Tbs Cumin seeds

5 g/1¾ Tsp Black Cumin seeds (Shahi Jeera)

5 g/1½ Tsp Black Peppercorns

Salt

150 g/¾ cup Ghee

Whole Garam Masala

- 5 Green Cardamom
- 1 Black Cardamom
- 5 Cloves
- 1 stick Cinnamon (1-inch)
- 1 Bay Leaf
- A pinch Mace

250 g/1½ cups Onions

20 g/2 Tbs Ginger

4 Green Chillies

10 g/1 Tbs Green Peppercorns

½ g/1 Tsp Saffron

200 ml/¾ cup Cream

5 g/1 Tsp Fennel powder

Serves 4

Preparation time: 1:05 hours

Cooking time: 1:20 hours

This is a delectable lamb dish, done in a creamy, but 'hot' green peppercorn curry, flavoured with saffron and the rarely used fennel.

Preparation

Lamb: Clean, debone and cut into 1-inch *boti*.

Whole Spices: Pound coriander seeds, cumin seeds, black cumin seeds and black peppercorns with a pestle.

Vegetables: Peel, wash and slice onions. Scrape, wash and chop ginger. Remove stems, wash, slit, deseed and chop green chillies.

Marination: Whisk the yoghurt in a large bowl, add the pounded spices and salt, leave the *boti* in this marinade for at least 30 minutes.

Saffron: Dissolve in 30 ml/2 Tbs of lukewarm water.

Cooking

Heat ghee in a *handi*, add whole garam masala and saute over medium heat until it begins to crackle. Add onions and saute until golden brown. Then add ginger, green chillies and green peppercorns, saute for a minute, add the marinated lamb. Alongwith the marinade, add water (approx 800 ml/3⅓ cup), bring to a boil, cover and simmer until tender. Now add saffron and cream, bring to a boil. Adjust the seasoning. Sprinkle fennel powder and stir.

To Serve

Remove to a dish and serve with an Indian bread of your choice or *Pulao*.

Khade Masale ka Gosht

An eye-pleasing and colourful delicacy, recommended for those with strong stomachs. The *Khada Masala* is really 'hot'.

INGREDIENTS
1 kg/2¼ lb Leg of Spring Lamb
150 g/¾ cup Ghee
Whole Garam Masala
5 Green Cardamom
1 Black Cardamom
5 Cloves
1 stick Cinnamon (1-inch)
1 Bay Leaf
A pinch Mace
250 g/1½ cups Onions
50 g/5 Tbs Garlic
50 g/5 Tbs Ginger
12 Green Chillies
5 g/2½ Tsp Coriander seeds
4 Whole Red Chillies
5 g/1½ Tsp Black Peppercorns
5 g/1 Tsp Cumin powder
5 g/1 Tsp Black Cumin powder
300 g/1⅓ cups Yoghurt
300 g/1⅓ cups Tomatoes
Salt
20 g/⅓ cup Coriander
2 Eggs

Serves 4

Preparation time: 1 hour

Cooking time: 1:30 hours

Preparation

Lamb: Clean, debone and cut into 1-inch *boti.*

Vegetables: Peel, wash and chop onions. Peel garlic, Scrape, wash and shred ginger. Remove stems, wash, slit, deseed and chop only 10 green chillies. Wash and chop tomatoes. Clean, wash and chop coriander.

Whole Spices: Pound coriander seeds, red chillies and black peppercorns with a pestle.

Yoghurt: Whisk in a bowl.

Eggs: Hard boil, cool, shell and cut into quarters.

Cooking

Heat ghee in a *handi*, add whole garam masala and saute over medium heat until it begins to crackle. Add onions and saute until golden brown. Then add garlic, ginger and chopped green chillies, stir for 2 minutes, add lamb, the pounded spices and the cumin. *Bhunno* until the *boti* are brown. Remove the *handi*, add yoghurt, return to heat and *bhunno* for 5 minutes. Now add tomatoes, *bhunno* until the fat leaves the masala, add water (approx 600 ml/2½ cups), bring to a boil, cover and simmer until lamb is cooked and the gravy becomes semi-dry. Adjust the seasoning. Sprinkle coriander and stir.

To Serve

Remove to a dish, garnish with slit green chillies and egg quarters. Serve with buttered *Naan**.

*See section on Breads.

Methi Murgh

INGREDIENTS

1 kg/2¼ lb Chicken (2 birds)
225 g/1 cup Yoghurt
Salt
100 g/½ cup Ghee
Whole Garam Masala
- 5 Green Cardamom
- 1 Black Cardamom
- 5 Cloves
- 1 stick Cinnamon (1-inch)
- 1 Bay Leaf
- A pinch Mace

300 g/1¾ cups Onions
30 g/3 Tbs Garlic
50 g/5 Tbs Ginger
6 Green Chillies
3 g/½ Tsp Turmeric
5 g/1 Tsp Coriander powder
5 g/1 Tsp Red Chilli powder
250 g/1 cup Tomatoes
10 g/2 Tbs Fenugreek (Kasoori Methi)
15 g/¼ cup Coriander

Serves 4

Preparation time: 45 minutes

Cooking time: 35 minutes

Note: When using fresh fenugreek (60 g/1 cup), clean, wash and immerse in salted water for 30 minutes to remove the bitterness. Drain and add to the marinade.

As with almost every delicacy, *Methi* (Fenugreek) *Murgh* tastes best with fresh fenugreek. The world's finest fenugreek comes from Qasur, in Pakistan. Dried fenugreek powder is now, in tribute, referred to as *Kasoori Methi* or fenugreek from Qasur. The 'spice' is an adequate replacement for the fresh vegetable.

Preparation

Chicken: Clean, remove the skin and cut each into 8 pieces.

Marination: Whisk yoghurt in a large bowl, add salt and leave the chicken in this marinade for at least 30 minutes.

Vegetables: Peel, wash and chop onions. Peel and chop garlic. Scrape, wash and chop 30 g/3 Tbs ginger, cut the rest into juliennes for garnish. Remove stems, wash, slit, deseed and chop green chillies. Wash and chop tomatoes. Clean, wash and chop coriander.

Oven: Preheat to 350°F.

Cooking

Heat ghee in a *handi,* add whole garam masala and saute over medium heat until it begins to crackle. Add onions and saute until golden brown. Then add chopped garlic, ginger and green chillies, stir for 2 minutes, add turmeric, coriander powder and red chillies—dissolved in 60 ml/¼ cup of water—and stir for 30 seconds. Now add tomatoes and *bhunno* until the fat leaves the masala, add the marinated chicken alongwith the marinade and water (approx 180 ml/ ¾ cup), bring to a boil, cover and simmer until chicken is almost cooked and the fat leaves the masala once again. Adjust the seasoning. Sprinkle fenugreek, ginger juliennes and coriander. Cover with a lid.

Finishing

Seal the *handi* with *atta* (whole-wheat dough) and put it on *dum* in the pre-heated oven for 15 minutes.

To Serve

Open the *handi* at the table and serve with an Indian bread of your choice.

Achaar Korma

A whiff of *Achaar Korma* is enough to tickle the palate. A creative endeavour that owes much to Rajasthani cuisine, this Chef's original is a semi-dry lamb done in a combination of mustard oil, mustard seeds, *kalonji* and jaggery—ingredients that go into the making of pickles.

INGREDIENTS

1 kg/2¼ lb Leg of Spring Lamb
3 g/½ Tsp Turmeric
Salt
20 ml/4 Tsp Mustard Oil
100 g/½ cup Ghee
125 g/¾ cup Onions
8 whole Red Chillies
3 g/1 Tsp Mustard seeds
5 Cloves
A pinch Asafoetida
5 g/1 Tsp Red Chilli powder
3 g/1 Tsp Cumin seeds
3 g/1 Tsp Kalonji
25 g/1 oz Jaggery
15 g/5 Tsp Ginger
10 cloves Garlic
30 ml/2 Tbs Lemon juice
225 g/1 cup Yoghurt

Serves 4

Preparation time: 30 minutes
Cooking time: 1:25 hours

Preparation

Lamb: Clean, debone and cut into 1-inch *boti.* Put in a *handi,* add turmeric, salt and water (approx 1.6 litres/ 6⅔ cups), bring to a boil, reduce to low heat, cover and simmer until tender. Drain and reserve the stock.

Vegetables: Peel, wash and slice onions, Scrape, wash and shred ginger. Peel and chop garlic.

Yoghurt: Whisk in a bowl.

Cooking

Heat mustard oil in a *handi* to smoking point (in order to remove the pungency from the oil), reduce to medium heat and add ghee. When the ghee becomes hot, add onions and saute until brown. Remove onions for garnish. In the same fat, add whole red chillies and fry until black. Remove and discard the chillies (the frying of chillies helps to incorporate the flavour in the fat.)

Reheat this 'chilli oil', add mustard seeds, cloves and asafoetida, saute until the seeds begin to crackle. Add the cooked lamb, red chilli powder, cumin seeds, *kalonji,* jaggery, ginger and garlic, *bhunno* for 2–3 minutes until the *boti* acquires a brownish hue. Then add the reserved stock and lemon juice, simmer for a minute. Remove the *handi,* add yoghurt, stir, return to heat and *bhunno* until fat leaves the masala. Adjust the seasoning (the *handi* is removed from fire to prevent yoghurt from curdling).

To Serve

Remove to a dish, garnish with fried onions and serve with an Indian bread of your choice.

Veg

Khumb Hara Dhania

INGREDIENTS

600 g/1⅓ lb Mushroom (fresh)

150 g/¾ cup Ghee

Whole Garam Masala

- 5 Green Cardamom
- 1 Black Cardamom
- 5 Cloves
- 1 stick Cinnamon (1-inch)
- 1 Bay Leaf
- A pinch Mace

150 g/⅔ cup boiled onion paste*

25 g/4 Tsp Ginger paste

25 g/4 Tsp Garlic paste

30 g/3 Tbs Ginger

4 Green Chillies

5 g/1 Tsp Red Chilli powder

3 g/1½ Tsp Coriander powder

350 g/1½ cups Yoghurt

Salt

60 g/1 cup Coriander

50 g/3 Tbs Cashewnut paste

*See section on Pastes.

Serves 4

Preparation time: 40 minutes

Cooking time: 8–10 minutes

A rich vegetarian curry which highlights the importance of fresh coriander in Indian cooking. In a significant departure, use is made of boiled onion paste, which helps improve the texture and taste of the gravy in many a delicacy.

Preparation

Mushroom: Trim, wash, blanch and drain.

Vegetables: Scrape, wash and chop two-thirds of the ginger, cut the rest into juliennes. Remove stems, wash, slit, deseed and chop green chillies. Clean, wash and chop coriander.

Yoghurt: Whisk in a bowl.

Cooking

Heat ghee in a *handi*, add whole garam masala and saute over medium heat until it begins to crackle. Add boiled onion paste, *bhunno* for 2 minutes, add the ginger and garlic pastes—dissolved in 60 ml/¼ cup of water—stir for a minute. Add chopped ginger and green chillies, stir for 30 seconds, add red chillies and coriander powder, stir for 30 seconds. Remove *handi*, add yoghurt and salt, return to heat, add water (approx 180 ml/¾ cup), bring to a boil and then simmer until the fat leaves the masala. Now add 45 g/¾ cup chopped coriander, simmer for a minute, add mushroom, simmer for 2 minutes, add cashewnut paste and bring to a boil. Adjust the seasoning.

To Serve

Remove to a dish, garnish with the remaining chopped coriander and ginger juliennes. Serve with plain boiled rice, *Pulao* or an Indian bread of your choice.

Boti Kebab
Adraki Chaamp
Malai Seekh

Sofyani Biryani
Subz Khada Masala
Shikampuri Kebab

Murgh Navrattan

Kale Moti Biryani

Aloo Chutneywale

Veg

An outstanding work of culinary art, potatoes stuffed with *paneer* and simmered in a tangy chutney, this original dish is certain to leave the palate tingling.

Preparation

Potatoes: Peel, wash and make barrel shape. Heat oil in a *kadhai* and deep fry over medium heat until three-fourths cooked and light brown in colour. Remove, cool and scoop out the centre leaving ¼-inch from the sides.

Filling: Grate *paneer*. Remove stems, wash, slit, deseed and finely chop green chillies. Scrape, wash and finely chop ginger. Crush cashewnuts. Mix all these ingredients in a bowl, add salt and stuff the scooped potatoes with the filling.

Chutney: Clean and wash coriander and mint. Peel and roughly chop the mangoes. Put coriander and mangoes in a blender and make a paste, add mint and make a fine paste.

Gravy: Whisk yoghurt in a bowl. Wash and chop tomatoes.

Cooking

Heat ghee in a *handi*, add boiled onion paste, stir over medium heat for 30 seconds, add the ginger and garlic pastes—dissolved in 60 ml/¼ cup of water—and stir until the fat leaves the masala. Add cumin, stir for a minute, add the *chutney* and red chillies, stir for 30 seconds. Then add yoghurt and water (approx 400 ml/1⅔ cups), bring to a boil, reduce to low heat and simmer until fat leaves the masala. Now add stuffed potatoes, simmer until cooked. Add tomatoes, simmer for a minute, add cashewnut paste and garam masala, stir and bring to a boil. Adjust the seasoning. Do not cover the *handi* while cooking.

To Serve

Remove to a dish and serve with an Indian bread of your choice.

INGREDIENTS

750 g/1⅔ lb Potatoes (medium size)
Groundnut Oil for frying

Filling

125 g/¼ lb Paneer*
4 Green Chillies
5 g/1½ Tsp Ginger
10 Cashewnuts
Salt

Chutney

150 g/2½ cup Coriander
30 g/1 oz Raw Mangoes
75 g/1¼ cups Mint

Gravy

100 g/½ cup Ghee
150 g/½ cup boiled Onion paste**
25 g/4 Tsp Ginger paste
25 g/4 Tsp Garlic paste
5 g/1¾ Tsp Cumin seeds
5 g/1 Tsp Red Chilli powder
300 g/1⅓ cup Yoghurt
100 g/½ cup Tomatoes
50 g/3 Tbs Cashewnut paste
10 g/2 Tsp Garam Masala
Salt

*See section on Milk.
**See section on Pastes.

Serves 4
Preparation time: 1:10 hours
Cooking time: 25–30 minutes

'Raspberry' Mattar

INGREDIENTS

350 g/¾ lb Green Peas

Raspberries

350 g/¾ lb Paneer*
4 Green Chillies
10 g/1 Tbs Ginger
1 g/2 Tsp Saffron
60 ml/¼ cup Milk
3 g/½ Tsp Red Chilli powder
Salt
50 g/⅔ cup Cornflour
Groundnut Oil for frying

Gravy

120 g/⅔ cup Ghee
150 g/⅔ cup Boiled Onion paste**
15 g/2½ Tsp Ginger paste
15 g/2½ Tsp Garlic paste
10 g/1 Tbs Ginger
4 Green Chillies
5 g/1 Tsp Red Chilli powder
5 g/1 Tsp Coriander powder
100 g/3½ oz fresh Tomato Puree
225 g/1 cup Yoghurt
50 g/3 Tbs Cashewnut paste
60 ml/¼ cup Cream
5 g/1 Tsp Garam Masala
Salt
20 g/⅓ cup Coriander

*See section on Milk.
**See section on Pastes.

Serves 4
Preparation time: 1:20 hours
Cooking time: 10–12 minutes

A Chef's original vegetarian delight of *paneer* balls—'raspberries'—and peas, cooked in a mild and rich gravy, which penetrates the 'raspberries' to make them 'juicy' like the fruit.

Preparation

Green Peas: Boil and drain.

Raspberries: Mash *paneer* in a bowl. Remove stems, wash, slit, deseed and finely chop green chillies. Scrape, wash and finely chop ginger. Mix these ingredients with *paneer*. Boil milk, add saffron, reduce by half and then pour on half the reduced saffron milk on the *paneer* mixture. Add red chillies and salt, mix well. Make small raspberry-size balls and dust evenly with cornflour. Heat oil in a *kadhai* and deep fry the 'raspberries' over medium heat until golden brown.

Gravy: Scrape, wash and chop ginger. Remove stems, wash, slit, deseed and chop green chillies. Clean, wash and chop coriander. Whisk yoghurt in a bowl.

Cooking

Heat ghee in a *handi*, add boiled onion paste, ginger paste and garlic paste, stir over medium heat for 2 minutes. Add ginger and green chillies, stir for 2 minutes, add red chillies and coriander powder, *bhunno* until fat leaves the masala. Then add tomato puree, bring to a boil, reduce to low heat, simmer until fat leaves the masala again, add yoghurt and stir constantly until fat leaves the masala a third time. Now add green peas, boil for 2–3 minutes, add cashewnut paste and cream mixed with the remaining saffron milk and bring to a boil. Reduce to medium heat, add the 'raspberries', sprinkle garam masala, bring to a boil and remove immediately (Make sure that the 'raspberries' are boiled just once and stirred very gently or else they will crumble). Adjust the seasoning.

To Serve

Gently transfer to a dish, garnish with coriander and serve with an Indian bread of your choice.

Kale Moti Biryani

Veg

Kale Moti—black pearls—*Biryani* is truly a jewel in this collection of *handi* delicacies. Bengal gram simmered in gravy and *basmati* rice, layer upon layer, make for a royal treat.

Preparation

Rice: Pick, wash in running water and soak for 30 minutes. Drain.

Bengal Gram: Soak overnight in a pan. Drain. Replenish with fresh water, add salt and soda bi-carb and boil until cooked. Drain and keep aside.

Gravy: Whisk yoghurt in a bowl. Wash and chop tomatoes. Peel, wash and cut potatoes into 3/4-inch cubes. Remove stems, wash, slit, deseed and chop green chillies.

Garnish: Clean, wash and chop coriander and mint. Scrape, wash and cut ginger into juliennes. Remove stems, wash, slit and deseed green chillies. Wash and cut tomatoes into quarters. Whisk yoghurt in a bowl, add garam masala, cardamom powder and half saffron. Dissolve the remaining saffron in warm milk.

Oven: Pre-heat to 350°F.

Cooking

To prepare rice, boil water (approx 1 litre/4 cups) and milk together in a *handi,* add whole garam masala, salt and rice, cook until almost done (7–8 minutes).

To prepare Bengal gram, heat ghee in a *handi,* add ginger paste, garlic paste, red chillies and turmeric—all dissolved in 50 ml/3 Tbs of water—and saute over medium heat for two minutes. Remove *handi,* add yoghurt, tomatoes, potatoes and green chillies, return to heat and stir constantly until the gravy becomes thick and the fat leaves the masala. Then add the boiled gram and simmer until the gravy coats the gram and potatoes. Adjust the seasoning.

INGREDIENTS

250 g/2¼ cups Basmati Rice
800 ml/3⅓ cups Milk
Whole Garam Masala
- 5 Green Cardamom
- 1 Black Cardamom
- 5 Cloves
- 1 stick Cinnamon (1-inch)
- 1 Bay Leaf
- A pinch Mace

Salt

Kale Moti

250 g/1¼ cups Bengal Gram
Salt
A pinch Soda bi-carb
100 g/½ cup Ghee
15 g/2½ Tsp Ginger paste
10 g/1¾ Tsp Garlic paste
3 g/½ Tsp Red Chilli powder
2 g/⅓ Tsp Turmeric
200 g/¾ cup Yoghurt
125 g/½ cup Tomatoes
125 g/5 oz Potatoes
3 Green Chillies

Garnish

30 g/½ cup Coriander
20 g/⅓ cup Mint
15 g/4½ Tsp Ginger
6 Green Chillies
100 g/3½ oz Tomatoes
25 g/4 Tbs Fried Onions
100 g/½ cup Yoghurt
5 g/1 Tsp Garam Masala
A pinch Green Cardamom powder
1 g/2 Tsp Saffron
60 ml/¼ cup Milk

Serves 4

Preparation time: 45 minutes

Cooking time: 1:25 hours

Assembling

In the *handi* with the Bengal gram, sprinkle garnish of coriander, mint, ginger, green chillies, tomatoes and fried onions and pour spiced yoghurt on top. Spread rice evenly over the garnished gram. Sprinkle saffron milk, place a moist cloth on top, cover with a lid and seal with *atta*-dough.

Finishing

Put the sealed *handi* on *dum* in the pre-heated oven for 15–20 minutes.

To Serve

Break the seal, remove the moist cloth and shift the rice from one side (just enough to remove the cooked gram). Make a bed of gram on the serving dish, spread the rice on top and serve.

Kadhai Jhinga

Ajwain-flavoured prawns done in an abundance of tomatoes, as is most *kadhai* cooking, *Kadhai Jhinga* is a colourful dish.

INGREDIENTS

750 g/1⅔ lb Prawns (medium size)
90 g/7 Tbs Ghee
160 g/1 cup Onions
20 g/3½ Tsp Garlic paste
8 Whole Red Chillies
4 g/2 Tsp Coriander seeds
5 g/2 Tsp Ajwain
750 g/3⅓ cups Tomatoes
40 g/¼ cup Ginger
6 Green Chillies
Salt
10 g/2 Tsp Garam masala
5 g/1½ Tsp Fenugreek (Kasoori Methi)
60 ml/4 Tbs Lemon juice
20 g/⅓ cup Coriander

Serves 4

Preparation time: 40–45 minutes

Cooking time: 20 minutes

Preparation

Prawns: Shell, devein, wash and pat dry.

Vegetables: Peel, wash and chop onions. Wash and chop tomatoes. Scrape, wash and chop ginger. Remove stems, wash, slit, deseed and chop green chillies. Clean, wash and chop coriander.

Whole Spices: Pound red chillies and coriander seeds with a pestle.

Cooking

Heat ghee in a *kadhai,* add onions and saute over medium heat until golden brown. Add garlic paste, stir for 15 seconds, add the pounded spices and *ajwain,* stir for 30 seconds. Then add tomatoes, bring to a boil, add three-fourths of the ginger and green chillies, reduce to medium heat and *bhunno* until fat leaves the masala. Now add prawns and continue to *bhunno* until fat leaves the gravy and the prawns are cooked (In case there is some liquid left, reduce the gravy over high heat). Adjust the seasoning. Sprinkle garam masala, fenugreek and lemon juice, stir.

To Serve

Remove to a dish, garnish with the remaining ginger and coriander and serve with an Indian bread of your choice.

Kadhai Murgh

INGREDIENTS

1 kg/2¼ lb Chicken (2 birds)
90 g/7 Tbs Ghee
20 g/3½ Tsp Garlic paste
8 Whole Red Chillies
6 g/1 Tbs Coriander seeds
1 kg/2¼ lb Tomatoes
4 Green Chillies
40 g/¼ cup Ginger
30 g/½ cup Coriander
10 g/2 Tsp Garam Masala
4 g/1 Tsp Fenugreek (Kasoori Methi)
Salt

Serves 4

Preparation time: 45 minutes
Cooking time: 20–22 minutes

Kadhai cooking originated with this 'hot' chicken delicacy, cooked in tomatoes. The predominant flavour: fenugreek and coriander.

Preparation

Chicken: Clean, remove the skin and cut each into 8 pieces.

Vegetables: Wash and chop tomatoes. Remove stems, wash, slit, deseed and chop green chillies. Scrape, wash and chop ginger. Clean, wash and chop coriander.

Whole Spices: Pound red chillies and coriander seeds with a pestle.

Cooking

Heat ghee in a *kadhai,* add garlic paste and saute over medium heat until light brown. Add the pounded spices, stir for 30 seconds, add tomatoes, bring to a boil, add green chillies, three-fourths of the ginger and one-third of the chopped coriander, reduce the heat and simmer for 4–5 minutes. Then add chicken, bring to a boil, simmer, stirring occasionally, until fat leaves the masala, the gravy becomes thick and chicken is tender. Sprinkle garam masala and fenugreek, stir for 2 minutes. Adjust the seasoning.

To Serve

Remove to a dish, garnish with the remaining ginger and coriander, serve with an Indian bread of your choice.

Narial ka Gosht

Lamb cooked with coconut and flavoured with fennel—a rare aromatic combination.

Preparation

Lamb: Clean, debone and cut into 3/4-inch chunks.

Vegetables: Peel, wash and slice onions. Scrape, wash and cut ginger into juliennes. Remove stems, wash, slit, deseed and chop green chillies. Wash and finely chop tomatoes.

Coconut: Remove the brown skin and grate.

Curry Leaves: Wash and dry. Heat oil in a pan and deep fry, Remove.

Whole Red Chillies: Cut into juliennes for garnish.

Cooking

Heat ghee in a *kadhai,* add whole garam masala and saute over medium heat until it begins to crackle. Add garlic, stir for 15 seconds, add onions and saute until light brown, add ginger and green chillies, continue to saute until onions become golden brown. Then add red chillies, coconut (reserve a little for garnish) and the curry leaves, saute for a minute, add tomatoes and *bhunno* until fat leaves the masala. Now add the lamb chunks, *bhunno* for 5 minutes, add water (approx 800 ml/3⅓ cups), bring to a boil, cover and simmer until tender and the liquid has evaporated. Adjust the seasoning. Sprinkle fennel powder and stir.

To Serve

Remove to a dish, garnish with red chilli juliennes and the reserved coconut, serve with an Indian bread of your choice.

INGREDIENTS

1 kg/2¼ lb Leg of Spring Lamb

150 g/¾ cup Ghee

Whole Garam Masala

- 5 Green Cardamom
- 1 Black Cardamom
- 5 Cloves
- 1 stick Cinnamon (1-inch)
- 1 Bay Leaf
- A pinch Mace

20 g/3½ Tsp Garlic paste

400 g/2⅓ cups Onions

10 g/1 Tbs Ginger

6 Green Chillies

5 g/1 Tsp Red Chilli powder

150 g/2 cups Coconut

16 Curry Leaves

Groundnut Oil to fry

350 g/1½ cups Tomatoes

Salt

5 g/1 Tsp Fennel powder

4 Whole Red Chillies

Serves 4

Preparation time: 40 minutes

Cooking time: 1:15 hours

Kadhai Gosht Hussainee

INGREDIENTS

450 g/1 lb Leg of Spring Lamb

450 g/1 lb Lamb Liver

225 g/1 cup Yoghurt

5 g/1 Tsp Red Chilli powder

5 g/1 Tsp Coriander powder

Salt

150 g/¾ cup Ghee

200 g/1¼ cups Onions

30 g/3 Tbs Ginger

15 g/4½ Tsp Garlic

3 Green Chillies

5 g/1¾ Tsp Cumin seeds

5 g/1¾ Tsp Mustard seeds

5 g/2½ Tsp Coriander seeds

50 g/3 Tbs Almond paste

50 ml/3 Tbs Cream

½ g/1 Tsp Saffron

30 ml/2 Tbs Milk

3 g/1 Tsp Fenugreek (Kasoori Methi)

3 g/½ Tsp Green Cardamom powder

50 g/2 oz Capsicum

50 g/¼ cup Tomatoes

10 g/2 Tbs Coriander

Serves 4

Preparation time: 1 hour

Cooking time: 45-50 minutes

This is a Chefs original—a mild *kadhai* dish, which makes it unique. It is one of the few recipes of the genre which make use of yoghurt, almond paste and cream.

Preparation

Lamb: Clean, debone and cut into ¾-inch chunks.

Lamb Liver: Clean and cut into ¾-inch chunks.

Marination: Whisk yoghurt in a large bowl, add red chilli powder, coriander powder and salt, mix well. Leave the lamb chunks in this marinade for at least 30 minutes.

Vegetables: Clean, wash and slice three-fourths of the onions, cut the rest into dices. Scrape, wash and chop ginger. Peel and chop garlic. Remove stems, wash, slit and deseed green chillies. Remove stems, cut into halves, deseed and dice capsicum. Wash and dice tomatoes. Clean, wash and chop coriander.

Coriander Seeds: Pound with a pestle.

Saffron: Dissolve in warm milk.

Cooking

Heat ghee in a *kadhai,* add sliced onions and saute over medium heat until light brown. Add ginger, garlic and green chillies, continue to saute until onions become golden brown, add cumin, mustard seeds and pounded coriander, stir for 15 seconds, add the marinated lamb, alongwith the marinade, add water (approx 1 litre/4 cups), bring to a boil, cover and simmer until the chunks are three-fourths cooked. Then add liver and simmer until lamb is tender and the liquid has evaporated. Now add almond paste, dissolved in cream, bring to a boil, reduce to medium heat, add saffron, stir, sprinkle fenugreek and cardamom powder, stir. Adjust the seasoning. Add dices of onions and capsicum, stir for 2 minutes, add tomatoes and stir for a minute.

To Serve

Remove to a dish, garnish with coriander and serve with an Indian bread of your choice.

Dahi ka Kheema

A mince delicacy with a difference: cooked with yoghurt and flavoured with the unusual combination of cloves and cinnamon powder.

INGREDIENTS

1 kg/2¼ lb Lamb Mince
150 g/¾ cup Ghee
Whole Garam Masala
- 5 Green Cardamom
- 1 Black Cardamom
- 5 Cloves
- 1 stick Cinnamon (1-inch)
- 1 Bay Leaf
- A pinch Mace

200 g/1¼ cups Onions
25 g/4 Tsp Ginger paste
25 g/4 Tsp Garlic paste
10 g/2 Tsp Red Chilli powder
300 g/1⅓ cups Yoghurt
3 g/½ Tsp Cinnamon powder
2 g/⅓ Tsp Clove powder
Salt
20 g/⅓ cup Coriander
15 Green Chillies
Groundnut Oil to fry

Serves 4

Preparation time: 25 minutes
Cooking time: 20–22 minutes

Preparation

Vegetables: Peel, wash and finely chop onions. Clean, wash and chop coriander.

Yoghurt: Whisk in a bowl with cinnamon and clove powder.

Green Chillies: Remove stems, wash, slit and deseed. Heat oil in a pan and deep fry for 15–20 seconds. Remove.

Cooking

Heat ghee in a *kadhai,* add whole garam masala and saute over medium heat until it begins to crackle. Add onions, saute until brown, add the ginger and garlic pastes, dissolved in 60 ml/¼ cup of water, stir for 30 seconds, add red chillies and stir for 1½ minutes. Then add the mince and *bhunno* until dry and the liquid has evaporated. Now add the spiced yoghurt, bring to a boil, cover and simmer until the lamb is cooked. Adjust the seasoning. Sprinkle half each of the coriander and green chillies, stir.

To Serve

Remove to a dish, garnish with the remaining coriander and green chillies, serve with an Indian bread of your choice.

Veg

Laziz Khumb

INGREDIENTS

600 g/1⅓ lb Mushroom (fresh)
150 g/¾ cup Ghee
100 g/1 cup Cabbage
20 g/3½ Tsp Garlic paste
4 Whole Red Chillies
5 g/2½ Tsp Coriander seeds
750 g/3⅓ cups Tomatoes
4 Green Chillies
30 g/3 Tbs Ginger
20 g/⅓ cup Coriander
100 g/⅔ cup Onions
40 g/1½ oz Capsicum
Salt
10 g/2 Tsp Garam Masala

Serves 4

Preparation time: 40 minutes
Cooking time: 18 minutes

It is inconceivable not to create something for the vegetarians. *Laziz Khumb* is a combination of mushroom (*khumb*), cabbage and capsicum.

Preparation

Mushroom: Slice off earthy base of the stalk, cut into quarters and wash just prior to cooking. Heat 20 g/5 Tsp ghee in a pan and saute over medium heat for 4–5 minutes. Drain.

Cabbage: Wash and shred. Heat 20 g/5 Tsp ghee in a *kadhai* and saute over medium heat until the liquid has evaporated. Remove cabbage and reserve the ghee.

Remaining Vegetables: Wash and chop tomatoes. Remove stems, wash, slit, deseed and chop green chillies. Scrape, wash and chop ginger. Clean, wash and chop coriander. Peel, wash and slice onions. Remove stems, cut capsicum into halves, deseed and make juliennes.

Whole Spices: Pound red chillies and coriander seeds with a pestle.

Cooking

Reheat the reserved ghee (plus 50 g/¼ cup) in a *kadhai,* add garlic paste and stir over medium heat for 20 seconds. Add the pounded spices, stir for 30 seconds, add tomatoes and *bhunno* until fat leaves the masala. Then add green chillies, ginger and half the coriander, stir.

Heat the remaining ghee in a separate *kadhai,* add onions and saute over medium heat until transparent. Add capsicum and saute for 1½–2 minutes. Transfer the masala from the first *kadhai,* add mushrooms and cabbage, stir constantly for 3–4 minutes. Adjust the seasoning. Sprinkle garam masala and the remaining coriander, stir.

To Serve

Remove to a dish and serve with an Indian bread of your choice.

Makki-Khumb Masala

Veg

A colourful maize and mushroom combination cooked with fresh herbs. In a significant departure from traditional *kadhai* cooking, this vegetarian delicacy—another chef's original—is prepared without pounded spices and fenugreek.

INGREDIENTS

250 g/9 oz Corn
450 g/1 lb Mushroom (fresh)
150 g/¾ cup Ghee
200 g/1¼ cups Onions
30 g/3 Tbs Ginger
4 Green Chillies
25 g/4 Tsp Ginger paste
25 g/4 Tsp Garlic paste
10 g/2 Tsp Red Chilli powder
450 g/1 lb Tomatoes
Salt
30 g/1 oz Capsicum
10 g/2 Tsp Garam Masala

Serves 4

Preparation time: 6 hours
Cooking time: 20–22 minutes

Preparation

Corn: Soak the niblets in a pan full of water for 3–4 hours. Then boil until tender. If canned niblets are available, drain the brine and pat dry.

Mushroom: Slice off earthy base of the stalk and wash just prior to cooking.

Vegetables: Peel, wash and chop onions. Scrape, wash and chop ginger. Remove stems, wash, slit, deseed and chop green chillies. Wash and chop 400 g/14 oz tomatoes, cut the rest into quarters. Remove stems, wash, cut capsicum into halves, deseed and make dices.

Cooking

Heat ghee in a *kadhai,* add onions and saute over medium heat until golden brown. Add ginger and green chillies, stir for 15–20 seconds, add ginger paste, garlic paste and red chillies-all dissolved in 60 ml/¼ cup of water and stir for a minute. Then add tomatoes, *bhunno* until fat leaves the masala, add corn and mushrooms, bring to a boil and simmer until the liquid has evaporated. Adjust the seasoning. Now add capsicum, stir for a minute, add the remaining tomatoes and stir. Sprinkle garam masala and stir.

To Serve

Remove to a dish and serve with an Indian bread of your choice.

Veg

Kadhai Paneer

INGREDIENTS

600 g/1⅓ lb Paneer*
40 g/3 Tbs Ghee
25 g/1 oz Capsicum
5 whole Red Chillies
5 g/2½ Tsp Coriander seeds
15 g/4 Tsp Ginger
550 ml/19 oz Kadhai Gravy**
A pinch Fenugreek (Kasoori Methi)
5 g/1 Tsp Garam Masala
15 g/¼ cup Coriander
Salt

*See section on Milk.
**See section on Gravies.

Serves 4

Preparation time: 10 minutes (Plus time taken for Kadhai Gravy)

Cooking time: 8–10 minutes

The *piece de resistance* among vegetarian recipes in the *kadhai* genre of cooking, *Kadhai Paneer* is chilli-hot, semi-dry and colourful.

Preparation

Paneer: Cut into fingers.

Vegetables: Remove stems, wash, cut capsicum into halves, deseed and make juliennes. Scrape, wash and chop two-thirds of the ginger, cut the rest into juliennes for garnish. Clean, wash and chop coriander.

Whole Spices: Pound red chillies and coriander seeds with a pestle.

Cooking

Heat ghee in a *kadhai,* add capsicum and saute over medium heat for 30 seconds. Add the pounded spices and chopped ginger, stir for 30 seconds. Then add *Kadhai Gravy,* bring to a boil and *bhunno* until fat leaves the masala. Now add *paneer* and stir gently for 2–3 minutes. Sprinkle fenugreek and garam masala, stir. Adjust the seasoning.

To Serve

Remove to a dish, garnish with ginger juliennes and coriander, serve with *Naan, Paratha* or *Phulka.* ***

***See section on Breads.

Kadhai Chholey

Veg

White gram, cooked in the *kadhai,* is unquestionably the most versatile delicacy in the north of India. A veritable one-dish meal, it can be served at any time of day or night, for breakfast or high tea, as an entrée or a snack.

INGREDIENTS

250 g/1¼ cups White Gram

A pinch Soda bi-carb

Salt

100 g/½ cup Ghee

30 g/5 Tsp Garlic paste

8 whole Red Chillies

10 g/5 Tsp Coriander seeds

750 g/3⅓ cups Tomatoes

4 Green Chillies

40 g/¼ cup Ginger

30 g/½ cup Coriander

30 ml/2 Tbs Lemon juice

10 g/2 Tsp Garam masala

3 g/¾ Tsp Fenugreek (Kasoori Methi)

Serves 4

Preparation time: 45 minutes

Cooking time: 20–22 minutes

Preparation

White Gram: Pick, wash, soak overnight in a *handi,* drain and replenish with fresh water. Add soda bi-carb and salt, boil until tender. Drain.

Vegetables: Wash and chop tomatoes. Remove stems, wash, slit, deseed and chop green chillies. Scrape, wash and chop ginger. Clean, wash and chop coriander.

Whole Spices: Pound red chillies and coriander seeds with a pestle.

Cooking

Heat ghee in a *kadhai,* add garlic paste and stir over medium heat for a minute. Add the pounded spices and stir for 15–20 seconds. Then add tomatoes, bring to a boil, add green chillies, three-fourths of the ginger and one-third of the chopped coriander, reduce to medium heat and *bhunno* until fat leaves the masala. Now add the boiled white gram and *bhunno* for another 5 minutes. Adjust the seasoning. Sprinkle lemon juice, garam masala and fenugreek, stir.

To Serve

Remove to a dish, garnish with the remaining coriander and ginger, serve with *Pooris, Bhaturas**, even slices of bread.

*See section on Breads.

Veg Dal Kabila

A tomato-based lentil delicacy, remarkable for its fresh taste—thanks to the abundant use of coriander and ginger.

INGREDIENTS
250 g/1¼ cups Urad dal
50 g/¼ cup Ghee
30 g/5 Tsp Garlic paste
8 Whole Red Chillies
10 g/5 Tsp Coriander seeds
750 g/3⅓ cups Tomatoes
30 g/½ cup Coriander
4 Green Chillies
25 g/7½ Tsp Ginger
Salt
100 g/7 Tbs Butter
10 g/2 Tsp Garam Masala
5 g/1¼ Tsp Fenugreek (Kasoori Methi)
30 ml/2 Tbs Lemon juice

Serves 4

Preparation time: 2:45 hours

Cooking time: 15 minutes

Preparation

Lentil: Pick, wash in running water and soak in a *handi* for 2 hours. Drain, replenish with fresh water (approx 3 litres/ 12½ cups) and boil until tender. Drain.

Vegetables: Wash and chop tomatoes. Clean, wash and chop coriander. Remove stems, wash, slit, deseed and chop green chillies. Scrape, wash and chop ginger.

Whole Spices: Pound red chillies and coriander seeds with a pestle.

Cooking

Heat ghee in a *kadhai,* add garlic paste and saute over medium heat until golden brown. Add the pounded spices and stir for 15–20 seconds. Then add tomatoes, bring to a boil, add two-thirds of the chopped coriander, green chillies and ginger, reduce to medium heat and *bhunno* until fat leaves the masala, add the boiled lentil and *bhunno* for 5 minutes. Adjust the seasoning. Now add butter, stir, sprinkle garam masala, fenugreek, lemon juice and the remaining coriander, stir for 5 minutes, mashing the lentil with the back of the ladle occasionally.

To Serve

Remove to a dish and serve with an Indian bread of your choice.

Tawa

Jhinga Masala

INGREDIENTS

1 kg/2¼ lb Prawns (medium size)

75 g/6 Tbs Ghee

5 g/2 Tsp Ajwain

200 g/1¼ cups Onions

4 Green Chillies

10 g/1 Tbs Ginger

5 g/1 Tsp Red Chilli powder

20 g/⅓ cup Coriander

300 ml/11 oz Makhani Gravy*

Salt

30 ml/2 Tbs Lemon juice

5 g/1 Tsp Garam Masala

*See section on Gravies.

Serves 4

Preparation time: 20 minutes (Plus time taken for Makhani Gravy)

Cooking time: 8–9 minutes

Ajwain elevates this prawn delicacy from the ordinary to a gourmet's delight. The ease of preparation makes it all the more attractive.

Preparation

Prawns: Shell, devein, wash and pat dry.

Vegetables: Peel, wash and chop onions. Remove stems, wash, slit, deseed and chop green chillies. Scrape, wash and chop ginger. Clean, wash and chop coriander.

Cooking

Heat ghee on a large *tawa,* add prawns and saute over medium heat for 2–3 minutes. Remove from the centre of the *tawa* and place on the periphery. To the same ghee, add *ajwain* and when it begins to crackle, add onions, green chillies and ginger, saute for 3 minutes. Return the prawns to the centre, add red chillies and two-thirds of the coriander, *bhunno* for a minute. Add the *Makhani Gravy* and *bhunno* until prawns are cooked and napped in the gravy. Adjust the seasoning. Sprinkle lemon juice, garam masala and the remaining coriander, stir.

To Serve

Remove to a dish and serve with an Indian bread of your choice.

Samudri Khazana Tak-a-Tak

INGREDIENTS

250 g/9 oz Prawns (medium size)
250 g/9 oz Crab Meat
250 g/9 oz Fish
100 g/3½ oz Seafood Mince
75 g/6 Tbs Ghee
5 g/2 Tsp Ajwain
100 g/⅔ cup Onions
10 g/1 Tbs Ginger
4 Green Chillies
8 Whole Red Chillies
5 g/2½ Tsp Coriander seeds
150 g/1 cup Potatoes
300 ml/11 oz Kadhai Gravy*
Salt
30 ml/2 Tbs Lemon juice
5 g/1 Tsp Garam Masala
20 g/⅓ cup Coriander

*See section on Gravies.

Serves 4

Preparation time: 40 minutes (Plus time taken for Kadhai Gravy)

Cooking time: 9–10 minutes

This bountiful seafood delight owes its cute name to the sound that metal spatulae make (takka-tak, takka-tak ...) during the process of cooking.

Preparation

Seafood: Shell, devein, wash and pat dry prawns. Take a variety of non-fatty fish of your choice, remove scales, wash, debone and cut into 1-inch chunks. Use the trimmings to make the seafood mince.

Vegetables: Peel, wash and chop onions. Scrape, wash and chop ginger. Remove stems, wash, slit, deseed and chop green chillies. Boil, cool, peel and roughly cut potatoes. Clean, wash and chop coriander.

Whole Spices: Pound red chillies and coriander seeds with a pestle.

Cooking

Heat ghee on a large *tawa,* add prawns, crab and fish, saute over medium heat for 2 minutes. Remove from the centre of the *tawa* and place on the periphery. To the same ghee, add *ajwain* and when it begins to crackle, add onions, ginger and green chillies, reduce to low heat and saute for 2–3 minutes. Add the pounded spices and seafood mince, saute for 30 seconds, return prawns, crab and fish to the centre and add potatoes. With two metal spatulae, held vertically, chop the seafood and potatoes. After every few strokes, stir and fold the mixture. Now add the *Kadhai Gravy* and *bhunno* for 2–3 minutes until the gravy becomes thick. Adjust the seasoning. Sprinkle lemon juice, garam masala and chopped coriander, stir.

To Serve

Remove to a dish and serve with an Indian bread of your choice.

Murgh Tawa Masala

INGREDIENTS

1 kg/2¼ lb Chicken (2 birds)
30 g/5 Tsp Ginger paste
30 g/5 Tsp Garlic paste
Salt
75 ml/5 Tbs Groundnut Oil
100 g/½ cup Ghee
160 g/1 cup Onions
15 g/4½ Tsp Ginger
6 Green Chillies
5 g/1 Tsp Red Chilli powder
10 g/1 Tbs Black Peppercorns
300 ml/11 oz Makhani Gravy*
5 g/1 Tsp Garam Masala
20 g/⅓ cup Coriander

*See section on Gravies.

Serves 4

Preparation time: 25 minutes (Plus time taken for Makhani Gravy)
Cooking time: 15 minutes

A chicken meal with a difference—done in a smooth sauce with crushed peppercorns.

Preparation

Chicken: Clean, remove the skin and cut each into 16 pieces.

Marination: Mix the ginger paste, garlic paste and salt with groundnut oil in a tray and rub the chicken pieces with this marinade. Keep aside for at least 30 minutes.

Vegetables: Clean, wash and chop onions. Scrape, wash and chop ginger. Remove stems, wash, slit, deseed and chop green chillies. Clean, wash and chop coriander.

Peppercorns: Crush with a pestle or in a pepper-mill.

Cooking

Heat ghee on a large *tawa,* add the marinated chicken, along with the marinade, and stir over medium heat for 10 minutes. Remove from the centre of the *tawa* and place on the periphery. To the same ghee, add onions, ginger, green chillies, red chillies and black peppercorns, stir for a minute. Return the chicken to the centre and *bhunno* for 2 minutes (sprinkle a little water if the chicken tends to stick). Add *Makhani Gravy* and *bhunno* until chicken is tender and napped in the gravy. Sprinkle garam masala and coriander, stir. Adjust the seasoning.

To Serve

Remove to a dish and serve with an Indian bread of your choice.

Murgh Galouti

A galouti is a ball made from fine mince of any meat. *Murgh Galouti* is a delicacy of chicken balls simmered in a cream-based *Shahi* (royal) *Gravy.*

INGREDIENTS

Galouti

675 g/1½ lb Chicken (finely minced)

10 g/1 Tbs Ginger

3 Green Chillies

20 g/⅓ cup Coriander

5 g/1 Tsp Garam Masala

Salt

50 g/3 Tbs Cashewnut paste

50 g/⅔ cup Cornflour

Groundnut Oil for frying

Masala

100 g/½ cup Ghee

160 g/1 cup Onions

10 g/1 Tbs Ginger

3 Green Chillies

2 g/⅓ Tsp Turmeric

300 ml/11 oz Shahi Gravy*

90 ml/6 Tbs Cream

10 g/2 Tbs Coriander

2 g/⅓ Tsp Nutmeg and Mace powder

Salt

*See section on Gravies.

Serves 4

Preparation time: 20 minutes (Plus time taken for Shahi Gravy)

Cooking time: 5–6 minutes

Preparation

Galouti: Scrape, wash and finely chop ginger. Remove stems, wash, slit, deseed and finely chop green chillies. Clean, wash and chop coriander. Mix the vegetables with the chicken mince, add garam masala, salt and cashewnut paste, knead well. Divide the mixture into 24 equal portions to make *galouti* of 1-inch diameter. Roll in cornflour.

Heat oil in a *kadhai* and deep fry *galouti* until golden brown. Remove.

Masala: Peel, wash and chop onions. Scrape, wash and chop ginger. Remove stems, wash, slit, deseed and chop green chillies. Clean, wash and chop coriander.

Cooking

Heat ghee on a large *tawa,* add onions, ginger and green chillies, saute over medium heat for 2–3 minutes. Add turmeric, stir for 15 seconds, add *Shahi Gravy* and *bhunno* for a minute. Then add the *galouti* and stir for a minute with extreme care as they are likely to crumble. Now add cream and stir gently for a minute. Sprinkle coriander and nutmeg and mace powder, stir gently. Adjust the seasoning.

To Serve

Gently remove *galouti* to a dish and pour on the gravy. Serve with an Indian bread of your choice.

Gosht Pasanda *Paya Ras*

INGREDIENTS

1.2 kg/2⅔ lb Leg of Spring Lamb
25 g/4 Tsp Ginger paste
25 g/4 Tsp Garlic paste
10 g/2 Tsp Garam masala
5 g/1 Tsp Red Chilli powder
Salt
75 ml/5 Tbs Groundnut Oil

Paya Ras

8 Lamb Trotters
30 g/1 oz Carrots
40 g/¼ cup Onions
Whole Garam Masala
- 5 Green Cardamom
- 1 Black Cardamom
- 5 Cloves
- 1 stick Cinnamon (1-inch)
- 1 Bay Leaf
- A pinch Mace

Masala

100 g/½ cup Ghee
100 g/⅔ cup Onions
10 g/1 Tbs Ginger
3 Green Chillies
Salt
5 g/1 Tsp Garam Masala
30 ml/2 Tbs Lemon juice
20 g/⅓ cup Coriander

Serves 4

Preparation time: 2 hours
Cooking time: 10–12 minutes

A delicacy of lamb *picatta,* napped in a masala rich in herbs and spices, simmered in *paya ras* (trotter stock) and cooked on a *tawa.* It is light and its freshness is guaranteed to stimulate the palate.

Preparation

Lamb: Clean, debone and cut into 1½-inch chunks. Flatten the chunks into ⅛-inch thick *picatta—pasanda.*

Marination: Mix the ginger and garlic pastes, garam masala, red chillies and salt with the groundnut oil and rub the *picatta* with this marinade. Keep aside for at least 1½-hours.

Paya Ras: Clean, wash and blanch trotters in a large pan. Drain. Peel, wash and dice carrots. Peel, wash and chop onions. Add the carrots and onions to the trotters, along with whole garam masala, and refill the pan with 4 litres/16⅔ cups of water. Bring to a boil, cover and simmer for 2 hours. Discard the trotters. Strain the stock, skim off the fat and allow it to simmer on the side.

Masala: Peel, wash and chop onions. Scrape, wash and chop ginger. Remove stems, wash, slit, deseed and chop green chillies. Clean, wash and chop coriander.

Cooking

Heat ghee on a large *tawa,* saute the marinated *pasanda* over low heat for approximately five minutes. Remove from the centre of the *tawa* and place on the periphery. To the same ghee add onions, ginger and green chillies, saute over medium heat for 2–3 minutes. Return the *picatta* to the centre, saute for a minute before pouring on the *paya ras* (approx 400 ml/ 1⅔ cups). Simmer until the *picatta* are tender and the stock is almost reduced. Adjust the seasoning. Sprinkle garam masala, lemon juice and half the coriander, stir.

To Serve

Arrange the *pasanda* overlapping on a flat dish, pour on the gravy, garnish with the remaining coriander and serve with *Kulcha* or *Phulka.**

*See section on Breads.

Gosht Banjara

The Hyderabadi style of cooking has in no small measure influenced this lamb delight, cooked in pounded spices.

INGREDIENTS

1 kg/2¼ lb Leg of Spring Lamb

5 g/1 Tsp Saltpetre

Whole Garam Masala

- 5 Green Cardamom
- 1 Black Cardamom
- 5 Cloves
- 1 stick Cinnamon (1-inch)
- 1 Bay Leaf
- A pinch Mace

100 g/½ cup Ghee

100 g/⅔ cup Onions

4 Green Chillies

30 g/3 Tbs Ginger

5 g/2½ Tsp Coriander seeds

4 Whole Red Chillies

15 g/¼ cup Coriander

300 ml/11 oz Kadhai Gravy*

Salt

2 g/½ Tsp Fenugreek (Kasoori Methi)

5 g/1 Tsp Garam Masala

*See section on Gravies.

Serves 4

Preparation time: 1 hour (Plus time taken for Kadhai Gravy)

Cooking time: 5–6 minutes

Preparation

Lamb: Clean, debone and cut into ¾-inch cubes. Put the cubes in a *handi,* add saltpetre, whole garam masala and water (approx 3 litres/12½ cups), bring to a boil, cover and simmer until lamb is tender.

Vegetables: Peel, wash and chop onions. Remove stems, wash, slit, deseed and chop green chillies, Scrape, wash and chop ginger. Clean, wash and chop coriander.

Whole Spices: Pound coriander seeds and red chillies with a pestle.

Cooking

Heat ghee on a large *tawa,* add onions, green chillies and ginger, saute over medium heat for 2 minutes. Add the pounded spices and chopped coriander, stir for 15 seconds, add lamb cubes, reduce to low heat and *bhunno* for a minute. Then add the *Kadhai Gravy* and *bhunno* until the gravy becomes thick and coats the cubes. Adjust the seasoning. Sprinkle fenugreek and garam masala, stir.

To Serve

Remove to a dish, serve with *Naan* or *Phulka***.

**See section on Breads.

Gosht-ke-Khaje

INGREDIENTS

2 Lamb Brain
200 g/7 oz Lamb Liver
200 g/7 oz Lamb Kidneys
200 g/7 oz Lamb Mince
2 g/⅓ Tsp Turmeric
Salt
100 g/½ cup Ghee
200 g/1¼ cups Onions
4 Green Chillies
10 g/1 Tbs Ginger
4 whole Red Chillies
5 g/2½ Tsp Coriander seeds
150 g/1 cup Potatoes
200 m/7 oz Kadhai Gravy*
60 ml/¼ cup Lemon juice
20 g/⅓ cup Coriander
10 g/2 Tsp Garam Masala

*See section on Gravies.

Serves 4

Preparation time: 55 minutes (Plus time taken for Kadhai Gravy)

Cooking time: 12–13 minutes

Gosht-ke-Khaje is a rare delicacy made from brain, liver and kidneys.

Preparation

Offals: Clean, wash and pat dry brain, liver and kidneys. Put kidneys in a *handi,* add turmeric, salt, and water, boil for 5 minutes. Then add the remaining offals and boil for a minute. Drain and dice liver and kidneys.

Vegetables: Peel, wash and chop onions. Remove stems, wash, slit, deseed and chop green chillies. Scrape, wash and chop ginger. Boil, cool, peel and roughly cut potatoes. Clean, wash and chop coriander.

Whole Spices: Pound red chillies and coriander seeds with a pestle.

Cooking

Heat ghee on a large *tawa,* add onions, green chillies and ginger, saute over medium heat for 3 minutes. Add the pounded spices, stir for 30 seconds, add the mince and *bhunno* for 5 minutes, stirring constantly. Now transfer the offals and potatoes to the *tawa* and roughly chop the mixture with two metal spatulae held vertically. For the following 2–3 minutes, stir and fold the mixture. Then add *Kadhai Gravy* and lemon juice, *bhunno* until the gravy becomes thick. Adjust the seasoning. Sprinkle chopped coriander and garam masala, stir.

To Serve

Remove to a dish and serve with an Indian bread of your choice.

Paneer Tawa Masala

Veg

A delectable vegetarian dish made from Indian cottage cheese, *Paneer Tawa Masala* is simmered in a rich gravy and flavoured with *ajwain.*

Preparation

Paneer: Cut into ½-inch cubes.

Vegetables: Peel, wash and chop onions. Scrape, wash and chop ginger. Remove stems, wash, slit, deseed and chop green chillies. Clean, wash and chop coriander.

Cooking

Heat ghee on a large *tawa,* add *ajwain* and saute over medium heat until it begins to crackle. Add onions, ginger and green chillies, saute for 2 minutes. Then add red chillies and coriander powder, stir for a minute, add *paneer* and stir for a minute. Now add *Makhani Gravy* and *bhunno* until the gravy becomes thick and coats the *paneer.* Adjust the seasoning. Sprinkle garam masala and coriander, stir.

To Serve

Remove to a dish and serve with an Indian bread of your choice.

INGREDIENTS

750 g/1⅔ lb Paneer*
120 g/⅔ cup Ghee
5 g/2 Tsp Ajwain
200 g/1¼ cups Onions
10 g/1 Tbs Ginger
4 Green Chillies
5 g/1 Tsp Red Chilli powder
5 g/1 Tsp Coriander powder
300 ml/11 oz Makhani Gravy**
Salt
10 g/2 Tsp Garam Masala
20 g/⅓ cup Coriander

* See section on Milk.
** See section on Gravies.

Serves 4

Preparation time: 10–12 miuutes (plus time taken for Makhani Gravy)

Cooking time: 6–7 minutes

Pao-Bhaji

Veg

INGREDIENTS

675 g/1½ lb Potatoes
100 g/½ cup Ghee
4 Green Chillies
15 g/5 Tsp Ginger
250 g/1 cup Tomatoes
4 whole Red Chillies
5 g/1 Tsp Ginger paste
5 g/1 Tsp Garlic paste
Salt
75 g/5 Tbs Butter
10 g/2 Tsp Garam Masala
20 g/⅓ cup Coriander
30 ml/2 Tbs Lemon juice
4 Buns

Serves 4

Preparation time: 35 minutes

Cooking time: 10–12 minutes

The simple potato 'n' tomato dish, made famous on the side streets of Bombay, the city that loves to eat out. Essentially a poor man's late-night meal, it has universal appeal.

Preparation

Potatoes: Boil, cool, peel and dice.

Remaining Vegetables: Remove stems, wash, slit, deseed and chop green chillies. Scrape, wash and chop ginger. Wash and chop tomatoes. Clean, wash and chop coriander.

Red Chillies: Pound with a pestle.

Buns: Cut into halves, horizontally.

Cooking

Heat ghee on a large *tawa,* add green chillies, ginger and tomatoes, saute over medium heat for 2–3 minutes, add red chillies and potatoes, reduce to low heat and with a metal spatula simultaneously mash and stir for 5 minutes. Whilst stirring keep sprinkling the ginger and garlic paste, dissolved in 90 ml/6 Tbs of water. Adjust the seasoning. Increase to medium heat, add two-thirds of the butter and stir constantly until the butter is incorporated. Sprinkle garam masala, coriander and lemon juice, stir.

To Serve

Apply the remaining butter on the bun-halves, place them on the *tawa* (without scraping off the *bhaji* that sticks to it to ensure that some of it clings to the bread) and grill until golden brown. Remove the *bhaji* to a dish and serve with the buns.

Dal Be-Aab

Veg

A dry lentil delicacy, cooked in butter and spiced with cumin.

Preparation

Lentil: Pick, wash in running water and boil (in approx 1.6 litres/6⅔ cups of water) along with turmeric, red chillies and salt until cooked. Drain.

Vegetables: Peel, wash, and slice onions. Remove stems, wash, slit, deseed and cut green chillies into ¼-inch pieces. Scrape, wash and cut ginger into juliennes. Wash and chop tomatoes. Clean, wash and chop coriander.

Cooking

Melt two-thirds of the butter on a large *tawa,* add cumin and saute over medium heat until it begins to crackle. Add onions, green chillies and ginger, saute until onions are light brown, add *dal.* reduce the heat and stir for 2–3 minutes. Now add garam masala, tomatoes, coriander and lemon juice, *bhunno* for a minute. Sprinkle the ginger and garlic pastes—dissolved in 30 ml/2 Tbs of water, stir constantly for a minute, add the remaining butter and stir.

To Serve

Remove to a dish and serve with *Paratha**.

*See section on Breads.

INGREDIENTS

300 g/1½ cups Urad dal
5 g/1 Tsp Turmeric
5 g/1 Tsp Red Chilli powder
Salt
150 g/⅔ cup Butter
5 g/1¾ Tsp Cumin seeds
100 g/⅔ cup Onions
6 Green Chillies
10 g/1 Tbs Ginger
10 g/2 Tsp Garam Masala
120 g/½ cup Tomatoes
10 g/2 Tbs Coriander
60 ml/¼ cup Lemon juice
5 g/1 Tsp Ginger paste
5 g/1 Tsp Garlic paste

Serves 4

Preparation time: 40 minutes

Cooking time: 7–8 minutes

Kadhai Jhinga

Kadhai Murgh

Pao-Bhaji

Badal Jaam

Khuroos-e-Potli

Dum Pukht and Avadh

With Mohammed Imtiaz Qureshi

Many scholars believe there is no such thing as 'Mughlai' cuisine. Mughals or Mongols, according to them, were nomads and the only food they knew was meat hung to roast on a spit. Those barbaric hordes, they add, had neither the time nor the subtlety to create an elaborate meal. What is called 'Mughlai' cuisine is actually the food of Hindustan, particularly the North. While this theory may be arguable, it certainly merits consideration. What brooks no argument, however, is the fact that once the Mughals made India their home, they became the only conquerors to appreciate the cuisine of this ancient land. More important, they provided patronage to—and became connoisseurs of—our culinary art. It was, perhaps, to honour the royal patrons that the cuisine came to be called 'Mughlai'.

In any event, the Indian kitchen flourished like never before and nowhere did it prosper more than in Avadh or what is today the Lucknow District of the State of Uttar Pradesh. Here two great cuisines—one innovative and the other traditional—became classic art forms.

Mohammed Imtiaz Qureshi: The illustrious scion of a family of Master Chefs, what sets Qureshi apart from the rest is his willingness to take culinary risks. He is almost compulsive about combining ingredients that others, more timid, might consider mutually exclusive. While he does not deviate from the classic form, his culinary philosophy is the more you innovate, the tastier will be the delicacy. His pioneering effort in reviving *Dum Pukht* is his unique contribution to Indian cooking.

The innovative *Dum Pukht* came into vogue during the reign of the benevolent Nawab Asaf-ud-Daulah. *Dum Pukht,* literally choking off the steam, has been described as the 'maturing of a prepared dish'. *Dum Pukht* originated in Persia, where a prepared dish was sealed and buried in hot sand to *mature.* In India, *Dum Pukht* was born a little over 200 years ago. To feed his starving subjects during the famine of 1784, Nawab Asaf-ud-Daulah decided to provide jobs by building the Bara Imambara. The monument was built by day and destroyed at night. During its build-and-destroy stages, huge quantities of food were cooked, sealed in *degs* (gigantic *handis)* and then kept warm in massive double-walled *bukhari* or ovens. As a result, the prepared food would get steamed in the gentle heat of the *bukhari.*

One day, the Nawab decided to sample the food—he relished every morsel. He adapted the *bukhari* for use at royal banquets and hunts. His chefs used exotic spices and herbs, to impart subtle flavours and aromas, before putting the delicacies on *dum.* Dishes prepared for the humble Avadhis became delicacies fit for their Sovereign.

The traditional *Avadh* cuisine found a champion in India's best-known gourmet, Nawab Wajid Ali Shah. Legend has it that his chefs vied with each other to create exotic delights—aromatic, embellished with dry fruits and, hold your breath, veritable aphrodisiacs capable of fulfilling the most insatiable of harems.

Dum Pukht

Gulnar Jalpari

A delicacy of succulent 'jumbo' prawns, marinated in a unique batter and then put on *dum.*

INGREDIENTS

12 Prawns (king size)
Groundnut Oil to deep fry
50 g/3 Tbs Ginger paste
50 g/3 Tbs Garlic paste
Salt
60 ml/4 Tbs Lemon juice
100 ml/7 Tbs Malt Vinegar

Batter

100 g/¾ cup Flour
300 g/1⅓ cups Yoghurt
5 g/1¾ Tsp Black Cumin seeds
20 g/⅓ cup Coriander
5 Green Chillies
2 Eggs
Salt

Serves 4

Preparation time: 1:15 hours
Cooking time: 10 minutes

Preparation

Prawns: Shell (but retain the tails), devein, wash and pat dry.

Marination: Mix ginger paste, garlic paste, salt and lemon juice with vinegar in a large bowl and leave the prawns in this marinade for an hour.

Batter: Hang yoghurt in muslin until reduced by two-thirds, then whisk in a large bowl. Clean, wash and chop coriander. Remove stems, wash, slit, deseed and finely chop green chillies. Mix these vegetables with yoghurt, add the remaining ingredients and make a batter of coating consistency (add a little water if the batter is too thick).

Oven: Pre-heat to 300°F.

Cooking

Heat oil in a *kadhai,* remove prawns from the marinade, squeeze out excess marinade, dip in the batter and deep fry over medium heat until light golden.

Finishing

Grease a roasting tray, arrange the prawns in it without overlapping, cover with silver foil and put it on *dum* in the pre-heated oven for 6–7 minutes.

To Serve

Tear off the foil, remove prawns to a silver platter and serve with lemon wedges and mint chutney.

Note: To make the prawns retain their original shape—and for decorative purposes as well—skewer on 3″ wooden sticks and then dip in the batter.

Khuroos-e-Tursh

INGREDIENTS

12 Breasts of Chicken
225 g/1 cup Yoghurt
50 g/3 Tbs Ginger paste
50 g/3 Tbs Garlic paste
200 g/1¼ cups Onions
2 Capsicum (medium size)
5 Green Chillies
5 g/1¾ Tsp Black Cumin seeds
5 g/1 Tsp White Pepper powder
Salt
50 g/3 Tbs Almond paste
30 ml/2 Tbs Lemon Juice
60 g/4 Tbs White Butter
½ g/1 Tsp Saffron
15 ml/1 Tbs Milk
10 Mint leaves

Serves 4

Preparation time: 50 minutes
Cooking time: 30 minutes

A tangy chicken delicacy, saffron flavoured and spiced with black cumin, popularly called *Shahi Jeera* or Royal Cumin in India.

Preparation

Chicken: Clean, remove the skin, debone but retain the wing bones.

Vegetables: Peel, wash and cut onions into roundels to make rings. Remove stems, wash and cut capsicum into roundels, deseed. Remove stems, wash, slit, deseed and finely chop green chillies. Clean, wash and chop mint.

Marination: Hang yoghurt in muslin until reduced by half, then whisk in a large bowl. Add the remaining ingredients, except saffron, milk, mint and butter, and leave the chicken breasts in this marinade for at least 30 minutes.

Saffron: Dissolve in warm milk.

Oven: Pre-heat to 300°F.

Cooking

Grease a shallow casserole with 10 g/2 Tsp of butter, arrange the chicken breasts in it without overlapping, spread the marinade evenly, place little knobs of the remaining butter on top and roast in the pre-heated oven for 20 minutes. Remove, sprinkle saffron and mint, cover with silver foil and put on *dum* in the pre-heated oven for 10 minutes.

To Serve

Tear off the foil and serve from the casserole with *Phulka**.

*See section on Breads.

Khuroos-e-Potli

An unusual delicacy which makes use of chicken skins, which are usually discarded in Indian cooking. *Khuroos* or chicken, wrapped in a *potli* or bundle, has the makings of an international favourite.

INGREDIENTS

1.2 kg/2⅔ lb Chicken
50 g/3 Tbs Ginger paste
50 g/3 Tbs Garlic paste
5 g/1 Tsp Yellow Chilli powder
Salt
30 ml/2 Tbs Lemon juice
400 g/1¾ cups Yoghurt
3 g/1 Tsp Black Cumin seeds
3 g/½ Tsp White Pepper powder
5 g/1 Tsp Garam Masala
20 g/⅓ cup Coriander
15 g/¼ cup Mint
Butter for basting and to grease roasting tray
8 Chicken skins (from the neck)

Serves 4

Preparation time: 1:10 hours

Cooking time: 25–30 minutes

Preparation

Chicken: Clean, remove the skin, debone and cut into 1½-inch *tikka.*

First Marination: Add water (approx 50 ml/3 Tbs) to the ginger and garlic pastes, put in muslin and squeeze out the juice into a large bowl. Add yellow chillies, salt and lemon juice and rub the *tikka* with this marinade. Keep aside for 20 minutes.

Second Marination: Hang yoghurt in muslin until reduced by half, then whisk in a large bowl. Add cumin, white pepper, garam masala, coriander and mint, mix well. Squeeze out excess moisture from the *tikka,* if any, and leave in this marinade for 10 minutes,

Stuffing: Tie one end of each skin, stuff an equal quantity of the *tikka* in each and tie the other end. Prick the stuffed skins evenly with a tooth pick.

Oven: Pre-heat to 300°F.

Cooking

Grease a shallow casserole with butter, arrange the stuffed skins in it, baste with butter and roast in the pre-heated oven, turning constantly, until skins are golden. Remove, cover with silver foil and put on *dum* in the pre-heated oven for 10 minutes.

To Serve

Tear off the foil, remove the *potli,* slice off the ends to remove the strings, re-arrange in the casserole and serve with lemon wedges and onion rings.

Ahd-e-Changezi

INGREDIENTS

2 Legs of Spring Lamb (600 g/1 1/3 lb each)

3 Spring Onions

Marination

50 g/3 Tbs Ginger paste

50 g/3 Tbs Garlic paste

3 g/½ Tsp Red Chilli powder

Salt

150 ml/⅔ cup Malt Vinegar

Gravy

100 ml/3½ oz Tomato Puree (or 50 ml/2 oz Tomato Sauce)

20 g/2 Tbs Black Peppercoms

A pinch Nutmeg powder

Salt

30 g/2 Tbs White Butter

60 ml/4 Tbs Cream

45 ml/3 Tbs Rum

Serves 4

Preparation time: 1 hour

Cooking time: 2 hours

A classic culinary tribute to Gengis Khan, the Great Mongol, the *Ahd* is a leg of lamb delicacy served with an exquisite peppery gravy.

Preparation

Lamb: Clean and prick with a needle.

Marination: Mix red chillies and salt with ginger and garlic pastes, rub this mixture evenly on the *raan,* arrange in a baking tray and douse with vinegar. Keep aside for at least 30 minutes.

Peppercorns: Broil on a *tawa* and pound with a pestle.

Onions: Clean, wash and cut bulbs into thin roundels. Finely chop 10 g/3 Tbs of the greens.

Oven: Pre-heat to 300°F.

Cooking

Add enough water to immerse three-fourths of the lamb legs, cover the baking tray with silver foil and put the *raan* on *dum* in the pre-heated oven for an hour and fifteen minutes. (Check at regular intervals to ensure that the meat is not over-cooked. The right time to remove is when the meat leaves the bone at both ends.) Tear off the foil, cool, remove *raan,* strain and reserve the *jus.*

To make the gravy, transfer the *jus* to a *handi,* bring to a boil, reduce to low heat, add tomato puree and reduce the gravy to a sauce consistency. Add pepper, nutmeg and salt, simmer for 2 minutes, add butter and stir constantly until the butter is incorporated. Remove, add cream and 30 ml/2 Tbs of rum, stir. Adjust the seasoning.

Finishing

Make a deep incision on each *raan*—right down to the bone—and carefully remove the bone. Make ¼-inch thick slices, arrange in a shallow casserole, sprinkle the remaining rum and return the *raan* to the pre-heated oven for 3–4 minutes.

To Serve

Remove the casserole from oven, pour on the gravy, sprinkle a little pepper from the pepper-mill, garnish with spring onions and serve with *Naan**.

*See section on Breads.

Zaqand-e-Kebabi

INGREDIENTS

24 Picatta of Lamb (50 g/1¾ oz each)

Ghee to shallow fry

Butter to grease casserole

Marination

150 g/⅔ cup Yoghurt

20 g/2 Tbs Ginger

20 g/2 Tbs Garlic

20 g/⅔ oz Raw Papaya

20 Cloves

10 g/2 Tbs Mint

100 g/⅔ cup Fried Onion paste*

3 g/½ Tsp Red Chilli powder

Salt

*See section on Pastes.

Serves 4

Preparation time: 1:30 hours

Cooking time: 1 hour

Clove-flavoured lamb *picatta* cooked on stone—marble or red—before being put on *dum.* Alternatively, the *picatta* can be cooked on a *tawa.*

Preparation

Picatta: Clean and flatten with a bat.

Marination: Hang yoghurt in muslin until reduced by half, then whisk in a large bowl. Scrape, wash and roughly chop ginger. Peel garlic. Peel, deseed and roughly cut raw papaya. Put the vegetables and the papaya in a blender, add water (approx 30 ml/2 Tbs) and make a fine paste. Broil the cloves on a *tawa* and grind into a powder. Clean, wash and chop mint. Put all these ingredients in a bowl, add fried onion paste, red chillies and salt, mix well and leave the *picatta* in this marinade for at least an hour.

Oven: Pre-heat to 275°F.

Cooking

Heat the stone slab (or the *tawa)* on a hot plate, gas or charcoals, apply a little ghee on the surface and shallow fry the marinated *picatta* over medium heat until tender.

Finishing

Grease a shallow casserole, arrange the cooked *picatta* in it, side-by-side, cover with silver foil and put on *dum* in the preheated oven for 5 minutes.

To Serve

Tear off the foil, garnish with onion rings and lemon wedges, serve with *Naan***.

**See section on Breads.

Firdaus-e-Barein

INGREDIENTS

Kofta

1 kg/2¼ lb Leg of Spring Lamb

15 g/5 Tsp Ginger

15 g/5 Tsp Garlic

50 g/⅓ cup Onions

5 g/1¾ Tsp Pomegranate seed powder

Salt

5 g/1¾ Tsp Sunflower seeds

15 g/5 Tsp Raisins

Gravy

125 g/⅔ cup Ghee

5 Green Cardamom

5 Cloves

1 stick Cinnamon (1-inch)

160 g/1 cup Onions

25 g/4 Tsp Ginger paste

25 g/4 Tsp Garlic paste

20 g/3½ Tsp Cashewnut paste

120 g/½ cup Tomatoes

5 g/1 Tsp Coriander powder

3 g/½ Tsp Red Chilli powder

Salt

1 g/¼ Tsp Mace powder

3 g/½ Tsp Garam Masala

Serves 4

Preparation time: 1:15 hours

Cooking time: 1 hour

A delicacy of meat balls stuffed with sunflower seeds and raisins, simmered in an aromatic gravy.

Preparation

Lamb: Clean, debone, mince and refrigerate for 15 minutes.

Meat Balls: Scrape, wash and finely chop ginger. Peel and chop garlic. Add both to the refrigerated mince and then mince the mixture. Peel, wash and finely chop onions. Add to the mince along with pomegranate seed powder and salt, mix well. Divide into 20 equal portions, flatten against the palms, place equal quantities of sunflower seeds and raisins in each, make *kofta* (balls) and refrigerate for 15 minutes.

Gravy: Peel, wash and chop onions. Wash and chop tomatoes, put in a blender and make a puree.

Oven: Pre-heat to 300°F.

Cooking

Heat ghee in a *handi,* add cardamom, cloves and cinnamon, saute over medium heat for 30 seconds. Add onions, saute until light brown, add ginger and garlic pastes, saute until onions are golden brown, add cashewnut paste and stir for a minute. Then add fresh tomato puree, *bhunno* until fat leaves the masala, add coriander, red chillies and salt, stir, add water (approx 400 ml/1⅔ cups) and bring to a boil. Gently add *kofta* to the gravy and cook until meat balls are firm. Reduce to low heat and simmer until *kofta* are three-fourths cooked. Adjust the seasoning.

Finishing

Grease an oven-proof *handi* (or casserole), transfer *kofta,* sprinkle mace and garam masala, cover with a lid, seal with *atta*-dough (or silver foil) and put on *dum* in the pre-heated oven for 8–10 minutes.

To Serve

Break the seal (or tear off the foil) and serve from the *handi* (or casserole) with boiled rice, *Pulao* or *Phulka**.

*See section on Breads.

Subz Gosht

The perfect combination of lamb, turnips (or zucchini) and spinach cooked in mustard oil.

INGREDIENTS

800 g/1¾ lb Leg of Spring Lamb
250 g/1¾ cups Turnips
500 g/18 oz Spinach
150 ml/⅔ cup Mustard Oil
100 g/⅔ cup Onions
40 g/7 Tsp Ginger paste
40 g/7 Tsp Garlic paste
5 g/1 Tsp Red Chilli powder
2 g/½ Tsp Turmeric
Salt
150 g/⅔ cup Tomatoes
1 g/¼ Tsp Clove powder
3 g/½ Tsp Green Cardamom powder
1 g/¼ Tsp Mace powder
30 g/½ cup Dill Leaves

Serves 4
Preparation time: 1 hour
Cooking time: 1 hour

Preparation

Lamb: Clean, wash, debone and cut into 1½-inch chunks.

Turnips: Peel, wash and cut into small pieces.

Spinach: Clean, wash and chop.

Remaining Vegetables: Peel, wash and chop onions. Wash and chop tomatoes. Clean, wash and chop dill.

Oven: Pre-heat to 275°F.

Cooking

Heat oil in a *handi* to smoking point, reduce to medium heat, add onions and saute until light brown. Add ginger and garlic pastes, saute until the moisture evaporates, add red chillies, turmeric and salt, stir. Then add turnips, stir, add lamb, stir, add spinach and water (approx 240 ml/1 cup), bring to a boil, cover and simmer until the meat is three-fourths cooked. Now add tomatoes and water (approx 120 ml/½ cup), cover and simmer until lamb is almost cooked.

Finishing

Grease an oven-proof *handi* (or casserole), transfer the cooked meat and vegetables, sprinkle clove, cardamom and mace powders, and dill, cover with a lid, seal with *atta*-dough (or silver foil) and put on *dum* in the pre-heated oven for 15 minutes.

To Serve

Break the seal (or tear off the foil) and serve from the *handi* (or casserole) with *Tandoori Roti** or boiled rice.

*See section on Breads.

Veg

Guncha-o-Bahar

INGREDIENTS

1 kg/2¼ lb Cauliflower
5 g/1 Tsp Turmeric
Salt
30 ml/2 Tbs Lemon juice
Groundnut Oil to deep fry

Marination

25 g/4 Tsp Ginger paste
25 g/4 Tsp Garlic paste
5 g/1 Tsp Red Chilli powder
Salt
100 ml/7 Tbs Malt Vinegar

Dusting

50 g/⅓ cup Gramflour
3 g/½ Tsp Cumin powder

Gravy

75 g/6 Tbs Ghee
50 g/⅓ cup Onions
30 g/5 Tsp Almond paste
60 g/2 oz Tomato puree
220 g/1 cup Yoghurt
120 g/4 oz Khoya*
5 g/1 Tsp Coriander powder
10 g/2 Tsp Fennel powder
3 g/½ Tsp Red Chilli powder
3 g/½ Tsp Turmeric
Salt
3 g/½ Tsp Garam Masala
½ g/1 Tsp Saffron
15 ml/1 Tbs Milk

*See section on Milk

Serves 4

Preparation time: 1 hour
Cooking time: 30 minutes

It is rare for Indians to cook vegetables with exotica like saffron and almonds. *Guncha-o-Bahar* is a rich exception.

Preparation

Cauliflower: Clean, cut into large florets and wash. Boil water (approx 2 litres/8⅓ cups) in a *handi,* add turmeric, salt and lemon juice, blanch for 5 minutes. Drain.

Marination: Mix red chillies and salt with ginger and garlic pastes, rub the blanched florets with this mixture, arrange in a shallow dish and douse with vinegar. Keep aside for 15 minutes. Drain off the excess marinade.

Dusting: Mix cumin with gramflour and dust the marinated florets with this mixture.

Florets: Heat oil in a *kadhai* and deep fry over medium heat until light golden.

Gravy: Peel, wash and chop onions. Whisk yoghurt in a bowl. Rub *khoya* gently between the palms to make a paste, blend with yoghurt, add coriander, fennel, red chillies, turmeric and salt, mix well. Dissolve saffron in warm milk.

Oven: Pre-heat to 300°F.

Cooking

Heat ghee in a *handi,* add onions and saute over medium heat until light brown. Add almond paste and tomato puree, *bhunno* until fat leaves the masala. Then add yoghurt mixture and reduce the gravy to a sauce consistency. Sprinkle garam masala and stir. Adjust the seasoning.

Finishing

Arrange the deep fried florets in a shallow casserole, pour on the gravy, sprinkle saffron, cover with silver foil and put on *dum* in the pre-heated oven for 8–10 minutes.

To Serve

Tear off the foil and serve from the casserole with *Phulka***.

**See section on Breads.

Phaldari Kofta

Veg

Raw banana-balls cooked in a rich gravy makes this a unique vegetarian delight.

Preparation

Bananas: Boil for 30 minutes, cool, peel and mash.

Kofta: Peel, wash and finely chop onions. Scrape, wash and finely chop ginger. Clean, wash and chop coriander. Remove stems, wash, slit, deseed and finely chop green chillies. Mix these chopped vegetables, white pepper and salt with the mashed bananas. Divide into 16 equal portions and make balls.

Heat ghee in a *kadhai* and deep fry the *kofta* over low heat until golden brown. Remove and keep aside.

Gravy: Peel, wash and chop onions. Wash and roughly chop tomatoes, put in a blender and make a puree.

Oven: Pre-heat to 275°F.

Cooking

Heat ghee in a *handi,* add cardamom, cloves and cinnamon, stir over medium heat for 30 seconds, add onions and saute until transparent. Add ginger and garlic pastes, saute until onions are light brown. Then add fresh tomato puree, red chillies and salt, *bhunno* until fat leaves the masala, add water (approx 400 ml/1⅔ cups) and bring to a boil. Remove, pass the gravy through a soup strainer into a separate *handi* and bring to a boil. Reduce to medium heat, add butter and stir until incorporated. Stir in cream, remove and add honey. Adjust the seasoning.

Finishing

Grease an oven-proof *handi* (or casserole), arrange the *kofta* in it, pour on the gravy, sprinkle mace and garam masala, cover with a lid, seal with *atta* dough (or silver foil) and put on *dum* in the pre-heated oven for 8–10 minutes.

To Serve

Break the seal (or tear off the foil) and serve from the *handi* (or casserole) with *Phulka** or boiled rice.

INGREDIENTS

Kofta

450 g/1 lb Raw Bananas
50 g/⅓ cup Onions
15 g/4 Tsp Ginger
5 g/¼ cup Coriander
5 Green Chillies
3 g/½ Tsp White Pepper powder
Salt
Ghee to deep fry

Gravy

75 g/6 Tbs Ghee
8 Green Cardamom
5 Cloves
1 stick Cinnamon (1-inch)
50 g/⅓ cup Onions
15 g/2½ Tsp Ginger paste
15 g/2½ Tsp Garlic paste
500 g/2¼ cups Tomatoes
5 g/1 Tsp Red Chilli powder
Salt
20 g/4 Tsp Butter
75 ml/⅓ cup Cream
1 Tsp Honey
1 g/¼ Tsp Mace powder
Garam Masala to sprinkle

*See section on Breads.

Serves 4
Preparation time: 1 hour
Cooking time: 30 minutes

Badal Jaam

An exotic and colourful aubergine delicacy, dressed in a creamy, coriander-flavoured yoghurt.

INGREDIENTS

- 2 Brinjals (375 g/13 oz each)
- Groundnut Oil to deep fry
- Chaat Masala* to sprinkle
- 2 kg/4½ lb Tomatoes
- 75 ml/⅓ cup Groundnut Oil
- 100 g/⅔ cup Onions
- 80 g/½ cup Garlic
- 20 g/2 Tbs Ginger
- 5 g/1 Tsp Red Chilli powder
- Salt
- 1 kg/4½ cups Yoghurt
- 20 g/⅓ cup Coriander
- 30 ml/2 Tbs Lemon juice

*See section on Masalas.

Serves 4

Preparation time: 1:05 hours

Cooking time: 5–6 minutes

Preparation

Brinjals: Remove stems, wash, slice ends, and cut each into 8 roundels of equal thickness. Heat oil in a *kadhai* and deep fry the roundels over medium heat until cooked. Remove. Lightly grease a roasting tray, arrange the slices in it without overlapping, and sprinkle *chaat masala.*

Tomato Sauce: Blanch tomatoes, remove the skin, deseed and roughly chop. Peel, wash and finely chop onions. Peel and finely chop garlic, reserve 10 g/1 Tbs for the yoghurt topping. Scrape, wash and finely chop ginger.

Heat oil in a *kadhai,* add onions and saute until light brown. Add garlic and ginger, saute until onions are golden brown. Then add tomatoes, red chillies and salt, *bhunno* until mashed. Reduce the masala to a thick sauce consistency. Adjust the seasoning.

Topping: Hang yoghurt in muslin until reduced by half, then whisk in a bowl. Clean, wash and chop coriander, add to the yoghurt, alongwith the reserved garlic and lemon juice, mix well.

Oven: Pre-heat to 275°F.

Cooking

Spoon out equal quantities of tomato sauce over each roundel, cover the roasting tray with silver foil and put on *dum* in the pre-heated oven for 5 minutes.

To Serve

Tear off the foil, transfer roundels to a silver platter, garnish each roundel with a dollop of the topping and serve as an accompaniment.

Avadh

Dudhia Bataer

A shade of the rich and cultured hues of game cooking is seen in this magnificent delicacy of fried quail.

Preparation

Quail: Clean and remove the skin.

Pepper: Pound with a pestle.

Batter: Dissolve saffron in warm milk, mix with the remaining ingredients and make a batter of fritter consistency.

Cooking

Boil milk in a *handi,* add pepper, boil for a minute, add quail and the remaining ingredients, except ghee, and boil over medium heat until tender. Remove the quail (but leave the coating on).

Heat ghee in a *kadhai,* dip the boiled quail in the batter and deep fry, three-at-a-time, until a crisp, cream-coloured layer is formed. (Ensure there is no browning whatsoever).

To Serve

Remove to a silver platter and serve with a salad of your choice.

INGREDIENTS

12 Quail
Ghee to deep fry
1 litre/4 cups Milk
5 g/1½ Tsp Black Peppercorns
10 g/4 Tsp Fennel seeds
12 Green Cardamom
6 Cloves
2 sticks Cinnamon (1-inch)
2 Bay Leaves
½ g/1 Tsp Saffron
Salt

Batter

100 g/⅔ cup Gramflour
3 g/½ Tsp Fennel powder
3 g/½ Tsp Red Chilli powder
Salt
½ g/1 Tsp Saffron
200 ml/7 oz Milk
30 ml/2 Tbs Lemon juice

Serves 4

Preparation time: 25 minutes
Cooking time: 1:20 hours

Peethiwali Machchi

INGREDIENTS

16 Steaks Sole
(60 g/2 oz each)
Mustard Oil to deep fry

Marination

25 g/4 Tsp Garlic paste
10 g/1¾ Tsp Ginger paste
60 ml/4 Tbs Lemon juice
3 g/½ Tsp Red Chilli powder
Salt

Peethi

50 g/¼ cup Basmati Rice
3 g/½ Tsp Red Chilli powder
Salt
50 g/3 Tbs Yoghurt

Gravy

100 ml/7 Tbs Mustard Oil
100 g/⅔ cup Onions
50 g/3 Tbs Fried Onion paste*
25 g/4 Tsp Ginger paste
50 g/3 Tbs Garlic paste
20 g/3½ Tsp Cashewnut paste
15 g/1 Tbs Coriander powder
3 g/½ Tsp Red Chilli powder
3 g/½ Tsp Turmeric
Salt
220 g/1 cup Yoghurt
3 g/½ Tsp Garam Masala
3 g/¾ Tsp Fenugreek
(Kasoori Methi)
2 drops Vetivier

Garnish

10 g/2 Tbs Coriander

*See section on Pastes.

Serves 4

Preparation time: 1:20 hours

Cooking time: 40 minutes

Sole, dipped in rice batter, fried in mustard oil and then simmered in a typical Avadhi gravy.

Preparation

Fish: Clean, wash and pat dry.

Marination: Mix all the ingredients and rub steaks with this mixture. Keep aside for 15 minutes. Remove and press gently to drain excess marinade.

***Peethi* (Batter):** Pick rice, wash in running water and soak for an hour. Drain, put in a blender, add red chillies, salt and water (approx 100 ml/7 lbs) and make a fine but thick paste. Remove. Whisk yoghurt in a bowl, add rice paste and mix well.

Steaks: Heat mustard oil in a *kadhai* to smoking point, reduce to medium heat, dip fish steaks in the batter and deep fry until light golden. Remove and reserve the oil.

Gravy: Peel, wash and roughly chop onions. Put in a blender, make a fine paste, add fried onion paste and mix well. Whisk yoghurt in a bowl.

Garnish: Clean, wash and chop coriander.

Cooking

Heat 100 ml/7 Tbs of mustard oil in a *handi* (use the oil in which fish was deep fried), add mixed onion paste and stir over medium heat for a minute. Add ginger, garlic and cashewnut pastes, stir, add coriander powder, red chillies, turmeric and salt, stir. Then add yoghurt, bring to a boil, reduce to medium heat and *bhunno* until fat leaves the masala. Now add water (approx 450 ml/2 cups), bring to a boil and simmer for 10 minutes. Remove, pass the gravy through a soup strainer into a separate *handi,* return strained gravy to the heat and bring to a boil. Reduce to low heat, add the fried fish, sprinkle garam masala, *Kasoori Methi* and vetivier, cover and simmer for 3–4 minutes. Adjust the seasoning.

To Serve

Remove and arrange fish gently in a shallow dish, pour on the gravy, garnish with coriander and serve with boiled rice or *Kulcha***.

**See section on Breads.

Murgh Mussalam

The most famous dish created by the chefs of the Royal House of Avadh—to say more would be to blaspheme, except the *Mussalam* is very, very rich.

INGREDIENTS
1.6 kg/3½ lb Chicken (2 birds)
Ghee to shallow fry chicken and for basting
Marination
50 g/3 Tbs Ginger paste
50 g/3 Tbs Garlic paste
5 g/1 Tsp Red Chilli powder
3 g/½ Tsp Turmeric
Salt
Filling
200 g/1 cup Chicken Mince
30 g/7½ Tsp Ghee
60 g/⅓ cup Onions
20 g/2 Tbs Ginger
5 g/1 Tsp Garam Masala
Salt
4 Eggs
12 Almonds
16 Pistachios
12 Cashewnuts
10 g/1 Tbs Raisins
20 g/⅓ cup Coriander

Preparation

Chicken: Clean and remove the skin.

Marination: Mix red chillies, turmeric and salt with the ginger and garlic pastes and rub the chicken with this mixture. Keep aside for 30 minutes.

Frying: Heat ghee in a *kadhai* and shallow fry each bird individually, turning constantly to ensure each is evenly light brown. Remove and keep aside, reserve the oil.

Filling: Peel, wash and finely chop onions. Scrape, wash and finely chop half the ginger, cut the rest into juliennes for garnish. Hard boil eggs, cool, shell and slice 2 for garnish. Blanch almonds and pistachio, cool, peel, make slivers and reserve half for garnish. Chop cashewnuts. Clean, wash and chop coriander, reserve two-thirds for garnish.

Heat ghee in a *kadhai* (use the ghee in which chicken was shallow fried), add onions and saute over medium heat until transparent. Add chicken mince, ginger and garam masala, *bhunno* until mince is cooked (add a little water if necessary). Remove, cool, add the remaining ingredients, except eggs, and mix well. Divide into 2 equal portions.

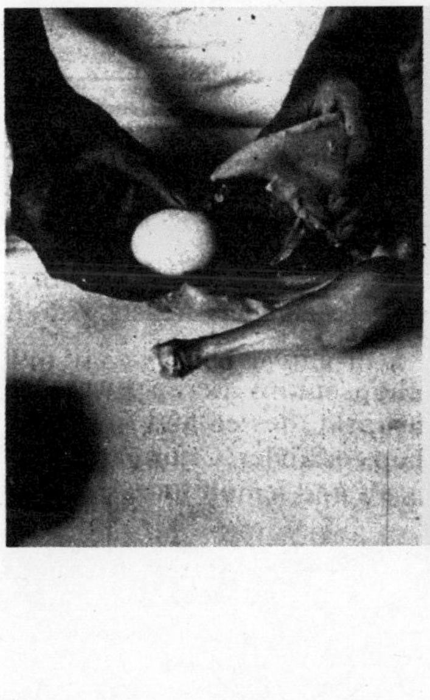

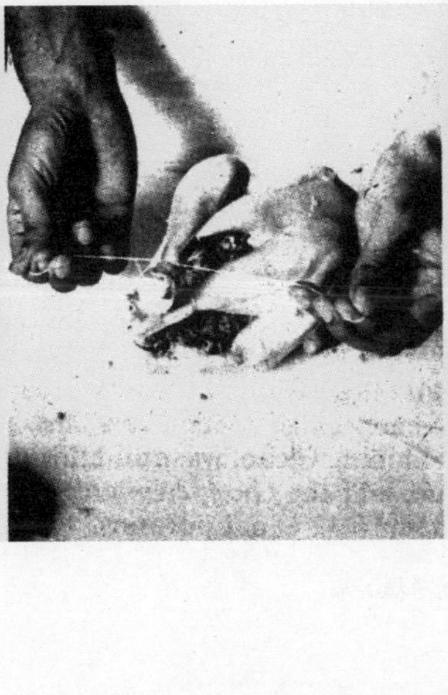

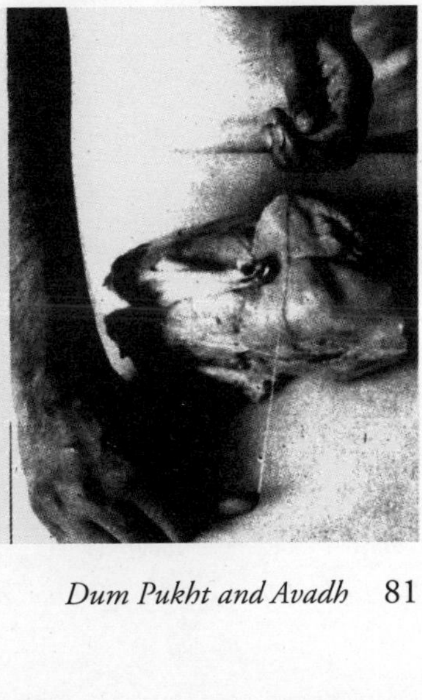

Coating

220 g/1 cup Yoghurt

60 g/4 Tbs Almond paste

3 g/½ Tsp Green Cardamom powder

1 g/¼ Tsp Mace powder

1 g/2 Tsp Saffron

30 ml/2 Tbs Milk

Serves 4

Preparation time: 2 hours

Cooking time: 30 minutes

Stuffing: Stuff the abdominal cavity of each bird from the tail end as follows: half of one portion of the mince, a whole boiled egg, followed by the remaining half of one portion of the mince. Then double up the legs, ensuring that the drumsticks cover the opening through which the filling was stuffed and tie firmly with a string *(see photographs in previous page).*

Coating: Whisk yoghurt in a bowl. Dissolve saffron in warm milk. Mix both, add remaining ingredients, make a paste and apply it evenly on the stuffed chicken.

Oven: Pre-heat to 300°F.

Cooking

Arrange the chicken on a greased roasting tray, spread the remaining coating paste on top, baste (use the ghee in which chicken was shallow fried) and roast in the pre-heated oven, basting with the drippings at regular intervals, until the coating becomes brown.

To Serve

Remove the tray, transfer the chicken to a silver platter, untie and discard the string. Skim off the fat and pour the drippings on the chicken. Garnish with the remaining ginger, coriander, almonds and pistachio, arrange egg slices along the border of the platter and serve with *Naan* or *Phulka**.

*See section on Breads.

Ahd-e-Changezi
Khuroos-e-Tursh

Murgh Mussalam

Murgh Wajid Ali
Chandi Kaliyan

Goa Curry

Murgh Wajid Ali

A befitting tribute to Avadh's best-known gourmet, Nawab Wajid Ali Shah, this delicacy of saffron-flavoured chicken breasts is done in a rich almond-based gravy.

INGREDIENTS

12 Breasts of Chicken

Butter to grease roasting tray

Marination

25 g/4 Tsp Ginger paste

25 g/4 Tsp Garlic paste

3 g/½ Tsp Yellow Chilli powder

3 g/½ Tsp Garam Masala

Salt

Filling

150 g/5 oz Khoya*

175 g/1 cup Onions

20 g/2 Tbs Ginger

5 Green Chillies

20 g/⅓ cup Coriander

Salt

30 ml/2 Tbs Lemon juice

Preparation

Chicken: Clean, remove the skin, debone and flatten with a bat *(see photographs).*

Marination: Mix yellow chillies, garam masala and salt with the ginger and garlic pastes and rub the flattened chicken breasts with this mixture. Keep aside for 15 minutes.

Filling: Peel, wash and finely chop onions. Scrape, wash and finely chop ginger. Remove stems, wash, slit, deseed and finely chop green chillies. Clean, wash and finely chop coriander. Crumble *khoya* in a bowl, add the chopped ingredients, salt and lemon juice, mix well. Divide into 12 equal portions.

Stuffing: Place a portion of the filling at the narrower end of each breast and roll *(see photographs).*

Oven: Pre-heat to 300°F.

Roasting: Grease a roasting tray with butter, arrange the breasts with loose ends touching the tray and roast in the pre-heated oven until evenly light golden.

Gravy: Peel, wash and chop onions. Put cashewnuts and coconut in a blender, add water (approx 100 ml/7 Tbs) and make a fine paste. Whisk yoghurt in a bowl. Dissolve saffron in warm milk.

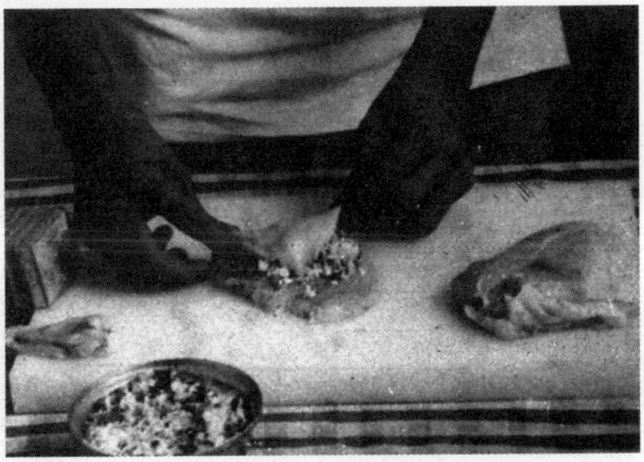

Gravy

100 g/½ cup Ghee

100 g/⅔ cup Onions

25 g/4 Tsp Ginger paste

25 g/4 Tsp Garlic paste

50 g/⅓ cup Cashewnuts

10 g/5 Tsp Dessicated Coconut

220 g/1 cup Yoghurt

5 g/1 Tsp Garam Masala

Salt

½ g/1 Tsp Saffron

15 ml/1 Tbs Milk

Garnish

20 Almonds

½ g/1 Tsp Saffron

15 ml/1 Tbs Milk

15 g/¼ cup Coriander

*See section on Milk.

Serves 4

Preparation time: 1 hour

Cooking time: 30 minutes

Garnish: Blanch almonds, cool, peel and split into halves. Dissolve saffron in warm milk and soak almonds in it. Clean, wash and chop coriander.

Cooking

Heat ghee in a *handi,* add onions and saute over medium heat until transparent. Add ginger and garlic pastes and saute until moisture has evaporated. Then add the cashewnut-coconut paste and *bhunno* for 5 minutes. Reduce to low heat, add yoghurt and simmer for 2–3 minutes, add garam masala and salt, stir, add saffron and stir. Transfer the roasted chicken breasts carefully, one-at-a-time, and simmer until napped in the gravy. Adjust the seasoning.

To Serve

Remove to a silver dish, garnish with almonds and saffron. Sprinkle coriander and serve with *Naan***.

**See section on Breads.

Gosht Korma

The extraordinary thing about a *korma*—which is a thin gravy—is that it is cooked *without* turmeric.

Preparation

Lamb: Clean and cut breast and saddle into 1½-inch chunks, clean chops.

Onions: Peel, wash and chop.

Yoghurt: Whisk in a bowl.

Saffron: Dissolve in warm milk.

Almonds: Pound with a pestle.

Cooking

Heat ghee in a *handi,* add cardamom, cloves, cinnamon and bay leaves, saute over medium heat until they begin to crackle. Add onions, saute until light brown, add ginger and garlic pastes and saute until moisture has evaporated. Then add coriander, red chillies and salt, stir, add lamb, *bhunno* for 5 minutes, add yoghurt, bring to boil, add water (approx 800 ml/3⅓ cups), cover and simmer, stirring occasionally, until lamb is almost cooked. Now add garam masala, mace and cardamom powder, and pepper, stir, add vetivier, stir, cover and simmer for 8–10 minutes. Adjust the seasoning. Add saffron and stir.

To Serve

Remove to a bowl, garnish with *varq* and roasted almonds, serve with *Phulka** or *Pulao.*

*See section on Breads.

INGREDIENTS

1.2 kg/2⅔ lb Spring Lamb (assorted cuts)

150 g/¾ cup Ghee

10 Green Cardamom

5 Cloves

2 sticks Cinnamon (1-inch)

4 Bay Leaves

160 g/1 cup Onions

50 g/3 Tbs Ginger paste

50 g/3 Tbs Garlic paste

10 g/2 Tsp Coriander powder

5 g/1 Tsp Red Chilli powder

Salt

220 g/1 cup Yoghurt

5 g/1 Tsp Garam Masala

3 g/½ Tsp Mace and Green Cardamom powder

3 g/½ Tsp Black Pepper powder

2 drops Vetivier

½ g/1 Tsp Saffron

30 ml/2 Tbs Milk

Chandi-ka-Varq

20 Roasted Almonds

Serves 4

Preparation time: 40 minutes

Cooking time: 1 hour

Chandi Kaliyan

INGREDIENTS

1.2 kg/2⅔ lb Leg of Spring Lamb

150 g/⅔ cup White Butter

10 White Cardamom

30 g/3 Tbs Garlic

100 g/⅔ cup Onions

8 Green Chillies

20 Almonds

225 g/1 cup Yoghurt

Salt

120 ml/½ cup Cream

5 g/1 Tsp White Pepper powder

3 g/½ Tsp White Cardamom powder

Chandi-ka-Varq

5 g/1 Tbs Coriander

Serves 4

Preparation time: 55 minutes

Cooking time: 1:30 hours

A delicacy of cardamom-flavoured lamb which 'glows' like *chandi* or silver. It has a 'white' gravy.

Preparation

Lamb: Clean, debone and cut into 1½-inch chunks.

***Chandi* Paste:** Peel garlic. Peel, wash and roughly chop onions. Remove stems, wash, slit and deseed green chillies. Blanch, cool and peel almonds. Put these ingredients in a blender, add water (approx 50 ml/3 Tbs) and make a fine paste.

Yoghurt: Whisk in a bowl.

Coriander: Clean, wash and chop.

Cooking

Melt butter in a *handi,* add cardamom and stir over low heat for 30 seconds. Add the *Chandi* paste, *bhunno* for 5 minutes, add lamb, stir, add yoghurt, salt and water (approx 750 ml/ 3 cups), cover and simmer, stirring occasionally, until tender. Increase to medium heat, add cream, bring to a boil, sprinkle pepper, stir, add cardamom powder and stir. Adjust the seasoning.

To Serve

Remove to a bowl, garnish with *varq* and coriander, serve with *Pulao* or *Phulka**.

Note: At no stage should the masala be allowed to stick to the bottom of the pan—or else the gravy will change colour.

*See section on Breads.

Nahari Gosht

This was originally a breakfast food. In days gone by, this rural light-gravy lamb delicacy was eaten in the wee hours of the morning—before going to till the fields.

INGREDIENTS

700 g/1½ lb Leg of Spring lamb
450 g/1 lb Spring Lamb Chops
175 g/6 oz Ghee
250 g/1½ cups Onions
5 Green Cardamom
5 Cloves
2 sticks Cinnamon (1-inch)
2 Bay Leaves
10 g/2 Tsp Coriander powder
5 g/1 Tsp Red Chilli powder
3 g/½ Tsp Turmeric
Salt
50 g/3 Tbs Ginger paste
50 g/3 Tbs Garlic paste
150 g/⅔ cup Yoghurt
10 g/2 Tsp Flour
10 g/2 Tsp Gramflour
5 g/1 Tsp Garam Masala
3 g/½ Tsp Mace and Green Cardamom powder
2 drops Vetivier

Serves 4

Preparation time: 40 minutes

Cooking time: 1:30 hours

Preparation

Lamb: Clean and cut leg into 1½-inch chunks. Clean chops.

Onions: Peel, wash and slice half the onions, chop the rest.

Yoghurt: Whisk in a bowl.

Cooking

Heat 150 g/5 oz of ghee in a *handi,* add sliced onions, saute over medium heat until golden brown, add lamb, chopped onions, cardamom, cloves, cinnamon and bay leaves, *bhunno* until the liquid has evaporated. Add coriander, red chillies, turmeric and salt, stir, add ginger and garlic pastes and *bhunno* until fat leaves the masala. Then add yoghurt, bring to a boil, reduce to medium heat, *bhunno* for 10 minutes, add water (approx 750 ml/3 cups), bring to a boil again, cover and simmer, stirring occasionally, until lamb is tender. Remove the meat from the gravy and keep aside.

Heat the remaining ghee in a separate *handi,* add the two flours and *bhunno* over low heat, stirring constantly, until light brown. Add the gravy and stir (ensure there are no lumps). Pass the thickened gravy through a soup strainer into its original *handi* (make sure it is clean), return the meat to the strained gravy and bring to a boil. Add garam masala and the mace and cardamom powder, stir. Adjust the seasoning. Then add vetivier, cover and simmer for 8–10 minutes.

To Serve

Remove to a bowl and serve with *Khameeri Roti* or *Kulcha**.

*See section on Breads.

Lazeez Paslian

INGREDIENTS

24 Spring Lamb Chops (single rib)
125 g/⅔ cup Ghee
200 g/1¼ cups Onions
10 Green Cardamom
5 Cloves
2 sticks Cinnamon (1-inch)
2 Bay Leaves
50 g/3 Tbs Ginger paste
50 g/3 Tbs Garlic paste
10 g/2 Tsp Coriander powder
5 g/1 Tsp Red Chilli powder
3 g/½ Tsp Turmeric
Salt
20 g/3½ Tsp Cashewnut paste
225 g/1 cup Yoghurt
20 g/2 Tbs Ginger
20 g/⅓ cup Coriander

Serves 4

Preparation time: 30 minutes

Cooking time: 1 hour

A delicacy of single-rib lamb chops cooked in a thick, yoghurt-based gravy.

Preparation

Chops: Clean and remove excess fat.

Vegetables: Peel, wash and chop onions. Scrape, wash and cut ginger into juliennes. Clean, wash and chop coriander.

Yoghurt: Whisk in a bowl.

Cooking

Heat ghee in a *kadhai,* add onions and saute over medium heat until light brown. Add cardamom, cloves, cinnamon and bay leaves, stir for 30 seconds, add ginger and garlic pastes, saute until moisture has evaporated, add coriander powder, red chillies, turmeric and salt, stir. Then add the cashewnut paste, *bhunno* until fat leaves the masala, add yoghurt and stir. Now add chops, cover and simmer, stirring occasionally, until tender. Adjust the seasoning.

To Serve

Remove to a flat dish, garnish with ginger juliennes and chopped coriander, serve with *Phulka**.

*See section on Breads.

Lauki Mussalam

Veg

A vegetarian's dream: white marrow stuffed with a rich *khoya-nuts*-seeds-dry fruits filling, coated with yoghurt and gramflour, and then finished in the oven.

INGREDIENTS

2 White Marrow (450 g/1 lb each)

Ghee to deep fry

Marination

10 g/1¾ Tsp Ginger paste

10 g/1¾ Tsp Garlic paste

60 ml/4 Tbs Lemon juice

5 g/1 Tsp Red Chilli powder

3 g/½ Tsp Turmeric

Salt

Filling

300 g/2 cups Potatoes

100 g/3½ oz Khoya*

50 g/¼ cup Ghee

50 g/⅓ cup Onions

10 g/1 Tbs Ginger

15 g/¼ cup Coriander

4 Green Chillies

3 g/½ Tsp Garam Masala

12 Cashewnuts

12 Almonds

5 g/1½ Tsp Sunflower seeds

5 g/1½ Tsp Melon seeds

15 g/5 Tsp Raisins

Salt

30 ml/2 Tbs Lemon juice

Preparation

Marrow: Remove stems, wash, peel and cut the ends. Core the length of each marrow, leaving ½-inch walls to form tubes.

Marination: Mix all the ingredients and rub the marrow—inside and out—with this mixture. Keep aside for 15 minutes.

Frying: Heat ghee in a *kadhai* and deep fry the marinated marrow over medium heat until cooked (approx 5–7 minutes). (The marrow will become limp but that is no cause for worry.) Remove and cool.

Filling: Boil, cool, peel and mash potatoes. *Bhunno khoya* in a *kadhai* over medium heat until light brown. Peel, wash and finely chop onions. Scrape, wash and finely chop ginger. Clean, wash and chop coriander. Remove stems, wash, slit deseed and finely chop green chillies. Blanch almonds, cool, remove the skin and split.

Heat ghee in a *kadhai,* add onions and saute over medium heat until light brown. Add potatoes, *bhunno* for 5 minutes, add the remaining ingredients, except lemon juice, stir and *bhunno* for 3 minutes. Remove, cool, add lemon juice and mix well. Adjust the seasoning.

Stuffing: Gently prize open the fried marrow at one end, stuff the filling, compress to ensure it is firmly packed.

Coating: Heat butter in a *kadhai,* add yoghurt and bring to a boil thrice. Add roasted cashewnut paste and fried onion paste, stir. Then add water (approx 30 ml/2 Tbs) and the remaining ingredients, bring to a boil, reduce to medium heat and *bhunno* for 2 minutes.

Garnish: Chop the roasted cashewnuts.

Oven: Pre-heat to 275°F.

Coating

30 g/2 Tbs White Butter

120 g/½ cup Yoghurt

50 g/3 Tbs Roasted Cashewnut paste

20 g/4 Tsp Fried Onion paste**

3 g/½ Tsp Red Chilli powder

Salt

3 g/½ Tsp Garam Masala

Garnish

12 Roasted Cashewnuts

*See section on Milk.

**See section on Pastes.

Serves 4

Preparation time: 1:30 hours

Cooking time: 8–10 minutes

Cooking

Grease a roasting tray with ghee, arrange the stuffed marrows in it and roast in the pre-heated oven for 4–5 minutes. Remove, coat with the yoghurt-cashewnut mixture and roast for 4–5 minutes.

To Serve

Remove to a silver platter, cut into 1-inch thick slices, pour the drippings on top, garnish with roasted cashewnuts and serve with *Phulka* or *Tandoori Roti****.

***See section on Breads.

Dhingri Dulma

Veg

A colourful combination of mushrooms and *paneer,* cooked with tomatoes and tempered with black cumin.

INGREDIENTS

675 g/1½ lb Mushrooms
450 g/1 lb Paneer*
100 g/½ cup Ghee
3 g/1 Tsp Black Cumin seeds
100 g/⅔ cup Onions
25 g/4 Tsp Ginger paste
25 g/4 Tsp Garlic paste
3 g/½ Tsp Red Chilli powder
5 g/1 Tsp White Pepper powder
Salt
220 g/1 cup Tomatoes
3 g/½ Tsp Garam Masala
15 g/4½ Tsp Ginger
15 g/¼ cup Coriander

*See section on Milk.

Serves 4

Preparation time: 30 minutes

Cooking time: 20 minutes

Preparation

Mushrooms: Slice off earthy base of the stalk, slice and wash just prior to cooking.

Paneer: Grate coarsely.

Remaining Vegetables: Peel, wash and dice onions. Wash tomatoes, cut into quarters, deseed and dice. Scrape, wash and cut ginger into juliennes. Clean, wash and chop coriander.

Cooking

Heat ghee in a *kadhai,* add cumin and saute over medium heat until it begins to crackle. Add onions, saute until light brown, add ginger and garlic pastes and saute until moisture has evaporated. Then add red chillies, pepper and salt, stir, add mushrooms and stir for 3–4 minutes. Now add *paneer,* cook for 4–5 minutes, stirring occasionally, add tomatoes and *bhunno* for 4–5 minutes. Sprinkle garam masala and stir. Adjust the seasoning.

To Serve

Remove to a flat dish, garnish with ginger and coriander, serve with *Phulka**.

**See section on Breads.

West Coast Foods

With ARVIND SARASWAT

Goa

The most surprising aspect of Goa's food is that for so small a state, it offers an intriguing variety of cuisines—each as colourful and full of zest as its people. There is the Christian food and there is the Hindu food. There is the cuisine of the Brahmins (both Hindu and Christian) and that of the non-Brahmins (both Christian and Hindu). Then there are the various influences—Kashmiri (since the Saraswats, who derive their name from the river Saraswati, which originates in the Vale, came from there), Muslim (Goa was annexed by the Mohammedan rulers of Bijapur) and Portuguese (who came in the early Sixteenth Century and stayed until the middle of the Twentieth). The result is an exquisite cuisine—one of a rich variety of culinary styles, with each style boasting of a distinct flavour.

Rice, for example, is eaten by all—and at both meals—but the gravies of each style are at a complete variance. They use the same names and, more often than not, the same ingredients for a delicacy and yet their aroma, flavour, taste, texture and colour can be completely different. There are subtle differences notwithstanding all the commonness. The Christians use vinegar whereas the Hindus prefer to use *kokum* to provide the tang in their respective cuisines. The Goans from the northern part of the State grind their masalas and coconuts separately while the southerners prefer to grind them together before squeezing out the goodness through fine muslin. Even eating preferences can be different: Hindus like lamb and chicken, Christians prefer pork. Both, however, prefer fish to any other meat.

Goan food is easy to cook but, make no mistake, it is chilli-hot. That until a few years ago the men of Goa dominated the kitchens of the Nation's finest hostelries is eloquent testimony to their culinary skills.

Assisted by E.B. Almeida

Parsee

There is a saying among the Parsees that the community can be divided into two groups: one that loves good food and the other that loves eating. For one who has witnessed the gourmandizing of a gourmet spread, I know exactly what the saying means. The occasion: the *Lagan nu Bhonu* or wedding feast of a former colleague in Bombay. The nuptials were still in progress when some people started inching toward the dining area where long tables, covered with white sheets, were laid out with plantain leaves as table settings. They quietly proceeded to incline the chairs against the tables—to 'reserve seats' for their families. When the ceremonies were over, there was a virtual stampede followed by a rattling of chairs and a buzz of anticipation.

Unaware of the 'reservation system', all of us (the bride's colleagues) casually strolled to the tables, pulled the chairs and sat down. Imagine our surprise when this indignant Parsee lady stomped over and demanded in her singsong: "Don't you know these seats are reserved?" Embarrassed, we were ready to get up and slink away quietly when the bride's father came to our rescue. Within minutes, our agony turned into ecstasy as we saw a gourmet extravaganza unfold, course by course, before us. We lost count after the fourth or the fifth course. Saying 'No' was impossible! It was a memorable meal.

Parsee cuisine has spawned a superabundance of lavish delights, but if any dish can lay claim to being the 'national' dish of the Parsees, it is *Dhansak.* In fact, Parsees are often called *Dhansakias* because of their preference for this one-course meal of brown caramelized rice, served with a potpourri of three or five types of *dals,* vegetables (like red pumpkin and brinjals) and chunks of lamb cooked together in a rich, spicy gravy. The usual accompaniment is deep fried (until chocolate brown) *kavab* that look like *kofta* (meatballs)—and a *pinta* ager. It is usually prepared on holidays, not because of any religious taboos, but simply because it would be impossible to digest—and get back to work—on the other days of the week. As the Parsees say: "You need to sleep it off."

Assisted by Cyrus R. Todiwala

Goa

Goa Prawn Masala

A pungent seafood delicacy which also makes an excellent cocktail snack.

Preparation

Prawns: Shell, devein, wash and pat dry.

Onions: Peel, wash and slice.

Paste: Scrape, wash and roughly cut ginger. Put this and the remaining ingredients in a blender, add water (approx 90 ml/6 Tbs) and make a fine paste.

Cooking

Heat oil in a *kadhai,* add onions and saute over medium heat until golden brown. Add the paste and *bhunno* until fat leaves the masala. Then add prawns and *bhunno* until cooked and dry. Adjust the seasoning.

To Serve

Remove to a dish and serve with bread or skewered on toothpicks for cocktails.

INGREDIENTS

1 kg/2¼ lb Prawns (medium size)

120 ml/¼ cup Groundnut Oil

90 g/½ cup Onions

Salt

Paste

15 Whole Red Chillies

20 g/2 Tbs Cumin seeds

5 g/1 Tsp Turmeric

15 Cloves

2 sticks Cinnamon (1-inch)

30 g/3 Tbs Ginger

90 ml/6 Tbs Malt Vinegar

Serves 4

Preparation time: 25 minutes

Cooking time: 10 minutes

Prawn Balchao

INGREDIENTS

1 kg/2¼ lb Prawns (small size)
Groundnut Oil to deep fry prawns
150 ml/⅔ cup Groundnut Oil
160 g/1 cup Onions
120 g/½ cup Tomatoes
10 Curry Leaves
10 g/2½ Tsp Sugar
Salt

Paste

20 Whole Red Chillies
4 sticks Cinnamon (1-inch)
15 Green Cardamom
15 Cloves
3 g/1 Tsp Black Peppercorns
3 g/1 Tsp Cumin seeds
10 g/1 Tbs Garlic
30 g/3 Tbs Ginger
150 ml/¾ cup Malt Vinegar

Serves 4

Preparation time: 40 minutes
Cooking time: 12 minutes

The English loved it so much that they started bottling it as a pickle, but they added preservatives. This is how the real thing is made—it tastes best after it is allowed to 'pickle' for a day or two.

Preparation

Prawns: Shell, devein, wash and pat dry. Heat oil in a *kadhai* to smoking point and deep fry prawns for 2 minutes. Remove.

Vegetables: Peel, wash and chop onions. Wash and chop tomatoes. Wash curry leaves.

Paste: Peel garlic. Scrape, wash and roughly cut ginger. Put these and the remaining ingredients in a blender, make a fine paste.

Cooking

Heat oil in a *handi,* add onions and saute over medium heat until golden brown. Add tomatoes, stir for a minute, add the paste and *bhunno* for 2 minutes. Then add the prawns and stir until cooked. Now add curry leaves and sugar, stir. Adjust the seasoning.

To Serve

Remove to a dish and serve with boiled rice or a bread of your choice.

Goa Curry

The traditional fish curry of the Konkan, the *Goa Curry* like most Goa cooking is chilli 'hot' but delicious.

Preparation

Fish: Clean, wash and make darnes.

Vegetables: Peel, wash and slice onions. Wash and chop tomatoes. Remove stems, wash, slit and deseed green chillies.

Paste: Peel and roughly chop garlic. Scrape, wash and roughly cut ginger. Deseed tamarind. Put these and the remaining ingredients in a blender, add water (approx 120 ml/½ cup) and make a fine paste.

Cooking

Heat oil in a *handi,* add onions and saute over medium heat until golden brown. Add tomatoes and the paste, *bhunno* for 2 minutes, add the second extract of coconut milk and water (approx 400 ml/1⅔ cups) and bring to a boil. Then add fish and green chillies, simmer for 5 minutes. Adjust the seasoning. Now add the first extract of coconut milk and bring to a boil.

To Serve

Remove to a bowl and serve with boiled rice.

INGREDIENTS

750 g/1⅔ lb Pomfret
120 ml/½ cup Groundnut Oil
60 g/⅓ cup Onions
60 g/¼ cup Tomatoes
100 ml/7 Tbs Coconut Milk (First extract)*
100 ml/7 Tbs Coconut Milk (Second extract)*
4 Green Chillies
Salt

Paste

15 whole Red Chillies
15 g/7½ Tsp Coriander seeds
5 g/1¾ Tsp Cumin seeds
5 g/1 Tsp Turmeric
5 g/1½ Tsp Garlic
20 g/2 Tbs Ginger
40 g/1½ oz Tamarind

*See section on Coconuts.

Serves 4

Preparation time: 40 minutes
Cooking time: 15 minutes

Galina Xacutti

INGREDIENTS

800 g/1¾ lb Chicken (2 birds)
100 ml/7 Tbs Groundnut Oil
100 g/⅔ cup Onions
100 g/½ cup Tomatoes
200 ml/¾ cup Coconut Milk (First extract)*
30 ml/2 Tbs Lemon juice
Salt
150 g/1 cup Potatoes
25 g/⅓ cup Coconut
Groundnut Oil to fry
Potatoes and coconut

Paste

30 g/3 Tbs Poppy seeds
3 g/1 Tsp Ajwain
4 g/1 Tsp Mustard seeds
4 g/1 Tsp Fenugreek seeds
45 ml/3 Tbs Groundnut Oil
2 sticks Cinnamon (1-inch)
10 Cloves
100 g/⅔ cup Onions
50 g/⅔ cup Coconut
6 Whole Red Chillies
10 g/5 Tsp Coriander seeds
3 g/1 Tsp Black Peppercorns
6 Green Cardamom
5 Phulpatri
1 g/¼ Tsp Nutmeg powder
1 g/¼ Tsp Mace powder

*See section on Coconuts.

Serves 4

Preparation time: 1:20 hours

Cooking time: 22–23 minutes

A combination of three sets of masalas—whole spice, dry roasted and tempered—all ground into a fine paste—go into the making of this speciality of chicken in a very rich gravy.

Preparation

Chicken: Clean, remove the skin and cut each into 8 pieces.

Vegetables: Peel, wash and slice onions. Wash and chop tomatoes.

Potatoes and Coconut: Boil, cool, peel and cut potatoes into ½-inch cubes. Remove the brown skin, make ⅛-inch thick slices and then cut coconut into 1-inch pieces. Heat oil in a frying pan and saute both these ingredients over medium heat until brown.

Paste: Broil poppy seeds, *ajwain,* mustard seeds and fenugreek on a *tawa,* remove and cool.

Heat oil in a frying pan, saute cinnamon and cloves for 30 seconds, remove and cool.

Peel, wash and roughly chop onions. Slice coconut and cut into small pieces. In the oil used to saute cinnamon and cloves, add onions and coconut, saute until golden brown, add whole red chillies and coriander seeds, stir until the chillies begin to crackle. Remove and cool.

Put the broiled spices, the sauteed spices and the remaining ingredients in a blender, add water (approx 350 ml/1½ cups) and make a fine paste.

Cooking

Heat oil in a *handi,* add onions and saute over medium heat until golden brown. Add tomatoes and the paste, *bhunno* for 2 minutes, add chicken, stir, add water (approx 400 ml/ 1⅔ cups), bring to a boil and simmer until tender. Now add coconut milk and lemon juice, bring to a boil. Adjust the seasoning.

To Serve

Remove to a bowl, garnish with the fried potatoes and coconut and serve with boiled rice.

Vindaloo

One of the many tasty—though 'hot'—pork dishes from Goa, *Vindaloo,* too, tastes better if it is allowed to 'pickle' for a day.

Preparation

Pork: Clean, remove the excess fat, debone and cut into 1-inch cubes.

Vegetables: Peel, wash and finely chop onions. Peel, wash and cut potatoes into cubes; heat oil in a *kadhai* and deep fry potatoes over medium heat until golden brown. Clean, wash and chop coriander.

Marination: Pound pepper with a pestle. Remove stems, wash, slit and deseed green chillies. Mix these and the remaining ingredients in a bowl and leave the pork cubes in this marinade for at least 1 hour.

Paste: Peel and roughly chop garlic. Scrape, wash and roughly chop ginger. Put these and the remaining ingredients in a blender, add water (approx 60 ml/1/4 cup) and make a fine paste.

Cooking

Heat oil in a pan, add onions and saute over medium heat until golden brown. Add the paste and *bhunno* until fat leaves the masala. Then add the pork, along with the marinade, stir for 2 minutes, add water (approx 1.2 litres/ 5 cups), bring to a boil, cover and simmer until pork is tender. Now add potatoes and pickled onions, cook until the potatoes are soft. Adjust the seasoning.

To Serve

Transfer to a dish, garnish with coriander and serve with boiled rice.

INGREDIENTS

675 g/1½ lb Leg of Pork
100 g/7 Tbs Groundnut Oil
60 g/⅓ cup Onions
200 g/1⅓ cups Potatoes
Groundnut Oil to fry potatoes
100 g/3½ oz Pickled Onions
Salt
15 g/¼ cup Coriander

Marination

120 ml/½ cup Malt Vinegar
5 g/1½ Tsp Black Peppercorns
5 g/1¾ Tsp Sugar
8 Green Cardamom
8 Cloves
3 Green Chillies
Salt

Paste

8 Whole Red Chillies
10 sticks Cinnamon (1-inch)
3 g/1 Tsp Cumin seeds
10 g/5 Tsp Coriander seeds
3 g/½ Tsp Turmeric
10 g/1 Tbs Garlic
30 g/3 Tbs Ginger
100 ml/7 Tbs Malt Vinegar

Serves 4

Preparation time: 40 minutes
Cooking time: 45 minutes

Sorpotel

INGREDIENTS

675 g/1½ lb Leg of Pork
225 g/½ lb Pork Liver
3 g/½ Tsp Turmeric
Salt
Groundnut Oil to shallow fry pork and liver
300 g/1⅓ cups Butter
160 g/1 cup Onions
100 g/½ cup Tomatoes
100 ml/7 Tbs Pork Blood (optional)
15 ml/1 Tbs Vinegar

Paste

5 Whole Red Chillies
5 g/1½ Tsp Black Peppercorns
3 g/1 Tsp Cumin seeds
3 Cloves
3 Green Cardamom
5 g/1½ Tsp Garlic
30 g/3 Tbs Ginger

Serves 4

Preparation time: 40 minutes
Cooking time: 1 hour

A pork and pork-liver delicacy, cooked in butter in a significant departure from the traditional medium of fat—groundnut oil.

Preparation

Pork and Pork Liver: Clean, remove the excess fat, debone and cut pork into 1-inch cubes. Clean and cut liver into 1-inch cubes. Put liver in a *handi,* add turmeric, salt and water, blanch and drain. Heat oil in a frying pan and shallow fry pork and pork liver separately over high heat until golden brown.

Vegetables: Peel, wash and slice onions. Wash and chop tomatoes.

Blood: Mix 15 ml/1 Tbs of vinegar with 15 ml/1 Tbs of water in a *handi,* bring to a boil, add blood and boil until it becomes very thick. Remove, cool, refrigerate until it solidifies and grate.

Paste: Peel and roughly chop garlic. Scrape, wash and roughly chop ginger. Put these and the remaining ingredients in a blender, add water (approx 60 ml/¼ cup) and make a fine paste.

Cooking

Melt butter in a *handi,* add onions and saute over medium heat until golden brown. Add tomatoes, stir for a minute, add the paste and *bhunno* until fat leaves the masala. Then add pork, stir, add water (approx 1.4 litres/5⅔ cups), bring to a boil, cover and simmer until pork is nearly cooked. Now add liver, cook for 10 minutes, add the grated blood and stir. Adjust the seasoning.

To Serve

Remove to a bowl and serve with boiled rice.

Parsee

Kolmino Patio

One of the more popular Parsi delicacies, the prawn *patio* is a rare curry. It is sharp (chillies), sweet (jaggery) and sour (tamarind and lemon juice).

Preparation

Prawns: Shell, devein, wash and pat dry.

Vegetables: Peel, wash and chop onions. Peel garlic. Clean, wash and chop coriander.

Paste: Put garlic, whole red chillies, coriander seeds, cloves, cinnamon, turmeric, cumin seeds and red chilli powder in a blender, add water (approx 60 ml/¼ cup) and make a fine paste.

Cooking

Heat ghee in a *handi,* add onions and saute over medium heat until golden brown. Add the paste and *bhunno* until fat leaves the masala. Then add prawns, *bhunno* for a minute, add water (approx 500 ml/2 cups), bring to a boil and simmer until prawns are cooked. Now add tamarind, jaggery, the chopped coriander and lemon juice, stir for 2 minutes. Adjust the seasoning.

To Serve

Remove to a dish and serve with brown rice *(see recipe for* Dhansak).

INGREDIENTS

800 g/1¾ lb Prawns (medium size)
100 g/½ cup Ghee
160 g/1 cup Onions
20 g/2 Tbs Garlic
5 Whole Red Chillies
10 g/5 Tsp Coriander seeds
5 Cloves
1 stick Cinnamon (1-inch)
5 g/1 Tsp Turmeric
5 g/1¾ Tsp Cumin seeds
5 g/1 Tsp Red Chilli powder
50 g/2 oz Tamarind pulp
30 g/1 oz Jaggery
15 g/¼ cup Coriander
20 ml/4 Tsp Lemon juice
Salt

Serves 4

Preparation time: 40 minutes

Cooking time: 15 minutes

Dhan-Dal Patio

INGREDIENTS

450 g/1 lb Pomfret
100 g/½ cup Ghee
120 g/¾ cup Onions
10 g/1 Tbs Garlic
10 Whole Red Chillies
8 g/2¾ Tsp Cumin seeds
3 g/½ Tsp Turmeric
15 g/¼ cup Coriander
5 g/1 Tsp Dhansak Masala*
120 g/½ cup Tomatoes
Salt
50 g/2 oz Tamarind pulp
10 g/1 Tbs Jaggery
100 g/3½ oz Brinjals
Salt

Mori Dal

150 g/¾ cup Tur dal
3 g/½ Tsp Turmeric
Salt
120 g/⅔ cup Ghee
120 g/¾ cup Onions
5 g/1 Tsp Garlic

*See section on Masalas.

Serves 4

Yield:

Mori dal—400 g/14 oz
Patio—1.1 kg/2½ lb

Preparation time: 1 hour
Cooking time:
Mori dal—20 minutes
Patio—20 minutes

Dhan is rice, *dal* is lentil and *Dhan-dal Patio* is a fish curry served with rice and lentils.

Preparation

Fish: Clean, wash and cut into darnes.

Vegetables: Peel, wash and slice onions. Peel garlic. Clean, wash and chop coriander. Wash and chop tomatoes, Remove stems, wash and cut brinjals into ¾-inch cubes, immerse in water.

Paste: Put garlic, red chillies and cumin seeds in a blender, add water (approx 60 ml/¼ cup) and make a fine paste.

Mori Dal: Pick and wash lentil in running water. Peel, wash and slice onions. Peel and chop garlic.

Cooking

Heat ghee in a *handi,* add onions and saute over medium heat until brown. Add the paste and turmeric, *bhunno* for a minute, add coriander and *dhansak masala,* stir for 30 seconds, add tomatoes and *bhunno* until the masala becomes smooth. Then add water (approx 400 ml/1⅔ cup) bring to boil, cover and simmer for 5 minutes. Adjust the seasoning. Now add tamarind and jaggery, simmer for 2–3 minutes, add brinjals and when half-cooked add fish and simmer until cooked.

Put the *dal* in a *handi,* add turmeric, salt and water (approx 800 ml/3⅓ cups) and boil until the lentil is soft. Force through a sieve.

Heat ghee in a separate *handi,* add onions and saute over medium heat until light brown. Remove half the onions for garnish, add garlic to the remaining half and saute until brown. Add the pureed *dal* and stir for 2 minutes. Adjust the seasoning.

To Serve

Remove the fish and the *dal* to separate bowls and serve with boiled rice in individual plates as follows: make a bed of boiled rice, pour the *mori dal,* top with fish *patio* and garnish with fried onions.

Patrani Machchi

A weight-watchers' dream, the *Patrani Machchi* is a Parsi delicacy cooked without *any fat* whatsoever. No Parsi banquet is complete without it.

INGREDIENTS

800 g/1¾ lb Fish

90 ml/6 Tbs Malt Vinegar

Salt

Banana leaves to wrap each fillet separately

30 ml/2 Tbs Groundnut Oil

3 Lemons

Coconut Chutney

100 g/1¼ cup Fresh Coconut

50 g/1 cup Coriander

6 Green Chillies

20 g/2 Tbs Garlic

5 g/1 Tsp Red Chilli powder

15 g/7½ Tsp Coriander seeds

15 g/5 Tsp Cumin seeds

60 ml/4 Tbs Lemon juice

Salt

25 g/2 Tbs Sugar

Serves 4

Preparation time: 40 minutes

Cooking time: 30 minutes

Preparation

Fish: Clean, wash, pat dry, make fillets and cut each fillet into two. Make horizontal slits in the pieces to create pockets. Sprinkle vinegar and salt, marinate for 30 minutes.

Banana Leaves: Trim, wash and wipe.

Chutney: Remove the brown skin and grate coconut. Clean, wash and chop coriander. Remove stems, wash, slit and deseed green chillies. Peel and roughly chop garlic. Put these and the remaining ingredients in a blender and make a fine paste.

Wrapping: Stuff the pockets in the fish pieces with chutney and spread the rest on both sides. Apply oil on banana leaves and wrap each piece separately.

Lemons: Wash and cut into wedges.

Cooking

Steam the fish in a steamer or an *Idli* maker for 30 minutes.

To Serve

Unwrap the fish, arrange on a platter and serve with lemon wedges.

Kheema-Sali

INGREDIENTS

75 g/1⅔ lb Lamb Mince
250 g/1⅔ cups Potatoes
Ghee to deep fry Sali
120 g/⅔ cup Ghee
160 g/1 cup Onions
10 g/1 Tbs Garlic
10 g/1 Tbs Ginger
8 Whole Red Chillies
10 g/1 Tbs Cumin seeds
5 g/1 Tsp Red Chilli powder
3 g/½ Tsp Turmeric
90 g/⅓ cup Tomatoes,
Salt
30 ml/2 Tbs Worcester Sauce
30 ml/2 Tbs Vinegar
10 g/2½ Tsp Sugar

Serves 4

Preparation time: 50 minutes
Cooking time: 30 minutes

A spicy lamb mince topped with *sali* or straw potatoes.

Preparation

Potatoes: Peel, wash, cut into match-sticks and immerse in water. Drain. Heat ghee in a *kadhai* and deep fry over medium heat until golden brown. Remove.

Remaining Vegetables: Peel, wash and slice onions. Peel garlic. Scrape, wash and roughly cut ginger. Wash and chop tomatoes.

Paste: Put garlic, ginger, whole red chillies and cumin in a blender, add water (approx 20 ml/4 Tsp) and make a fine paste.

Cooking

Heat ghee in a *handi,* add onions and saute over medium heat until brown. Add the paste, red chilli powder and turmeric, stir for a minute, add tomatoes and *bhunno* until the masala becomes smooth. Then add the mince, *bhunno* until the liquid has evaporated, add water (approx 200 ml/ ¾ cup), cover and simmer until cooked and the liquid has evaporated. Adjust the seasoning. Now add Worcester sauce, vinegar and sugar, stir for 2 minutes.

To Serve

Transfer to a dish, sprinkle the straw potatoes and serve with an Indian bread of your choice.

Dhansak

The Parsi 'National' dish, this mutton, lentil and vegetable potpourri, served with brown rice, is essentially a lunch-time delicacy, consumed with a pint of lager.

INGREDIENTS

Dhansak

750 g/1⅔ lb Leg of Spring Lamb
100 g/½ cup Tur dal
100 g/½ cup Masoor dal
200 g/1 cup Ghee
200 g/1¼ cups Onions
10 g/1 Tbs Ginger
10 g/1 Tbs Garlic
50 g/2 oz Potatoes
100 g/3½ oz Brinjals
100 g/3½ oz Red Pumpkin
300 g/1⅓ Cups Tomatoes
5 g/1 Tsp Red Chilli powder
3 g/½ Tsp Turmeric
Salt
2 Green Chillies
10 Black Peppercorns
50 g/2 oz Tamarind pulp
50 g/2 oz Butter
3 g/1 Tsp Cumin seeds
2 whole Red Chillies
20 g/4 Tsp Dhansak Masala*
30 g/½ cup Coriander

Preparation

Lamb: Clean and cut into 1-inch chunks.

Lentils: Pick, wash in running water and soak the *dals* together for 30 minutes. Drain.

Vegetables: Peel, wash and slice onions. Scrape, wash and chop ginger. Peel and chop garlic. Peel, wash and cut potatoes into cubes. Remove stems, wash and cut brinjals into cubes. Immerse potatoes and brinjals in water. Peel and cut red pumpkin into cubes. Wash and chop tomatoes. Remove stems, wash, slit and deseed green chillies. Clean, wash and chop coriander.

Dry Masala: Broil cumin and whole red chillies on a *tawa*. Cool and grind.

Kavab: Peel, wash and finely chop onions. Clean, wash and chop coriander and mint. Remove stems, wash, slit, deseed and finely chop green chillies. Slice off the edges, soak bread in water and squeeze. Mix well all the ingredients, except breadcrumbs and ghee. Divide into 20 equals portions, make balls and roll in breadcrumbs.

Heat ghee in a *kadhai* and deep fry the *kavab* over low heat until cooked and brown.

Oven: Pre-heat to 375°F.

Brown Rice: Pick, wash in running water and soak rice for 30 minutes. Drain. Peel, wash and slice onions. Put sugar in a pan, caramelize until brown, add water (approx 180 ml/¾ cup) and simmer until smooth. Heat ghee in a *handi,* add onions and saute over medium heat until brown. Remove half the onions for garnish. Add cinnamon, cloves, salt and rice to the remaining half, stir for a minute, add the caramel and water (approx 600 ml/2½ cups), bring to a boil. Then simmer until the liquid has evaporated. Place a wet cloth on

Kavab

300 g/⅔ lb Lamb Mince

90 g/½ cup Onions

15 g/2½ Tsp Ginger-Garlic paste

2 g/⅓ Tsp Turmeric

15 g/¼ cup Coriander

10 g/2 Tbs Mint

4 Green Chillies

30 ml/2 Tbs Worcester Sauce

60 g/3 Slices Bread

1 Egg

Salt

150 g/1½ cups Breadcrumbs

Ghee-to deep fry

Rice

40 g/2 cups Basmati Rice

100 g/½ cup Ghee

120 g/¾ cup Onions

2 sticks Cinnamon (1-inch)

10 Cloves

Salt

20 g/5 Tsp Sugar

*See section on Masalas.

Serves 4

Preparation time: 1:50 hours

Cooking time: 1:25 hours

top, cover with a lid and put on *dum* in the pre-heated oven for 15 minutes.

Cooking

Heat ghee in a pan, add onions, ginger and garlic and saute over medium heat for 2 minutes. Add lamb and *bhunno* for 10 minutes. Then add the *dals,* potatoes, brinjals, pumpkin, tomatoes, red chillies, turmeric, salt, green chillies and black peppercorns, *bhunno* for 2–3 minutes, add water (approx 1.6 litres/6⅔ cups), bring to a boil, cover and simmer until the meat is tender and lentils and vegetables are mashed. Remove lamb pieces from the *handi* and force the lentils and vegetables through a strainer into a separate *handi.* Add tamarind and stir. Adjust the seasoning.

Heat butter in a separate *handi,* add the dry rnasala and *Dhansak masala,* stir over medium heat for 30 seconds. Add the cooked lamb and the strained mash, bring to a boil, reduce to low heat and cook for 5 minutes.

To Serve

Transfer to a dish, garnish with coriander and serve with *Brown Rice.*

Sorpotel
Vindaloo

Patrani Machchi in plantain leaves

Dhansak

Amritsari Machchi

Masalewalian Chaampan

Patialashahi Meat

Punjab

With MANJIT S. GILL

Punjab—the Land of Five Rivers. Punjab—the Land of Milk and Honey. Punjab—the Granary of the Subcontinent. Punjab—the Land of an Indomitable People, reflecting the Spirit of Man. Punjab—the Land of Virile Men, the symbol of India's Manhood. Punjab—Home of the *tandoor* and a superlative, robust cuisine. A cuisine richly influenced by all the invaders—from Alexander the Greek to Nadir Shah the Persian to Sher Shah the Afghan to Babar the Mongol.

A decade ago, on my first visit to London, I was overjoyed to see so many 'Indian' restaurants. Imagine my dismay when I discovered that almost all of them were Bangladeshi joints, miserable holes in the wall, selling *'curry* (made with curry powder—*sic*!) and *rice'* with *'poppadom'*. Then, just five years later, the city boasted of some of the finest Indian restaurants—anywhere. A new breed of restaurateurs—the Punjabi from India and Pakistan—had 'invaded' Blighty and had launched a 'campaign' across the Atlantic. Thanks to them the world discovered the joys of Indian cooking. If India's culinary art has, at last, found its rightful place among the great cuisines of the world, it is primarily because of the trail blazed by Punjabi food.

Punjab's other grand contribution is the *dhaaba*—the roadside eatery that is an important feature on our network of national and state highways. Once frequented exclusively by thousands of truckers, today it is fashionable to eat at a *dhaaba*—urban or roadside. Puran Singh's Dhaaba in Ambala has acquired a nationwide reputation for the excellence of its food. Moti Mahal in Delhi made *Tandoori Chicken* a truly international favourite.

Manjit Singh Gill: Star of *Queen Elizabeth* II's tenth world cruise (Singapore-India leg), this Executive Chef of the Welcomgroup *Maurya Sheraton**, New Delhi—a position he earned at 30—is obviously accustomed to leading the pack. Gill is widely acknowledged as the man who not only rejuvenated an indisciplined and disgruntled team but took it to such soaring heights—note the culinary success of *Bukhara* and *Mayur,* Delhi's leading Indian restaurants—that it established his as one of the finest kitchens in India.

*Designation subject to change.

What makes Punjabi food so special? In a word, the *tandoor.* The tandoor is much more than a versatile kitchen equipment—it is a social institution. In the villages of Punjab, the communal *tandoor,* dug in the ground, is a meeting place for the rural womenfolk—just like the village well—who bring kneaded *atta* and, occasionally, marinated meats to have them cooked and to have a chat. This is not a rural phenomenon alone. Until just a few years ago, every urban neighbourhood had its communal *tandoor* as well. Many have one even today.

Punjabi cuisine boasts of equally good non-*tandoori* food. The remarkable aspect of this 'other' cuisine is its simplicity. The Punjabis delight in the simplest food. The earthy *Sarson-da-Saag* (with knobs of white butter, *Makki-ki-Roti* and *Lassi* or churned yoghurt) is Punjab's eternal dish.

To go with their fine cuisine, the Punjabis have, *per se,* a wonderfully simple 'code' of eating. A meal of vegetables and lentils, for example, is eaten with a *choprhya* (spread with *desi ghee*—clarified butter—or plain butter) *Phulka* or *Tandoori Paratha.* On the other hand, a meat delicacy is usually eaten with a plain *Phulka* or *Tandoori Roti*—sans *ghee* or butter—accompanied by nothing more than a *raita* and onions split open by smashing them with a fist.

Traditionally, meat dishes are prepared by menfolk, mostly on holidays, with a great deal of flair. The women are, by and large, vegetarian though they are not averse to cooking meat. Other holiday favourites include stuffed *Paratha* with yoghurt, lentils *(dal* or red kidney beans) with *Pulao* and, occasionally, *Poori* with potatoes.

Assisted by Satinderpal S. Chaudhury

Amritsari Machchi

Flavoured with *ajwain,* this is a popular fish delicacy.

INGREDIENTS

- 1.2 kg/2⅔ lb Fish (centre-bone river fish)
- 120 ml/½ cup Malt Vinegar
- Salt
- 50 g/3 Tbs Ginger paste
- 50 g/3 Tbs Garlic paste
- 10 g/3 Tbs Ajwain
- 5 g/1 Tsp Red Chilli powder
- 3 g/½ Tsp Turmeric
- 3 g/½ Tsp White Pepper powder
- 150 g/1 cup Gramflour
- A few drops Orange Colour
- Ghee to deep fry
- 2 Lemons
- Chaat Masala* to sprinkle

*See section on Masalas.

Serves 4

Preparation time: 45 minutes

Cooking time: 5–6 minutes for each lot

Preparation

Fish: Clean, wash, cut into ½ inch thick darnes and pat dry.

First Marination: Dissolve salt in vinegar and leave the fish in this marinade for at least 25 minutes. Remove, place between two napkins and press gently to remove the excess moisture. (The moisture can ruin the second marinade by making it too sour.)

Second Marination: Mix the ginger and garlic pastes, *ajwain,* red chillies, turmeric, pepper and salt with gramflour, add water (approx 100 ml/7 Tbs) and orange colour, make a paste of coating consistency. Apply the paste on both sides of the darnes and arrange them on a tray at least an inch apart. Keep aside for 20 minutes.

Lemons: Wash and cut into wedges.

Cooking

Heat ghee in a *kadhai* and deep fry the fish over medium heat until crisp.

To Serve

Arrange on a flat dish, sprinkle *chaat masala* and serve with lemon wedges.

Note: Amritsari Machchi makes an excellent snack—tea-time and cocktail.

Mogewala Kukarh

INGREDIENTS

1.2 kg/2⅔ lb Breasts of Chicken

450 g/1 lb Tomatoes

225 g/½ lb Onions

225 g/½ lb Capsicum

25 Mint Leaves

100 g/½ cup Ghee

4 Bay Leaves

25 g/4 Tsp Ginger paste

25 g/4 Tsp Garlic paste

10 g/1 Tbs Kashmiri Deghi Mirch (or Paprika)

3 g/1 Tsp Black Cumin seeds

5 g/1 Tsp Garam Masala

Salt

Serves 4

Preparation time: 1 hour

Cooking time: 30 minutes

Tikka of chicken, skewered with tomatoes, onions, capsicum and mint leaves, cooked in a *shahi jeera*-flavoured masala.

Preparation

Chicken: Clean, remove the skin, debone and cut into 1-inch *tikka.*

Vegetables: Wash, cut 225 g/1 cup tomatoes into quarters, remove the pulp and make 1-inch pieces, chop the rest for masala. Peel, wash and quarter one-third of the onions, separate the layers, chop the rest for masala. Remove stems, wash, cut capsicum into halves, deseed and make 1-inch pieces. Clean and wash mint.

Skewering: Skewer the *tikka* and vegetables on 3-inch wooden sticks in the following order: *tikka,* tomato, mint leaf, *tikka,* onion, mint leaf, *tikka* and capsicum.

Cooking

Heat ghee in a *handi,* add onions and saute over medium heat until light brown. Add bay leaves and the ginger and garlic pastes, saute until onions are golden brown. Then add tomatoes and *deghi mirch* (or paprika), *bhunno* until fat leaves the masala. Place the skewers in the *handi* and *bhunno* until chicken is tender. Sprinkle cumin, stir, sprinkle garam masala and stir. Adjust the seasoning.

To Serve

Arrange the skewers on a flat dish and spread the masala on top. Serve with *Phulka**.

*See section on Breads.

Makhani Chooze

Also known as *Butter Chicken,* this is easily the most popular Indian poultry delicacy after *Murgh Tandoori* or *Tandoori Chicken.*

INGREDIENTS

2 Murgh Tandoori*

Gravy

250 g/9 oz Butter

50 g/3 Tbs Ginger paste

50 g/3 Tbs Garlic paste

1 kg/4½ cups Tomatoes

Salt

10 g/1 Tbs Ginger

8 Green Chillies

30 g/5 Tsp Cashewnut paste

3 g/½ Tsp Kashmiri Deghi Mirch (or Paprika)

150 ml/⅔ cup Cream

20 g/⅓ cup Coriander

*See section on Kebab.

Serves 4

Preparation time: 20 minutes (Plus time taken to roast chicken)

Cooking time: 45 minutes

Preparation

Chicken: Cut each into 8 pieces.

Vegetables: Wash, and roughly chop tomatoes. Scrape, wash and chop ginger. Remove stems, wash, slit, deseed and chop green chillies. Clean, wash and chop coriander.

Cooking

Melt half the butter in a *handi,* add the ginger and garlic pastes, stir over medium heat until the liquid evaporates. Add tomatoes, salt and water (approx 500 ml/2 cups), cover and simmer until mashed. Force the gravy through a finely meshed sieve (or food mill) into a separate *handi* and keep aside.

Melt the remaining butter in a *kadhai,* add chopped ginger and green chillies, saute over medium heat for a minute. Add cashewnut paste, *bhunno* until light brown, add *deghi mirch* (or paprika) and stir (the *mirch* is used to provide a brighter red colour). Then add the sieved gravy, bring to a boil, add *Murgh Tandoori* and simmer for 7–8 minutes. Stir-in cream. Adjust the seasoning.

To Serve

Remove to a bowl, garnish with coriander and serve with *Naan***.

**See section on Breads.

Patialashahi Meat

INGREDIENTS

1.2 kg/2⅔ lb Leg of Spring Lamb
125 g/⅔ cup Ghee
250 g/1½ cups Onions
Salt
25 g/4 Tsp Ginger paste
25 g/4 Tsp Garlic paste
4 Black Cardamom
5 Cloves
2 Bay Leaves
2 sticks Cinnamon (1-inch)
3 g/1 Tsp Black Peppercorns
5 g/1 Tsp Red Chilli powder
3 g/½ Tsp Turmeric
20 g/4 Tsp Coriander powder
250 g/1 cup Tomatoes
20 g/2 Tbs Ginger
12 g/4 Tsp Cumin seeds
20 g/⅓ cup Coriander

Serves 4

Preparation time: 30 minutes

Cooking time: 1:45 hours

A delicacy from the splendoured kitchen of the Royal House of Patiala—purportedly a favourite with the great gourmet Maharaja Bhupendra Singh.

Preparation

Lamb: Clean, debone and cut into 1-inch *boti.*

Vegetables: Peel, wash and chop onions. Wash and chop tomatoes. Scrape, wash and cut ginger into thin roundels. Clean, wash and chop coriander.

Pepper: Pound with a pestle.

Cumin: Put in a blender and make a fine powder.

Cooking

Heat ghee in a *handi,* add *boti,* onions and salt, *bhunno* over low heat until both are light brown. Add ginger and garlic pastes, *bhunno* for 8–10 minutes, add cardamom, cloves, bay leaves, cinnamon and pepper, stir for 30 seconds. Then add water (approx 750 ml/3 cups), cover and simmer, stirring occasionally, until lamb is tender. Remove the *boti* from the gravy and keep aside. Add red chillies and turmeric to the gravy, stir, add coriander powder and stir. Increase to medium heat, add tomatoes and *bhunno* until mashed, add water (approx 60 ml/¼ cup) and simmer.

Meanwhile, skewer a ginger roundel between 2 *boti* on 2-inch wooden sticks, place the skewers in the gravy and simmer for 5 minutes, turning the skewers at regular intervals. Add cumin powder and stir for a minute. Adjust the seasoning.

To Serve

Arrange the skewers on a flat dish, pour on the gravy, garnish with coriander and serve with *Tandoori Paratha**.

*See section on Breads.

Meat Belli Ram

An integral part of every banquet 'created' by Lahore's Masterchef Belli Ram—the undisputed King of Punjabi cooking prior to Partition—was this lamb delicacy. We have tried to reproduce it to the best of our ability—in tribute.

INGREDIENTS

1.2 kg/$2\frac{2}{3}$ lb Spring Lamb (assorted cuts)

600 g/$2\frac{2}{3}$ cups Yoghurt

500 g/3 cups Onions

70 g/7 Tbs Ginger

50 g/5 Tbs Garlic

10 Green Cardamom

5 Cloves

2 Sticks Cinnamon (1-inch)

Salt

10 g/2 Tsp Kashmiri Deghi Mirch (or Paprika)

125 g/$\frac{2}{3}$ cup Ghee

15 g/$7\frac{1}{2}$ Tsp Coriander seeds

Serves 4

Preparation time: 2 hours

Cooking time: 1:15 hours

Preparation

Lamb: Clean and cut breast and saddle into $1\frac{1}{2}$-inch chunks; clean chops.

Yoghurt: Whisk in a large bowl.

Vegetables: Peel, wash and slice onions. Scrape, wash and finely chop ginger. Peel and chop garlic.

Marination: Mix all the ingredients, except coriander seeds and ghee, with yoghurt and leave the lamb chunks in this marinade for 1:45 hours.

Cooking

Heat ghee in a *handi,* add coriander seeds and saute over mediun heat until they begin to crackle. Transfer the lamb, alongwith the marinade, bring to a boil, stirring constantly, then cover and simmer, stirring at regular intervals, until the meat is tender. Uncover, increase to medium heat and *bhunno* until fat leaves the masala. Adjust the seasoning.

To Serve

Remove to a dish and serve with *Tandoori Roti**.

*See section on Breads.

Masalewalian Chaampan

INGREDIENTS

1.2 kg/2⅔ lb Spring Lamb Chops

175 g/1 cup Onions

120 g/½ cup Tomatoes

50 g/3 Tbs Ginger paste

50 g/3 Tbs Garlic paste

225 g/1 cup Yoghurt

Salt

5 g/1 Tsp Red Chilli powder

6 g/2 Tsp Cumin seeds

5 g/1 Tsp Garam Masala

Garnish

20 g/2 Tbs Ginger

15 ml/1 Tbs Lemon juice

Serves 4

Preparation time: 25 minutes

Cooking time: 1:10 hours

A weight-watchers delight, these cumin-flavoured lamb chops cook in their own fat. This is a rare recipe—it does not list ghee, oil or butter as an ingredient.

Preparation

Lamb: Clean and make 2-rib chops.

Vegetables: Peel, wash and roughly chop onions. Wash and roughly chop tomatoes.

Yoghurt: Whisk in a bowl.

Cumin: Put in a blender and make a fine powder.

Garnish: Scrape, wash and cut ginger into fine juliennes and immediately marinate in lemon juice until the chops are ready to be served.

Cooking

Put all the ingredients, except cumin, garam masala and the garnish, in a *kadhai,* bring to a boil, cover and simmer until chops are tender. Remove the chops and keep aside. *Bhunno* the masala until half the liquid has evaporated. Add cumin, stir for a minute, return the chops to the *kadhai* and simmer for 3 minutes. Sprinkle garam masala and stir. Adjust the seasoning.

To Serve

Arrange the lamb chops on a flat dish, spread the masala on top, garnish with the marinated ginger juliennes and serve with *Phulka* or *Tandoori Roti**.

*See section on Breads.

Raarha Meat

To establish their credentials as amateur chefs, the men of Punjab love to prepare this lamb delicacy. It is also a classic example of the art of *bhunno* in Indian cooking:

INGREDIENTS

- 1.2 kg/2⅔ lb Spring Lamb (assorted cuts)
- 150 g/⅔ cup Yoghurt
- Salt
- 150 g/¾ cup Ghee
- 10 Green Cardamom
- 4 Black Cardamom
- 2 Bay Leaves
- 250 g/1½ cups Onions
- 50 g/3 Tbs Ginger paste
- 50 g/3 Tbs Garlic paste
- 25 g/5 Tsp Coriander powder
- 5 g/1 Tsp Red Chilli powder
- 3 g/½ Tsp Turmeric
- 400 g/¾ cup Tomatoes
- 20 g/2 Tbs Ginger
- 20 g/2 Tbs Garlic
- 10 g/2 Tsp Cumin powder
- 4 Whole Red Chillies

Serves 4

Preparation time: 2 hours

Cooking time: 1:45 hours

Preparation

Lamb: Clean and cut breast and saddle into 1½-inch chunks; clean chops.

Marination: Whisk yoghurt in a large bowl, add salt, mix, and leave the lamb in this marinade for at least 90 minutes.

Vegetables: Peel, wash and chop onions. Wash and chop tomatoes. Scrape, wash and roughly chop ginger. Peel and roughly chop garlic.

Cooking

Heat ghee in a *handi,* add green cardamom, black cardamom and bay leaves, saute over medium heat for 10 seconds, add onions and saute until light brown, Add ginger and garlic pastes, stir until moisture has evaporated, add coriander, red chilli powder and turmeric, stir. Then add lamb, alongwith the marinade, bring to a boil, reduce to low heat, cover and simmer until tender. (Keep adding 30 ml/ 2 Tbs of water at regular intervals to ensure that the meat does not stick.) Now add tomatoes, chopped ginger and chopped garlic, stir and *bhunno* until lamb is napped in the masala. Add cumin and whole red chillies, stir for a minute. Adjust the seasoning.

To Serve

Remove to a flat dish and serve with *Tandoori Roti**.

*See section on Breads.

Peshawari Chhole

INGREDIENTS

150 g/¾ cup White Gram
A pinch Soda bi-carb
Salt
50 g/¼ cup Ghee
10 g/1¾ Tsp Ginger paste
10 g/1¾ Tsp Garlic paste
3 g/½ Tsp Red Chilli powder
Garam Masala to sprinkle

Bouquet Garni
2 Tea bags
4 Black Cardamom
2 sticks Cinnamon (1-inch)
2 Bay Leaves

Mince
400 g/14 oz Lamb Mince
75 g/6 Tbs Ghee
50 g/⅓ cup Onions
10 g/1¾ Tsp Ginger paste
10 g/1¾ Tsp Garlic paste
5 g/1 Tsp Coriander
120 g/½ cup Tomatoes
Salt
5 g/1 Tsp Garam Masala

Garnish
10 g/1 Tbs Ginger
4 Green Chillies
5 g/1 Tsp Mango powder (Amchur)
Salt
Ghee to shallow fry

Serves 4
Preparation time: 25 minutes
Cooking time: 1:45 hours

A white gram and lamb mince delicacy—from my mother's collection—perfected by my co-authors for this Section.

Preparation

Gram: Pick, wash in running water and soak overnight. Drain.

Bouquet Garni: Wrap all the ingredients in muslin and tie with a string.

Mince: Peel, wash and chop onions. Wash and chop tomatoes.

Garnish: Scrape, wash and cut ginger into fine juliennes. Wash green chillies, make a slit on one side. Mix mango powder and salt and stuff the slit chillies with this mixture.

Heat ghee in a frying pan and shallow fry ginger juliennes over medium heat until golden brown. Remove. In the same oil, shallow fry the stuffed chillies until they become bright green (approx 1 minute).

Cooking

Put the drained gram in a *handi,* add soda bi-carb, salt and water (approx 500 ml/2 cups), bring to a boil, reduce to low heat, immerse the *bouquet garni,* cover and simmer until gram is cooked. (The tea bags are used for colouring.) Discard the *bouquet garni.*

Heat ghee in a *kadhai,* add ginger and garlic pastes, stir over medium heat for 30 seconds. Add red chillies and water (approx 100 ml/7 Tbs), *bhunno* for 4–5 minutes. Then add boiled gram, stir gently for 3–4 minutes, add garam masala and stir gently for a minute. Cautious stirring is important or else the gram will split.

To prepare the mince, heat ghee in a separate *kadhai,* add mince and saute over medium heat for 2–3 minutes. Add water (approx 200 ml/¾ cup), stir and simmer until half the liquid has evaporated. Then add the remaining ingredients, except garam masala, and simmer. When all the liquid has evaporated, increase to medium heat and *bhunno* until fat leaves the mince. Now add a little more water (approx 75 ml/5 Tbs) and stir for a minute. (This last addition of water makes the mince soft and succulent.) Adjust the seasoning. Sprinkle garam masala and stir.

To Serve

Make a bed of gram in a bowl, spread the mince on top, garnish with ginger juliennes and stuffed chillies, serve with *Bhatura, Kulcha* or *Poori**.

*See section on Breads.

Sarson ka Saag

Veg

The Punjabi farmer's winter meal of mustard leaves cooked in white butter has become a national favourite. Mustard leaves are pungent—but robust and delicious.

INGREDIENTS

1 kg/2¼ lb Mustard leaves
250 g/9 oz Spinach
8 Green Chillies
60 g/2 oz Ginger
Salt
20 g/2 Tbs Makki-ka-Atta (maize flour)
5 g/1 Tsp Red Chilli powder
225 g/1 cup White Butter

Serves 4

Preparation time: 30 minutes

Cooking time: 2:30 hours

Preparation

Mustard and Spinach: Clean, wash in running water, roughly shred leaves and finely slice stems. Discard the hard stems.

Remaining Vegetables: Remove stems and wash green chillies. Scrape, wash and roughly cut two-thirds of the ginger, cut the rest into fine juliennes.

Cooking

Put the mustard, spinach and 4 green chillies in a *handi,* add roughly cut ginger, salt and water (approx 2 litres/8⅓ cups), bring to a boil, cover and simmer until tender (approx 1:45 hours). Remove, drain and reserve the excess liquid if any. Put the drained vegetables in a blender and make a coarse puree. Return the pureed vegetables to the *handi,* add *makki-ka-atta,* red chillies and remaining green chillies, mix well. Return to heat, add the reserved liquid and 100 g/7 Tbs of butter, cover and simmer, stirring occasionally, for 30 minutes. Adjust the seasoning.

Meanwhile, to prepare the tempering, melt 100 g/7 Tbs of butter in a frying pan, add the ginger juliennes and saute over medium heat for 2–3 minutes. Bring the simmering *sarson* to a boil and pour on the tempering, stir.

To Serve

Remove to a bowl, garnish with the remaining butter and serve with *Makki-ki-Roti. (Makki-ki-Roti* can be baked in the *tandoor* or on the *tawa.* Make a firm dough with maize flour, salt and lukewarm water. Follow the method for *Tandoori Roti* or *Phulka* as the case may be. However, the *Roti* made on the *tawa* will not puff up like a *Phulka.)*

Hara Chholia te Paneer

Veg

INGREDIENTS

600 g/1⅓ lb Chholia (Fresh Bengal Gram)
300 g/⅔ lb Paneer*
100 g/⅔ cup Ghee
100 g/⅔ cup Spring Onions
20 g/3½ Tsp Ginger paste
20 g/3½ Tsp Garlic paste
5 Green Chillies
3 g/½ Tsp Red Chilli powder
Salt
50 ml/2 oz Tomato puree
10 g/2 Tsp Cumin powder
3 g/½ Tsp Garam Masala
10 g/1 Tbs Ginger
20 g/⅓ cup Coriander

*See section on Milk.

Serves 4

Preparation time: 35 minutes (Plus time taken to shell Bengal gram, which is also available in cans)

Cooking time: 30 minutes

Every winter, the Punjabi housewife spends half the morning shelling fresh Bengal gram, to make one of her vast repertoire of *chholia* dishes—with potatoes, scrambled eggs, as stuffing in a *paratha* as the main ingredient in *pulao* or, most popularly, with Indian Cottage Cheese *(below).*

Preparation

Chholia: Shell and wash.

Paneer: Cut into ½-inch chunks.

Remaining Vegetables: Peel spring onions, wash and chop the bulbs, discard the greens, Remove stems, wash, slit, deseed and chop green chillies. Scrape, wash and cut ginger into juliennes. Clean, wash and chop coriander.

Cooking

Heat ghee in a *handi,* add onions, saute over medium heat until light brown, add ginger and garlic pastes and saute until onions are light brown. Add green chillies, stir, add red chillies and salt, stir, add tomato puree and *bhunno* until fat leaves the masala. Then add gram, *bhunno* for 5 minutes, add water (approx 240 ml/1 cup), bring to a boil, reduce to medium heat and cook until tender. Now add *paneer,* stir for a minute, reduce to low heat and cook for 5 minutes. Adjust the seasoning. Sprinkle cumin and garam masala, stir for a minute.

To Serve

Remove to a dish, garnish with ginger and coriander, serve with *Phulka* or *Tandoori Roti***.

**See section on Breads.

Masaledar Karele

Veg

A bitter gourd delicacy—an acquired taste to be sure—stuffed with the scrapings and onions, Bitter gourd is used in blood purifying *Ayurvedic* and *Unani* medicines and tonics, hence its popularity. It is the secret of the healthy—and envied—Indian skin.

INGREDIENTS

1 kg/2¼ lb Bitter Gourd (medium size)

Salt

16 Button Onions

Groundnut Oil to shallow fry

Filling

300 g/1¾ cups Onions

5 g/1 Tsp Mango powder (Amchur)

3 g/½ Tsp Black Pepper powder

3 g/½ Tsp Red Chilli powder

3 g/½ Tsp Turmeric

Serves 4

Preparation time: 1:15 hours

Cooking time: 40 minutes

Preparation

Bitter Gourd: Wash, peel, reserve the scrapings and slit on one side. Rub salt on gourd and mix with scrapings, keep aside for at least 30 minutes (preferably in the sun). Then squeeze the gourd and scrapings separately in napkins to ensure both are completely devoid of moisture. (The procedure ensures that the bitterness is considerably reduced.)

Button Onions: Peel and wash.

Filling: Peel, wash and pound onions to make a coarse paste. Add the remaining ingredients and mix.

Stuffing: Stuff equal quantities of three-fourths of the filling in the slit gourd and seal by wrapping with a string—to ensure that the filling does not spill out.

Cooking

Heat oil in a *kadhai*, shallow fry the stuffed gourd over medium heat, turning constantly, until cooked. Remove gourd and keep aside. In the same oil (at least 100 ml/7 Tbs, add more if necessary), shallow fry the remaining filling, the scrapings and button onions until cooked. Return the gourd to the *kadhai* and stir for 2 minutes.

To Serve

Arrange on a flat dish, use button onions to decorate and serve as an accompanying dish.

Note: Bitter gourd can be stuffed with a variety of fillings—the other popular ones being potatoes and lamb mince.

Bhartha

Veg

INGREDIENTS

1 kg/2¼ lb Brinjals (large and round)

150 g/¾ cup Ghee

3 g/1 Tsp Cumin seeds

120 g/¾ cup Onions

10 g/1 Tbs Ginger

5 g/1 Tsp Kashmiri Deghi Mirch (or Paprika)

Salt

100 g/2¼ cups Tomatoes

4 Green Chillies

20 g/⅓ cup Coriander

Serves 4

Preparation time: 25 minutes

Cooking time: 20 minutes

A charcoal-smoked aubergine delicacy, cooked with onions and tomatoes.

Preparation

Brinjals: Skewer the brinjals, baste with a little ghee and roast in a medium hot tandoor until the skin starts peeling off. (The process can also be performed on a charcoal grill, gas stove or oven. The only disadvantage with the latter two is that there will be no 'charcoal flavour'.) Remove from the skewer and immerse in water to cool. Then remove the skin and the stem, chop roughly. (Yield: approx 400 g/14 oz.)

Remaining Vegetables: Peel, wash and chop onions. Scrape, wash and finely chop ginger. Wash and finely chop tomatoes. Remove stems, wash, slit, deseed and chop green chillies. Clean, wash and chop coriander.

Cooking

Heat ghee in a *kadhai,* add cumin and saute over medium heat until it begins to crackle. Add onions, saute until transparent; add ginger and stir for 30 seconds. Reduce to low heat, add *deghi mirch* and salt, stir, add tomatoes and *bhunno* until fat starts to leave the sides. Now add the chopped brinjals and *bhunno* for 4–5 minutes, add green chillies and stir. Adjust the seasoning.

To Serve

Remove to a shallow dish, garnish with coriander and serve with *Tandoori Roti* or *Phulka**.

Note: A good *Bhartha* brinjal is light, large and round. A heavy piece means ripe seeds, which ruins the delicacy.

*See section on Breads.

Kadhi

Veg

A preparation of *Pakora*—gramflour dumplings—simmered in a yoghurt-based gravy.

Preparation

Yoghurt: Whisk in a bowl, add gramflour, red chillies, turmeric and salt, mix well.

Vegetables: Peel, wash and cut potatoes and onions into ¼-inch thick roundels.

Pakora: Scrape, wash and finely chop ginger. Remove stems, wash, slit, deseed and finely chop green chillies. Sieve gramflour and soda bi-carb together, add *ajwain, Kasoori methi* and enough water to make a thick batter. Add the remaining ingredients and mix well.

Heat ghee in a *kadhai,* make 1½-inch dumplings and deep fry until golden brown. Remove and keep aside.

Cooking

Heat ghee in a *handi,* add the yoghurt mixture and water (approx 800 ml/3⅓ cups), bring to a boil, reduce to low heat and simmer for 8–10 minutes, stirring constantly (or else yoghurt will curdle). Add potatoes, bring to a boil, reduce to low heat and simmer for 8–10 minutes. Then add onions and simmer until potatoes are cooked. Now add *Pakora* and stir for 2 minutes. Adjust the seasoning. Allow the *kadhi* to simmer.

Meanwhile, to prepare the tempering, heat ghee in a frying pan, add all the seeds and saute over medium heat until cumin begins to crackle. Add red chillies, stir and remove. Bring the simmering *kadhi* to a boil, pour on the tempering and stir.

To Serve

Remove to a bowl and serve with boiled rice.

Note: The Marwaris stir in a pinch of asafoetida in their *Kadhi* and do not use onions.

INGREDIENTS

350 g/1½ cups Yoghurt (1-day old)

60 g/6 Tbs Gramflour

50 g/¼ cup Ghee

5 g/1 Tsp Red Chilli powder

3 g/½ Tsp Turmeric

Salt

150 g/5 oz Potatoes

150 g/5 oz Onions

Pakora

75 g/½ cup Gramflour

A pinch Soda bi-carb

Salt

2 g/¾ Tsp Ajwain

2 g/1 Tsp Fenugreek (Kasoori Methi)

5 g/1½ Tsp Ginger

5 Green Chillies

Ghee to deep fry

Tempering

25 g/5 Tsp Ghee

3 g/1 Tsp Cumin seeds

1 g/¼ Tsp Fenugreek seeds

1 g/¼ Tsp Mustard seeds

4 whole Red Chillies

Serves 4

Preparation time: 45 minutes

Cooking time: 35 minutes

Veg

Punj Rattani Dal

INGREDIENTS

30 g/7 Tsp Moong dal (whole)

30 g/7 Tsp Masoor dal (whole)

30 g/7 Tsp Urad dal (whole)

30 g/7 Tsp Channa dal

30 g/7 Tsp Tur dal

75 g/6 Tbs Ghee

3 g/1 Tsp Black Cumin seeds

50 g/⅓ cup Onions

50 g/2 Tsp Coriander powder

3 g/½ Tsp Red Chilli powder

3 g/½ Tsp turmeric

Salt

5 g/1 Tsp Cumin powder

5 g/1 Tsp Fennel powder

20 g/⅓ cup Coriander

Tempering

60 g/4 Tbs White Butter

60 g/¼ cup Tomatoes

60 g/¼ cup Yoghurt

3 g/½ Tsp Garam Masala

Serves 4

Preparation time: 1 hour

Cooking time: 2:30 hours

A combination of five lentils is used to prepare this rarely made delicacy.

Preparation

Lentils: Pick, wash in running water and immerse for an hour. Drain.

Vegetables: Peel, wash and chop onions. Clean, wash and chop coriander.

Tempering: Wash and finely chop tomatoes. Whisk yoghurt in a bowl.

Cooking

Heat ghee in a *handi,* add cumin seeds and saute over medium heat until they begin to crackle. Add onions, saute until light brown, add lentils and *bhunno* for 4–5 minutes. Then add water (approx 2 litres/8⅓ cups), bring to a boil, reduce to low heat and remove the scum. Now add coriander powder, red chillies, turmeric and salt, cover and simmer until lentils are cooked and two-thirds of the liquid has evaporated. Mash the lentils lightly against the sides with a wooden spoon. Sprinkle cumin powder and fennel powder, stir for 2–3 minutes. Adjust the seasoning.

To prepare the tempering, melt butter in a *kadhai,* add tomatoes, yoghurt and garam masala, *bhunno* over medium heat until fat leaves the sides. Transfer the cooked lentils and stir for 3–4 minutes.

To Serve

Remove to a bowl, garnish with coriander and serve with *Phulka**, boiled rice or as an accompaniment.

*See section on Breads.

Dal Amritsari

Veg

A lentil delicacy made famous by a *dhaaba*—roadside eatery—outside the Golden Temple in the Holy City of the Sikhs. The Chefs have perfected the original. A rare, slow-cooked delicacy, which has no spices whatsoever.

INGREDIENTS

200 g/1 cup Urad dal (whole)
50 g/¼ cup Channa dal
Salt
20 g/2 Tbs Ginger
20 g/2 Tbs Garlic
25 ml/5 Tsp Groundnut Oil
30 g/3¼ Tbs Onions
5 Green Chillies
60 g/¼ cup Tomatoes
5 g/1 Tbs Mint
100 g/7 Tbs White Butter

Serves 4

Preparation time: 45 minutes

Cooking time: 3 hours

Preparation

Lentils: Pick, wash in running water and soak for at least 30 minutes. Drain.

Vegetables: Scrape, wash and chop ginger. Peel and chop garlic. Peel, wash and chop onions. Remove stems, wash, slit, deseed and chop green chillies. Wash and chop tomatoes. Clean and wash mint.

Cooking

Put drained lentils in a *handi,* add salt and water (approx 2 litres/8⅓ cups), bring to a boil, reduce to low heat and remove the scum. Add two-thirds each of ginger and garlic, cover and simmer until the *dals* are cooked and two-thirds of the liquid has evaporated. Mash the lentils lightly against the sides with a wooden spoon. Adjust the seasoning.

Heat oil in a *kadhai,* add onions and saute over medium heat until light brown. Add remaining ginger and garlic and saute until onions are brown. Then add green chillies, stir for a minute, add tomatoes and *bhunno* until tomatoes are mashed. Transfer the lentils, stir for 2 minutes, then cook until of medium thick consistency.

To Serve

Remove to four individual bowls, garnish with mint, top with a knob of butter and serve as an accompaniment.

Veg

Dal Makhani

INGREDIENTS

120 g/⅔ cup Urad dal (whole)
30 g/3 Tbs Red Kidney Beans
Salt
20 g/3½ Tsp Ginger paste
20 g/3½ Tsp Garlic paste
120 ml/4½ oz Tomato puree
5 g/1 tsp Red Chilli powder
120 g/4½ cup White Butter
120 ml/½ cup Cream

Serves 4

Preparation time: 15 minutes

Cooking time: 3 hours

The Nation's favourite lentil delicacy, the *Dal Makhani* for reasons unknown always tastes best after a day in the refrigerator. However, do not splurge—the black lentil can cause quite a rumble.

Preparation

Lentils: Pick, wash in running water and soak overnight. Drain.

Cooking

Put the drained lentils in a *handi,* add salt and water (approx 1.5 litres/6¼ cups), bring to boil, cover and simmer until the lentils are cooked and two-thirds of the liquid has evaporated. Mash the lentils lightly against the sides with a wooden spoon. Add ginger paste, garlic paste, tomato puree, red chillies and 100 g/7 Tbs of butter, stir and cook for 45 minutes. Then add cream, stir and cook for 10 minutes. Adjust the seasoning.

To Serve

Remove to a bowl, garnish with the remaining butter and serve with *Tandoori Roti* or *Phulka**.

*See section on Breads.

Rajasthan

With Manu Mehta and
Late Rani Meena Ranawat Bambulia Kotah

The desert has challenged man since antiquity and has, in fact, spawned the earliest civilizations. The centuries old battle with nature is what makes the denizens of the desert a breed apart—the only people on earth with *joie de vivre.*

No one reflects this zest for life better than the Rajasthanis. Their home is the Thar or the Great Indian Desert. A hundred holidays or even a thousand celebrations elsewhere cannot match the year-round excitement of the festivals and fairs of Rajasthan, where myth and history intermingle in explosion after explosion of merriment. With celebration constantly in the air, could exotic cuisine be far behind? No!

Many a fine kitchen flourishes in the Land of the Princes—within the palaces and without. The love for *shikar* has made game a particular favourite with royalty. In the world of good eating, game cooking is easily the most respected art form—largely because the skills required to clean, cut and cook game are not the most easily acquired. Wild boar, venison, pheasant, peacock, quail, duck are all found in the desert and their *shikar* has spawned incomparable exotic delicacies. There are as many ways of cooking game as there are Maharajas. *Sule,* the 'smoked' Rajasthani *kebab,* for example, is barbecued in eleven different ways. So prized is game meat that what is not immediately consumed is pickled and preserved, including the rind of boar. Pickled rind is usually kept under lock and key—produced only before honoured guests and close friends.

At the other end of the spectrum is the vegetarian cuisine of the Maheshwaris of Marwar or Jodhpur, who eschew even roots—like garlic and onions—because they excite passions.

Manu Mehta: Not only is he a sound technician—something to do with his interest in Science and Computers—but also a fine culinary craftsman. Mehta is currently Executive Chef at the Welcomgroup *Vadodara**, Baroda.

*Designation subject to change.

The sparse rainfall allows minimal vegetation and only a handful of vegetables grow in the desert. The enterprising Marwaris have made most of the limited resources—they sun-dry the vegetables and preserve them for the remainder of the year. Remarkably, despite the constraints, they have created a superlative cuisine. Unfortunately, the non-availability of several sun-dried vegetables—*kehar* (a small, berry-like fruit), *sangri* (akin to beans), *phog* and many others—pre-empt the inclusion of many delicacies in this book.

Lentils, in their myriad forms—*Moong Dal Khilma, Mongodi Ki Subzi, Besan Ke Gatte*—are the principal source of proteins. Another feature of Maheshwari cooking is the use of mango powder—a suitable substitute for tomatoes (which are scarce in the desert)—and asafoetida, used to enhance the taste in the absence of garlic and onions.

Maas ke Sule

This is the quintessential Rajput *kebab* made from game (venison, wild boar, sand grouse, quail, partridge), lamb, chicken and fish. There are 11 different ways of making *Sule,* some simple, others exotic (*below*).

INGREDIENTS

1.2 kg/2⅔ lb Venison* (lean)
Clarified Butter for basting

First Marination
75 g/½ cup Raw Papaya
30 g/5 Tsp Garlic paste
10 g/2 Tsp Red Chilli powder
Salt

Second Marination
120 g/½ cup Yoghurt
120 g/¾ cup Onions
30 g/3 Tbs Garlic
Clarified Butter to deep fry
15 g/5 Tsp Ginger
2 g/½ Tsp Clove powder
Salt

'Smoking'
10 Cloves
A little Charcoal
15 g/1 Tbs Clarified Butter

Preparation

Venison: Clean, debone and cut into 1½-inch *boti.*

First Marination: Peel papaya, deseed, roughly cut, put in a blender and make a fine paste. Remove, mix with garlic paste, red chillies and salt. Rub *boti* with this mixture and refrigerate for 10 hours. Drain off the excess moisture. (Marinate lamb for 2 hours.)

Second Marination: Whisk yoghurt in a bowl. Peel, wash and evenly slice onions. Peel and evenly slice garlic. Heat clarified butter in a flying pan and separately deep fry onions and garlic over medium heat until golden brown. Scrape, wash and roughly cut ginger, put in a blender, add fried onions and garlic, clove powder, salt and water (approx 30 ml/2 Tbs), make a fine paste. Mix the paste with yoghurt and rub marinated meat with this mixture. Keep aside for 2 hours.

Oven: Pre-heat to 350°F.

Skewering: Skewer the marinated *boti* at least an inch apart. Keep a tray underneath to collect the drippings.

Serves 4

Preparation time: 12:30 hours

Cooking time: 1 hour

*The other meats that can be used are wild boar, spring lamb and fish.

Cooking

Roast in a moderately hot *tandoor* or charcoal grill for 10–12 minutes, in a pre-heated oven for 18–20 minutes. Remove and hang the skewers to allow the excess moisture to drip off (approx 5–6 minutes). Baste with clarified butter and roast again for 8–10 minutes.

Finishing

Put a live piece of charcoal in a *katori* (small metal bowl), place the *katori* in the middle of a large pre-heated casserole. Remove *boti* from the skewers and arrange around the *katori*, drop cloves over the coals, pour on the clarified butter and quickly cover with a lid. Allow *boti* to smoke for 3–5 minutes (*see photographs*).

To Serve

Uncover, remove *katori* and serve *Sule* in the same casserole.

Safed Maas

INGREDIENTS

1.2 kg/2⅔ lb Leg of Spring Lamb

Salt

225 g/1 cup Yoghurt

125 g/⅔ cup Ghee

5 g/1 Tsp White Pepper powder

20 g/2 Tbs Ginger

60 g/½ cup Almonds

30 g/⅓ cup Coconut

4 Green Chillies

3 g/½ Tsp White Cardamom powder

120 ml/½ cup Cream

15 ml/1 Tbs Lemon juice

15 ml/1 Tbs Rosewater

Serves 4

Preparation time: 30 minutes

Cooking time: 1:30 hours

Safed Maas, literally 'white meat', is an ancient Rajasthani delicacy.

Preparation

Lamb: Clean and cut into 1½-inch chunks. Put in a *handi,* add salt and water (approx 1.5 litres/6¼ cups) and boil for 5 minutes. Drain and wash the chunks.

Yoghurt: Whisk in a bowl, add white pepper and mix well.

Ginger: Scrape, wash and cut into juliennes.

Almond Paste: Blanch almonds, cool and remove the skin. Remove the brown skin and roughly cut coconut. Remove stems, wash, slit and deseed green chillies. Put these ingredients in a blender, add water (approx 60 ml/¼ cup) and make a fine paste.

Oven: Pre-heat to 275°F.

Cooking

Heat ghee in a *handi,* add the blanched meat, the spiced yoghurt, ginger, salt and water (approx 800 ml/3⅓ cups), cover and simmer, stirring occasionally, until the lamb is tender and four-fifths of the liquid has evaporated. Add the paste and stir for 2 minutes. Sprinkle cardamom powder and stir. Then add cream, lemon juice and rosewater, stir. Adjust the seasoning.

Finishing

Cover the *handi* with a lid, seal with *atta*-dough and put it on *dum* in a pre-heated oven for 15 minutes.

To Serve

Break the seal, remove the cooked meat to a shallow dish and serve with *Phulka**.

*See section on Breads.

Lal Maas

Rajasthan's favourite lamb preparation is only for those with steel-lined stomachs—it is easily the 'hottest' dish in this collection of recipes.

INGREDIENTS

1.2 kg/2⅔ lb Leg of Spring Lamb
30 Whole Red Chillies
150 g/¾ cup Ghee
60 g/⅓ cup Garlic
200 g/1¼ cups Onions
5 Black Cardamom
5 Green Cardamom
3 g/1 Tsp Cumin seeds
225 g/1 cup Yoghurt
20 g/4 Tsp Coriander powder
3 g/½ Tsp Turmeric
Salt
20 g/⅓ cup Coriander

Serves 4

Preparation time: 30 minutes

Cooking time: 1:45 hours

Preparation

Lamb: Clean and cut into 1½-inch chunks.

Chillies: Remove stems, slit and deseed.

Vegetables: Peel and slice garlic. Peel, wash and finely slice onions. Peel, wash and chop coriander.

Cumin: Broil the seeds on a *tawa.*

Yoghurt: Whisk in a bowl, add red chillies, cumin, coriander powder, turmeric and salt, mix well and keep aside for 10 minutes.

Cooking

Heat ghee in a *handi,* add garlic and saute over medium heat until golden brown. Add onions and the black and green cardamom, saute until onions are golden brown. Then add meat, *bhunno* for 4–5 minutes, add yoghurt mixture and *bhunno* until liquid has evaporated. Now add water (approx 800 ml/3⅓ cups), bring to a boil, cover and simmer, stirring occasionally, until meat is tender. Adjust the seasoning.

To Serve

Remove to a bowl, garnish with the chopped coriander and serve with *Phulka**. (The Rajasthanis make a bed of *Phulka,* pour on the *Lal Maas,* crumble a papad on top and eat when the *Phulka* has soaked as much of the gravy as possible.)

*See section on Breads.

Makki ka Soweta

INGREDIENTS

750 g/1⅔ lb Spring Lamb (assorted cuts)
450 g/1 lb Corn on the Cob
150 g/¾ cup Ghee
3 g/1 Tsp Cumin Seeds
4 Green Cardamom
4 Black Cardamom
8 Cloves
2 sticks Cinnamon (1-inch)
2 Bay Leaves
300 ml/1¼ cups Milk
30 ml/2 Tbs Lemon juice
20 g/⅓ cup Coriander

Paste

160 g/1 cup Onions
50 g/5 Tbs Garlic
8 Green Chillies

Marination

225 g/1 cup Yoghurt
10 g/2 Tsp Coriander Powder
5 g/1 Tsp Red Chilli Powder
3 g/½ Tsp Turmeric
Salt

Serves 4

Preparation time: 1:25 hours
Cooking time: 1:30 hours

The Rajasthanis proudly claim that no other people can match their ability to create corn dishes. The *Soweta* is a spicy combination of corn and lamb.

Preparation

Lamb: Clean and cut breast and saddle into 1½-inch chunks. Clean chops.

Corn: Boil, cool and grate the kernels on the cob. (If using canned corn, roughly chop.)

Paste: Peel, wash and roughly cut onions. Peel garlic. Remove stems, wash, slit and deseed green chillies. Put these ingredients in a blender and make a fine paste.

Marination: Whisk yoghurt in a large bowl, add the paste, coriander powder, red chillies, turmeric and salt, mix well. Leave the meat in this marinade for at least 45 minutes.

Coriander: Clean, wash and chop.

Cooking

Heat ghee in a *handi,* add cumin seeds, cardamom, cloves, cinnamon and bay leaves, saute over medium heat until the seeds begin to crackle. Add lamb chunks, alongwith the marinade, and *bhunno* until evenly brown and the moisture has evaporated. Then add water (approx 750 ml/3 cups), bring to a boil, cover and simmer until meat is almost cooked. Now add grated corn and milk, cook, stirring constantly, for 8–10 minutes. Remove, add lemon juice and stir. Adjust the seasoning.

To Serve

Remove to a shallow dish, garnish with coriander and serve as a meal.

Besan ke Gatte

Maas ki Kadhi

Bati
Mongodi ki Subzi
Lal Maas
Khad

Kerala Nandu Masala
Erha Kari

Milagu Kozhi Chettinad

Maas ki Kadhi

An uncommon lamb delicacy, done in a gramflour 'n' yoghurt gravy.

INGREDIENTS

- 1 kg/2¼ lb Leg of Spring Lamb
- 100 g/½ cup Ghee
- 5 g/1¾ Tsp Cumin seeds
- A generous pinch Asafoetida
- 100 g/½ cup Boiled Onion paste*
- 50 g/3 Tbs Garlic paste
- 400 g/1¾ cups Yoghurt (1-day old)
- 50 g/⅓ cup Gramflour
- 5 g/1 Tsp Red Chilli powder
- 3 g/½ Tsp Turmeric
- Salt
- 8 Green Chillies
- 20 g/⅓ cup Coriander

*See section on Pastes.

Serves 4

Preparation time: 35 minutes

Cooking time: 2:15 hours

Preparation

Lamb: Clean, debone and cut into 1-inch *boti.*

Cumin: Broil half the seeds on a *tawa,* cool, put in a grinder and make a powder.

Yoghurt: Whisk yoghurt in a bowl, add gramflour, red chillies, turmeric and salt, mix well. Add water (approx 800 ml/3⅓ cups) and whisk again.

Vegetables: Remove stems, wash, slit, deseed and finely chop green chillies. Clean, wash and chop coriander.

Cooking

Heat ghee in a *kadhai,* add cumin seeds and asafoetida, saute over medium heat until the seeds begin to crackle. Add lamb chunks and salt, *bhunno* until evenly light brown, add boiled onion and garlic pastes, *bhunno* for 3–4 minutes. Then add water (approx 600 ml/2½ cups), bring to a boil, cover and simmer, stirring occasionally, until meat is almost tender. Now add the yoghurt mixture, bring to a boil, reduce to medium heat and cook, stirring constantly, until the gravy starts getting thick (approx 8–10 minutes). Add cumin powder and green chillies, stir and cook for 2–3 minutes. Adjust the seasoning.

To Serve

Remove to a bowl, garnish with coriander and serve with boiled rice.

Note: Buttermilk (1.2 litres/5 cups) is better suited for *Kadhi* than a mixture of yoghurt and water.

Khad

INGREDIENTS

800 g/1¾ lb Lamb Mince
300 g/11 oz Potatoes
120 g/⅔ cup Ghee
350 g/12 oz Onions
100 g/3½ oz Yoghurt
20 g/3½ Tsp Ginger paste
20 g/3½ Tsp Garlic paste
20 g/4 Tsp Coriander powder
5 g/1 Tsp Red Chilli powder
3 g/½ Tsp Turmeric
Salt
20 g/⅓ cup Coriander
4 Green Chillies
15 ml/1 Tbs Lemon juice
12 Phulka* (Thin)

*See section on Breads.

Serves 4

Preparation time: 30 minutes

Cooking time: 1:05 hours

A multi-tiered 'cake' of lamb mince and *Phulka*—a magnificent meal in itself. *Khad* means a hole in the ground. Originally, the 'cake' was baked in a hole in the ground with charcoals and hot sand providing the heat. Today, electric ovens have taken over.

Preparation

Vegetables: Peel, wash and dice potatoes. Peel, wash and chop 100 g/4 oz of onions; roughly cut the rest, put in a blender and make a rough paste. Clean, wash and chop coriander. Remove stems, wash, slit, deseed and finely chop green chillies.

Mince: Whisk yoghurt in a large bowl, add mince, onion, ginger and garlic pastes, coriander powder, red chillies, turmeric and salt, mix well and keep aside for 10 minutes.

Oven: Pre-heat to 275°F.

Cooking

Heat ghee in a *kadhai,* add chopped onions and saute over medium heat until golden brown. Reduce to low heat, add the mince mixture and *bhunno* for 5 minutes. Then add potatoes and *bhunno* until cooked and the liquid has evaporated (add a little water if necessary). Remove, add coriander and green chillies, stir. Sprinkle lemon juice and stir. Divide into 11 equal portions.

Finishing

Prepare the 'cake' as follows: Spread a portion of the cooked mince on a *Phulka.* Place the second *Phulka* on the mince and spread another portion of the cooked mince... and so on until all the *Phulka* are stacked one on top of the other. Wrap the stack in greased silver foil, place on a baking tray and bake in the pre-heated oven for 8–9 minutes. Remove, turn over and bake for 8–9 minutes.

To Serve

Tear off the foil, cut into wedges of desired size and serve with *Kachumbar***, Mint Chutney and lemon wedges.

Note: Khad can be made in single *Chappati* rolls or balls. Divide the mince into 12 equal portions and wrap in individual *Chappati* and then in foil.

**See section on Salads.

Amrud ki Subzi

Veg

An exquisite delicacy of guavas—yes, the fruit—simmered in a tangy tomato and yoghurt masala.

INGREDIENTS

1 kg/2¼ lb Guavas (semi-ripe)
125 g/⅔ cup Ghee
5 g/1¾ Tsp Cumin seeds
A pinch Asafoetida
25 g/5 Tsp Coriander powder
3 g/½ Tsp Red Chilli powder
5 g/1 Tsp Turmeric
Salt
120 g/½ cup Tomatoes
225 g/1 cup Yoghurt
3 g/½ Tsp Garam Masala
10 g/2 Tsp Mango powder
10 g/2 Tsp Fennel powder
75 g/⅓ cup Sugar
30 ml/2 Tbs Lemon juice

Serves 4

Preparation time: 25 minutes

Cooking time: 40 minutes

Preparation

Guavas: Peel, cut into quarters, deseed and halve.

Tomatoes: Wash and chop.

Yoghurt: Whisk in a bowl.

Cooking

Heat ghee in a *handi,* add cumin and saute over medium heat until it begins to crackle. Add asafoetida, stir, add coriander powder, red chillies, turmeric and salt, stir. Then add tomatoes and yoghurt, *bhunno* until fat leaves the masala, add water (approx 250 ml/1 cup) and bring to a boil. Now add guavas, bring to a boil, reduce to medium heat, cover and cook, stirring occasionally, until tender. Sprinkle garam masala, mango powder and fennel powder, stir, add sugar and cook for 5 minutes. Adjust the seasoning. Sprinkle lemon juice and stir.

To Serve

Remove to a dish and serve with Poori*.

*See section on Breads.

Mongodi ki Subzi

INGREDIENTS

Dumplings

240 g/1¼ cups Moong Dal (washed)

5 g/1 Tsp Red Chilli powder

Salt

Ghee to shallow fry

Masala

60 g/5 Tbs Ghee

2 g/1 Tsp Coriander seeds

3 g/1 Tsp Cumin seeds

A pinch Asafoetida

20 g/4 Tsp Coriander powder

3 g/½ Tsp Red Chlilli powder

3 g/½ Tsp Turmeric

10 g/2 Tsp Mango powder (Amchur)

Salt

Garnish

15 g/¼ cup Coriander

Serves 4

Preparation time: 10 minutes (Plus time taken to prepare dumplings)

Cooking time: 1 hour

Grape-sized dumplings of *moong dal—Mongodi*—napped in a spicy masala, can also be served with *Kadhi.*

Preparation

Dumplings: Pick, wash in running water and soak *dal* for *not* more than 30 minutes. Drain, put in a blender, add red chillies and salt, make a coarse paste. Make grape-sized dumplings with a spoon and place them on a tray evenly spaced out. Dry in the sun until hard (at least 2 days). *Mongodi* has a shelf life of 6 months in an airtight container.

Yield: Approx 250 g/9 oz.

Coriander: Clean, wash and chop.

Cooking

Heat ghee in a *kadhai,* add dumplings and shallow fry over medium heat until golden brown. Remove dumplings and reserve the fat.

Reheat 60 g/4 Tbs of reserved ghee, add coriander and cumin seeds, saute over medium heat until they begin to crackle, add asafoetida and stir. Add coriander powder, red chillies, turmeric and mango powder—all dissolved in water (approx 120 ml/½ cup)—and stir constantly until the liquid has almost evaporated. Then add water (approx 600 ml/ 2½ cups) and bring to a boil. Now add fried *Mongodi* and salt, bring to a boil, cover and simmer until soft and coated with gravy. Adjust the seasoning.

To Serve

Remove to a dish, garnish with coriander and serve with *Poori* or *Phulka**.

Note. To make *Mongodi* with *Kadhi*, use 100 g/3½ oz of dumplings to be fried and added half-way through the cooking process of *Kadhi* (see *Punjab Section*). However, to make the Marwari *Kadhi* use 50 g/⅓ cup of gramflour and black salt instead of table salt.

*See section on Breads.

Besan ke Gatte

Veg

Besan Ke Gatte or gramflour dumplings cooked in a sharp cumin-and-asafoetida gravy.

INGREDIENTS

Gatte (Dumplings)

350 g/2½ cups Gramflour
A pinch Soda bi-carb
5 g/1¾ Tsp Cumin seeds
3 g/½ Tsp Red Chilli powder
Salt
15 g/4 Tsp Ginger
5 g/1 Tbs Mint
60 g/¼ cup Yoghurt
30 g/7½ Tsp Ghee
Ghee to deep fry

Gravy

100 g/½ cup Ghee
3 g/1 Tsp Cumin seeds
6 Cloves
2 sticks Cinnamon (1-inch)
2 Bay Leaves
A generous pinch Asafoetida
220 g/1 cup Yoghurt
20 g/4 Tsp Coriander powder
3 g/½ Tsp Red Chilli powder
3 g/½ Tsp Turmeric
Salt
5 g/1 Tbs Mint
4 Green Chillies
3 g/½ Tsp Garam Masala

Garnish

15 g/¼ cup Coriander
15 g/4 Tsp Ginger

Serves 4

Preparation time: 1 hour

Cooking time: 30 minutes

Preparation

Gatte: Scrape, wash and finely chop ginger. Clean, wash and chop mint. Whisk yoghurt in a bowl, add the remaining ingredients and warm water (approx 180 ml/¾ cup) to make a hard but pliable dough. Divide into 8 equal portions, make balls and roll into cylinders (½-inch diameter).

Heat water (approx 1.5 litres/6¼ cups) in a *handi,* add the cylinders and boil for 20 minutes. Remove the cylinders and reserve the liquid. Cool the cylinders and cut into ½-inch pieces. Heat oil in a *kadhai* and deep fry *gatte* over medium heat until golden brown.

Gravy: Whisk yoghurt in a bowl, add coriander powder, red chillies, turmeric and salt. Keep aside for 10 minutes. Clean, wash and chop mint. Remove stems, wash, slit, deseed and chop green chillies.

Garnish: Clean, wash and chop coriander. Scrape, wash and cut ginger into juliennes.

Cooking

Heat ghee in a *handi,* add cumin seeds, cloves, cinnamon and bay leaves, saute over medium heat until the seeds begin to crackle. Add asafoetida, stir for a few seconds, reduce to low heat, add the yoghurt mixture and stir, without increasing the heat, until it starts boiling. Then add 500 ml/2 cups of the reserved liquid, bring to a boil, cover and simmer for 5 minutes. Now add the dumplings, bring to a boil and then simmer for 10 minutes, add mint and green chillies, stir. Sprinkle garam masala and stir. Adjust the seasoning.

To Serve

Remove to a bowl, garnish with coriander and ginger and serve with *Phulka** or boiled rice.

*See section on Breads.

Veg

Moong Dal Khilma

INGREDIENTS

300 g/1½ cups Green Moong dal

10 g/1 Tbs Ginger

10 g/2 Tbs Coriander

Tempering

75 g/6 Tbs Ghee

3 g/1 Tsp Cumin seeds

A pinch Asafoetida

3 g/½ Tsp Red Chilli powder

3 g/½ Tsp Turmeric

Salt

3 g/½ Tsp Garam Masala

15 ml/1 Tbs Lemon juice

Serves 4

Preparation time: 20 minutes

Cooking time: 1:35 hours

A dry preparation of pulses, tossed in a tempered mixture of spices.

Preparation

Lentil: Pick and wash in running water.

Vegetables: Scrape and wash ginger. Clean, wash and chop coriander.

Cooking

Put *dal* and ginger in a *handi,* add water (approx 750 ml/ 3 cups), bring to boil, cover and simmer until almost cooked. Ensure that the lentil is not mashed, it should be *just* soft. Drain and discard ginger.

To prepare the tempering, heat ghee in a *kadhai,* add cumin and saute over medium heat until it begins to crackle. Add asafoetida, stir, add red chillies, turmeric and salt, stir. Then add the cooked *dal* and toss (or stir carefully) for 5 minutes, ensuring that the lentil does not get mashed. Sprinkle garam masala and lemon juice, toss. Adjust the seasoning.

To Serve

Remove to a shallow dish, garnish with coriander and serve as an accompaniment.

South India

With J. Ramesh Babu and Syed Nasir

Before I am 'arraigned', I plead 'guilty' to the 'charge' of being unfair. Unfair because I have clubbed the cuisines of our Southern states—including Hyderabad—in one chapter. My only 'excuse' is that the rich variety of foods from the South should be covered in a separate book—a project I propose to undertake. There are many superb culinary styles—Malabari, Tulu, Coorg, Syrian Christian, Cochin Jewish—which I have *had* to leave out. Many of the recipes penned are common—with minor differences, of course—to every genre of Southern cooking. In any event, this chapter is only a 'palate-teaser'—a hint of things to come.

There are some inexcusable—and unforgivable—misconceptions about the food of the South. While the West only knew of 'curry', the ubiquitous *Madras Soup* and *Mulligatawny,* what was even worse was that most Indians themselves were unaware that the region's cuisine was much more than *Dosai, Idli, Bonda, Vadai, Sambhar* and *Rasam,* which are all breakfast foods, snacks and/or accompaniments. Without taking anything away from these delights, it must be said that each state has a cuisine as rich and varied as that of the other states in the country.

J. Ramesh Babu: Botanist (a B.Sc. from Madras University), sportsman (badminton and soccer star at school and college) and amateur pilot (possibly the only Indian chef with a pilot's license), Ramesh Babu is the Chef of the Welcomgroup Maurya Sheraton*. Besides Southern, he specialises in French and Italian cooking.

Syed Naseer: At 12, he dropped out of school—despite parental disapproval and "innumerable thrashings"—and apprenticed with Hyderabad's redoubtable Ustad Noor Khan. He was such a great success that as soon as he "graduated", the Oberoi's snapped him up and made him Chef of the *Mughal Room* at the *Oberoi Towers**, Bombay.

*Designation subject to change.

Just as inaccurate is the belief that Southern food is 'strictly' vegetarian. While it is true that the South remained largely untouched by the Muslim invasions and has remained, more or less, vegetarian, it is just as true that the variety of non-vegetarian—especially seafood—delicacies is unmatched. A noteworthy feature of the region's non-vegetarian food is the manner of slaughtering animals—they are drowned before being put under the knife.

The bewildering array of meat dishes notwithstanding, rice and *dal* remain the heart and soul of a Southern vegetarian meal. The grain is consumed in some form or the other at breakfast, lunch, dinner and everything in between. Lentils are the major source of protein. The consumption of wheat and breads though not altogether unknown is quite limited. The most popular form of bread is *Poori,* which is usually served with sweets on festive occasions like *Pongal.* With their undoubted imagination and ingenuity, Southern chefs have produced a plethora of vegetarian delights to supplement their various rice and *dal* dishes.

Other notable features of Southern cooking are the liberal use of coconut, *kari* (curry) leaves, fenugreek seeds, tamarind and asafoetida. Contrary to popular belief, the food of the South is not 'chilli-hot'. The notable exceptions are the cuisines of Andhra (terribly 'hot') and Kerala (tolerably 'hot').

Incidentally, 'curry' is an oversimplified form of the Tamil word, *kari,* which means sauce. The word 'curry' does not even exist in any Indian culinary dictionary. However, thanks to the Raj legacy—and much to the disgust of all Indians—the word became synonymous with our cuisine. The insipid, colourless and tasteless stew a handful of *khansamah* prepared to pander to the *Sahibs'* taste became India's culinary shame. The confusion was worse confounded when the *Sahibs* themselves started cooking the stuff using, what else, 'curry powder', which again is non-existent in the list of Indian condiments. Fortunately, the world is learning to distinguish between the different styles of Indian cooking and between different gravies—not 'curries'.

A traditional Southern feast is eaten sitting cross-legged on the floor and out of banana leaves. The food is served in copious quantities from stainless steel pails and each delicacy is topped with a spoonful of *desi ghee* (clarified butter). The *ghee* is prepared by simmering butter over very low heat. When the butter starts frothing, a small piece of turmeric root and some turmeric leaves are added. The butter is simmered until clarified, removed from the heat, cooled to room temperature and then carefully decanted. Yoghurt is eaten at the end of every meal—to sooth the innards after the spices.

Assisted by Ponnapatti Papaiah

Iggaru Royya

A home-style sea-food delicacy, spiced with cumin, fenugreek and pepper.

INGREDIENTS
1 kg/2¼ lb Prawns (medium size)
125 ml/½ cup Groundnut Oil
200 g/1¼ cups Onions
20 g/3½ Tsp Garlic paste
10 g/1¾ Tsp Ginger paste
400 g/1¾ cups Tomatoes
Salt
75 g/1 cup Coconut
10 Curry leaves
5 g/1¾ Tsp Cumin seeds
2 g/½ Tsp Fenugreek seeds
10 g/1 Tbs Black Peppercorns
20 g/⅓ cup Coriander

Serves 4

Preparation time: 1 hour

Cooking time: 15 minutes

Preparation

Prawns: Shell, devein, wash and pat dry.

Vegetables: Peel, wash and chop onions. Wash and chop tomatoes. Wash curry leaves. Clean, wash and chop coriander.

Coconut Paste: Remove the brown skin and grate coconut, put in a blender, add 60 ml/¼ cup of coconut water and make a fine paste.

Spices: Pound cumin seeds, fenugreek seeds and peppercorns with a pestle.

Cooking

Heat oil in a *kadhai,* add onions and saute over medium heat until light brown. Add garlic and ginger pastes, stir until the liquid has evaporated. Then add tomatoes and salt, *bhunno* until semi-mashed, reduce to low heat, add coconut paste and curry leaves, stir for 2 minutes. Now add prawns, stir, add the pounded spices, stir, increase to medium heat and *bhunno* until prawns are cooked. Adjust the seasoning.

To Serve

Remove to a flat dish, garnish with coriander and serve with boiled rice.

Erha Kari

INGREDIENTS

1 kg/2¼ lb Prawns (medium size)

100 ml/7 Tbs Groundnut Oil

200 g/1¼ cups Onions

20 g/3½ Tsp Garlic paste

10 g/1¾ Tsp Ginger paste

10 g/2 Tsp Coriander powder

10 g/2 Tsp Red Chilli powder

3 g/½ Tsp Turmeric

Salt

300 g/1⅓ cups Tomatoes

75 g/1 cup Coconut

10 Curry leaves

20 g/⅓ cup Coriander

Serves 4

Preparation time: 1 hour

Cooking time: 15 minutes

A coconut-flavoured prawn curry redolent with coriander—the powder as well as the herb.

Preparation

Prawns: Shell, devein, wash and pat dry.

Vegetables: Peel, wash and chop onions. Wash and chop tomatoes. Wash curry leaves. Clean, wash and chop coriander.

Coconut Paste: Remove the brown skin and grate coconut, put in a blender, add 60 ml/¼ cup of coconut water and make a fine paste.

Cooking

Heat oil in a *handi,* add onions and saute over medium heat until transparent. Add garlic and ginger pastes, stir until the liquid has evaporated, add coriander powder, red chillies, turmeric and salt, stir. Then add tomatoes and *bhunno* until mashed. Reduce to low heat, add coconut paste and curry leaves, stir for 2 minutes. Now add prawns and water (approx 400 ml/1¾ cups), bring to a boil, reduce to low heat and simmer, stirring occasionally, until cooked. Adjust the seasoning.

To Serve

Transfer to a bowl, garnish with coriander and serve with boiled rice.

Kerala Nandu Masala

A coconut-flavoured crab curry. Extracting the meat from the shell is an easily acquired art and that is half the fun of eating this mild delicacy.

INGREDIENTS
8 Crab (medium size)
100 ml/7 Tbs Groundnut Oil
2 g/½ Tsp Mustard seeds
2 Whole Red Chillies
120 g/⅔ cup Onions
50 g/3 Tbs Ginger paste
50 g/3 Tbs Garlic paste
3 g/½ Tsp Red Chilli powder
3 g/½ Tsp Turmeric
Salt
400 g/1¾ cups Tomatoes
75 g/1 cup Coconut
2 Green Chillies
10 Curry leaves
20 g/⅓ cup Coriander

Serves 4

Preparation time: 30 minutes

Cooking time: 40 minutes

Preparation

Crab: Rinse in running water, remove and retain claws, cut each into 2 pieces.

Vegetables: Peel, wash and chop onions. Wash and chop tomatoes. Clean and wash curry leaves. Clean, wash and chop coriander.

Coconut Paste: Remove the brown skin and grate coconut. Remove stems, wash, slit, deseed and chop green chillies. Put both ingredients in a blender, add 75 ml/⅓ cup of coconut water and make a fine paste.

Cooking

Heat oil in a *handi,* add mustard seeds, saute over medium heat until they begin to crackle, add whole red chillies and stir for 5 seconds. Add onions, saute until light golden, add ginger and garlic pastes, stir until the liquid has evaporated. Then add red chilli powder, turmeric and salt, stir for 30 seconds, add tomatoes and *bhunno,* until fat leaves the masala. Now add the paste, reduce to low heat, stir for 2 minutes, add crab, curry leaves and water (approx 300 ml/ 1¼ cups), bring to a boil, cover and simmer, stirring occasionally, for 20 minutes. Adjust the seasoning.

To Serve

Remove to a bowl, garnish with coriander and serve with boiled rice and lemon wedges.

Pomfret Mappas

INGREDIENTS

12 Fillet of Fish
75 g/⅓ cup Tamarind pulp*
Salt
150 ml/⅔ cup Coconut Oil
4 g/1 Tsp Mustard seeds
75 g/½ cup Onions
20 g/2 Tbs Ginger
30 g/3 Tbs Garlic
3 g/½ Tsp Turmeric
10 Curry leaves
4 Green Chillies
5 g/1 Tsp Coriander powder
5 g/1 Tsp Fennel powder
1 g/¼ Tsp Clove powder
2 g/½ Tsp Cinnamon powder
100 ml/½ cup Coconut Milk (First extract)**
100 ml/½ cup Coconut Milk (Second extract)**
10 ml/2 Tsp Malt Vinegar

*See section on Tamarind.
**See section on Coconuts.

Serves 4

Preparation time: 30 minutes
Cooking time: 30 minutes

Fillet of pomfret (or sole or halibut), marinated in tamarind and then simmered in a delicately spiced gravy.

Preparation

Fish: Wash, pat dry and cut fillets into halves.

Marination: Dissolve tamarind pulp in 100 ml/7 Tbs of water for 10 minutes, add salt and leave the fish in this marinade for 15 minutes.

Vegetables: Peel, wash and chop onions. Scrape, wash and chop ginger. Peel and chop garlic. Wash curry leaves. Remove stems, wash, slit, deseed and chop green chillies.

Cooking

Heat oil in a *handi,* add mustard seeds, stir over medium heat until they begin to crackle, add onions and saute until light brown. Add ginger and garlic, stir for 2–3 minutes, add turmeric and salt, stir for 30 seconds. Then add curry leaves and green chillies, stir for a minute, add coriander, fennel, clove and cinnamon powders, stir for a minute, add the second extract of coconut milk and simmer for 5 minutes. Now add the fish, bring to a boil, add vinegar and the first-extract of coconut milk, bring to a boil, cover and simmer until fish is cooked. Adjust the seasoning.

To Serve

Remove to a bowl and serve with boiled rice.

Kozhi Vartha Kari

Tender boneless chicken cubes cooked in a palate-tickling combination of herbs and spices.

Preparation

Chicken: Clean, remove the skin, debone and cut-into 1½-inch *tikka.*

Marination: Mix red chillies, turmeric and salt with half each of ginger and garlic pastes and rub this mixture on the *tikka.* Keep aside for 30 minutes.

Sauteeing: Heat oil in a *kadhai,* add the marinated chicken and saute over medium heat until evenly light brown. Remove the *tikka* and reserve the oil.

Vegetables: Wash curry leaves. Peel, wash and slice onions. Wash and chop tomatoes. Clean, wash and chop coriander.

Tamarind: Dissolve in 25 ml/5 Tsp of water.

Pepper: Pound with a pestle.

Cooking

Reheat the reserved oil, add curry leaves, stir over medium heat for 30 seconds, add onions and saute until light brown. Add the remaining ginger and garlic pastes, stir for a minute, add tomatoes and *bhunno* until fat leaves the masala. Then add coriander, cardamom and clove and cinnamon powders, stir for a minute, add tamarind and cook for 5 minutes. Now add the sauteed chicken, *bhunno* for 8–10 minutes, add water (approx 240 ml/1 cup) and bring to a boil. Reduce to medium heat and *bhunno,* stirring constantly, until the moisture has evaporated and the masala coats the *tikka.* Sprinkle pepper and lemon juice, stir. Adjust the seasoning.

To Serve

Remove to a dish, garnish with coriander and serve with *Dosai**, Paratha* or *Poori****. It can also be served as a cocktail snack—skewered on toothpicks.

**See section on Snacks.

***See section on Breads.

INGREDIENTS

1.2 kg/2¾ lb Chicken
45 g/7½ Tsp Ginger paste
30 g/5 Tsp Garlic paste
3 g/½ Tsp Red Chilli powder
5 g/1 Tsp Turmeric
Salt
120 ml/½ cup Groundnut Oil
10 Curry leaves
150 g/1 cup Onions
100 g/½ cup Tomtoes
3 g/½ Tsp Coriander powder
2 g/⅓ Tsp Green Cardamom powder
2 g/⅓ Tsp Clove and Cinnamon powder
25 g/4 Tsp Tamarind pulp*
3 g/1 Tsp Black Peppercorns
15 ml/1 Tbs Lemon juice
20 g/⅓ cup Coriander

*See section on Tamarind.

Serves 4
Preparation time: 1 hour
Cooking time: 30 minutes

Milagu Kozhi Chettinad

INGREDIENTS

1.2 kg/2⅔ lb Chicken (2 birds)
25 g/⅓ cup Coriander

Marination

20 g/2 Tbs Black Peppercorns
125 g/½ cup Yoghurt
25 g/4 Tsp Ginger paste
25 g/4 Tsp Garlic paste
30 ml/2 Tbs Lemon juice
Salt

Gravy

100 ml/7 Tbs Groundnut Oil
175 g/1 cup Onions
25 g/4 Tsp Ginger paste
25 g/4 Tsp Garlic paste
150 g/⅔ cup Tomatoes
Salt
5 g/⅔ Tsp Garam Masala

Serves 4

Preparation time: 45 minutes
Cooking time: 25 minutes

The authentic recipe for a 'devilled' chicken curry—done to perfection in a black pepper sauce. Remember, it was South India which 'exported' black pepper to the world.

Preparation

Chicken: Clean, remove the skin and cut each into 8 pieces.

Coriander: Clean, wash and chop.

Marination: Pound peppercorns with a pestle. Whisk yoghurt in a large bowl, add the pounded pepper, the ginger and garlic pastes, lemon juice and salt, mix well. Leave the chicken pieces in this marinade for at least 30 minutes.

Gravy: Peel, wash and chop onions. Wash and chop tomatoes.

Cooking

Heat oil in a *handi,* add onions and saute over medium heat until light golden. Add ginger and garlic pastes, saute until onions are golden brown. Then add tomatoes and *bhunno* until fat leaves the masala. Now add chicken, alongwith the marinade, stir for 4–5 minutes, add water (approx 250 ml/ 1 cup) bring to a boil, cover and simmer, stirring occasionally, until chicken is tender. Adjust the seasoning. Sprinkle garam masala and stir.

To Serve

Remove to a shallow dish, garnish with coriander and serve with boiled rice or *Paratha**.

*See section on Breads.

Vendakka Masala Pachchadi

Veg

Okra simmered in a thick, coconut-flavoured, yoghurt-based gravy.

INGREDIENTS

800 g/1¾ lb Okra
Groundnut Oil to deep fry
3 g/1 Tsp Cumin seeds
4 g/1 Tsp Mustard seeds
20 g/2 Tbs Urad dal
3 whole Red Chillies
10 Curry leaves
125 g/¾ cup Onions
250 g/1 cup Tomatoes
5 g/1 Red Chilli powder
3 g/½ Tsp Turmeric
15 g/1 Tbs Coriander powder
Salt
75 g/1 cup Coconut
15 g/2 Tbs Cashewnuts
100 g/½ cup Yoghurt

Serves 4

Preparation time: 30 minutes

Cooking time: 30 minutes

Preparation

Okra: Slice off the ends (without exposing the tubes), wash, pat dry and cut into l-inch pieces. Heat oil in a *kadhai* and deep fry over medium heat until crisp (approx 5–6 minutes). Drain and reserve the oil.

Remaining Vegetables: Wash curry leaves. Peel, wash and chop onions. Wash and chop tomatoes.

Lentil: Pick, wash in running water and pat dry.

Coconut Paste: Remove the brown skin and grate coconut. Split cashewnuts. Put both in a blender, add 60 ml/¼ cup of coconut water and make a fine paste.

Yoghurt: Whisk in a bowl.

Cooking

Heat 75 ml of the reserved oil in a *handi,* add cumin and mustard seeds, *urad dal,* whole red chillies and curry leaves, saute over medium heat until the seeds begin to crackle. Add onions and saute until golden brown. Then add tomatoes, stir, add red chilli powder, turmeric, coriander and salt, *bhunno* until fat leaves the masala. Reduce to low heat, add coconut paste and *bhunno* for 2 minutes. Remove the *handi,* add yoghurt, stir, add water (approx 400 ml/1⅔ cups), return to heat and bring to a boil. Now add the deep fried okra and simmer until napped in the gravy. Adjust the seasoning.

To Serve

Remove to a shallow dish and serve with boiled rice.

Veg

Bataani Kaal Kari

INGREDIENTS

750 g/1¾ lb Green Peas
750 g/1¾ lb Mushroom (fresh)
150 ml/⅔ cup Groundnut Oil
6 g/2 Tsp Cumin seeds
4 g/1 Tsp Mustard seeds
1 g/¼ Tsp Fenugreek seeds
20 g/2 Tbs Urad dal
125 g/¾ cup Onions
25 g/4 Tsp Ginger paste
25 g/4 Tsp Garlic paste
10 g/2 Tsp Coriander powder
5 g/1 Tsp Red Chilli powder
5 g/1 Tsp Turmeric
Salt
250 g/1 cup Tomatoes
60 g/¾ cup Coconut
30 g/¼ cup Cashewnuts
20 Curry leaves
20 g/⅓ cup Coriander

Serves 4

Preparation time: 1 hour

Cooking time: 30 minutes

A delicious combination of peas and mushrooms in a thick, rich gravy.

Preparation

Peas: Boil and drain.

Mushroom: Slice off the earthy base of the stalk, wash and cut into quarters. Heat 50 ml/3 Tbs of oil in a *kadhai* and saute over medium heat for 4–5 minutes.

Lentil: Pick, wash in running water and pat dry.

Remaining Vegetables: Clean, wash and chop onions. Wash and chop tomatoes. Wash curry leaves. Clean, wash and chop coriander.

Coconut Paste: Remove the brown skin and grate coconut. Split cashewnuts. Put both in a blender, add 60 ml/¼ cup of coconut water and make a fine paste.

Cooking

Heat oil in a *kadhai,* add cumin seeds, mustard seeds, fenugreek seeds and *urad dal,* saute over medium heat until the seeds begin to crackle. Add onions, saute until light brown, add ginger and garlic pastes and stir until the liquid has evaporated. Then add coriander powder, red chillies, turmeric and salt, stir, add tomatoes and *bhunno* until fat leaves the masala. Reduce to low heat, add coconut paste and curry leaves, stir for a minute, add water (approx 500 ml/ 2 cups) and bring to a boil. Now add the boiled peas and sauteed mushroom, simmer for 5 minutes. Adjust the seasoning.

To Serve

Remove to a bowl, garnish with coriander and serve with boiled rice.

Murungakkai Sambhar

Veg

A must with every meal—breakfast, lunch and dinner—this lentil delicacy is flavoured with asafoetida. *Sambhar* can be made with okra, aubergines, radish, squash, pumpkin or any other vegetables except the 'starchies'. The most popular vegetable, however, is drumstick.

INGREDIENTS

200 g/1 cup Toor dal
200 g/7 oz Drumstick
5 g/1 Tsp Turmeric
5 g/1 Tsp Red Chilli powder
4 Green Chillies
175 g/1 cup Onions
300 g/1⅓ cups Tomatoes
Salt
5 ml/1 Tsp Groundnut Oil
15 g/2½ Tsp Tamarind pulp*
10 g/1 Tbs Jaggery
75 g/5 Tbs Coconut paste
20 g/⅓ cup Coriander

Tempering

30 ml/2 Tbs Groundnut Oil
4 g/1 Tsp Mustard seeds
6 g/2 Tsp Cumin seeds
2 g/1 Tsp Coriander seeds
3 g/1 Tsp Sesame seeds
10 g/1 Tbs Urad dal
15 Curry leaves
A generous pinch Asafoetida

*See section on Tamarind.

Serves 4

Preparation time: 55 minutes
Cooking time: 45 minutes

Preparation

Lentil: Pick, wash in running water and soak *toor dal* for 30 minutes. Drain.

Drumstick: Peele, wash and cut into 1-inch pieces.

Remaining Vegetables: Remove stems, wash, slit and deseed green chillies. Peel, wash and slice onions. Wash and cut tomatoes into quartets. Clean, wash and chop coriander.

Tamarind: Dissolve in 30 ml/2 Tbs of water.

Jaggery: Pound and soak in 30 ml/2 Tbs of coconut water.

Tempering: Pick, wash *urad dal* in running water and pat dry. Wash curry leaves.

Cooking

Put the drained lentil in a *handi,* add water (approx 1 litre/4 cups), drumstick, turmeric, red chillies, green chillies, onions, tomatoes, and salt, boil until the *dal* is cooked. Stir in oil. Remove.

To prepare the tempering, heat oil in a large *kadhai,* add mustard seeds, cumin seeds, coriander seeds, sesame seeds and *urad dal,* saute over medium heat until the seeds begin to crackle. Add curry leaves, stir, add asafoetida and stir. Transfer the cooked *dal* and tamarind, simmer for 5 minutes, add jaggery and bring to a boil. Reduce to low heat, add coconut paste and simmer for 5 minutes. Sprinkle chopped coriander and stir. Adjust the seasoning.

To Serve

Remove to a bowl and serve as an accompaniment.

Veg

Rasam

INGREDIENTS

350 g/1½ cups Tomatoes
75 g/7 Tbs Toor Dal
1 Green Chilli
A pinch Turmeric
Salt
15 ml/1 Tbs Groundnut Oil
4 g/1 Tsp Mustard seeds
6 g/2 Tsp Cumin seeds
3 whole Red Chillies
10 Curry leaves
A pinch Asafoetida
30 g/3 Tbs Garlic
5 g/1½ Tsp Black Peppercorns
100 g/5 Tbs Tamarind pulp*
20 g/⅓ cup Coriander

*See section on Tamarind.

Yield: 1 litre
Preparation time: 1:20 hours
Cooking time: 10 minutes

Rasam, literally, 'juice' or 'extract', is an appetizer-cum-digestive-cum-accompaniment. Its versatility apart, it comes in several flavours—the more popular ones being tomato and lemon.

Preparation

Tomatoes: Wash, roughly cut, put in a blender and make a puree.

Lentil Puree: Pick and wash *dal* in running water. Remove stem, wash, slit and deseed green chilli. Put both in a *handi,* add turmeric, salt and water (approx 800 ml/3⅓ cups), bring to a boil, cover and simmer until *dal* is mashed. Force the cooked *dal* through a soup strainer or a food mill into a separate *handi.*

Remaining Vegetables: Wash curry leaves. Peel and crush garlic. Clean, wash and chop coriander.

Pepper: Pound with a pestle.

Tamarind: Dissolve in 100 ml/7 Tbs of water.

Cooking

Heat oil in a *kadhai,* add mustard seeds and cumin seeds, saute over medium heat until they begin to crackle. Add whole red chillies and curry leaves, stir for a few seconds. Then add asafoetida, crushed garlic and salt, stir. Now add tomato puree, pepper and water (approx 750 ml/3 cups), bring to a boil. Transfer the lentil puree and tamarind, bring to a boil again and strain. Adjust the seasoning.

To Serve

Remove to a bowl and garnish with coriander

Note: For *Lemon Rasam,* use 100 ml/7 Tbs of lemon juice instead of the tamarind pulp and garnish with ginger juliennes (10 g/1 Tbs) besides coriander.

Bisi Bhela Huliyana

Veg

A rice 'n' *Sambhar* delicacy cooked with a special *Huliyana Masala,* garnished with cashewnuts.

Preparation

Rice and Lentil: Pick, wash in running water and soak for 30 minutes. Drain.

Vegetables: Wash and cut cauliflower into small florets. Wash and finely chop tomatoes. Wash curry leaves.

Tamarind: Dissolve in 50 ml/3 Tbs of water.

***Hullyana Masala*:** Pick lentils, wash in running water, drain, pat dry and broil each, separately, on a *tawa* until light brown. Broil each of the remaining ingredients separately on a *tawa* for 30 seconds. Put all these broiled ingredients in a blender and make a coarse powder.

Garnish: Heat oil in a *kadhai* and deep fry the cashewnuts over medium heat until golden brown.

Cooking

Put the drained *toor dal* in a handi, add water (approx 2.5 litres/10 cups), bring to a boil, cover and simmer until almost cooked. Add the drained rice, peas and cauliflower, boil for 10 minutes, stirring occasionally (to ensure that the rice grains do not stick to the bottom). Then add tomatoes, tamarind, asafoetida, stir, add red chillies, turmeric and salt, stir. Now add the *Huliyana Masala,* cover and simmer until rice and lentil are mashed and achieve a porridge consistency. Sprinkle curry leaves and continue to simmer.

Meanwhile, to prepare the tempering, heat oil in a frying pan, add mustard seeds and saute over medium heat until they begin to crackle. Add whole red chillies and stir for 15 seconds. Bring the simmering rice to a boil, pour on the tempering and mix. Adjust the seasoning.

To Serve

Remove to a bowl, garnish with cashewnuts and serve with *papad* and mango pickle.

INGREDIENTS

300 g/1½ cups Basmati Rice
150 g/¾ cup Toor dal
50 g/⅓ cup Green Peas
50 g/½ cup Cauliflower
400 g/1¾ cups Tomatoes
50 g/3 Tbs Tamarind pulp*
3 g/½ Tsp Asafoetida
3 g/½ Tsp Red Chilli powder
5 g/1 Tsp Turmeric
Salt
10 Curry leaves

Huliyana Masala

50 g/¼ cup Channa Dal
20 g/2 Tbs Urad Dal
5 Green Cardamom
5 Cloves
2 sticks Cinnamon (1-inch)
4 g/1 Tsp Fenugreek seeds
3 g/1 Tsp Cumin seeds

Tempering

75 ml/⅓ cup Groundnut Oil
2 g/½ Tsp Mustard seeds
3 whole Red Chillies

Garnish

50 g/⅓ cup Cashewnuts
Groundnut Oil to deep fry

*See section on Tamarind.

Serves 4

Preparation time: 40 minutes
Cooking time: 40 minutes

Hyderabad

Hyderabadi Murgh Korma

INGREDIENTS

800 g/1¾ lb Chicken (1 bird)
225 g/1 cup Yoghurt
60 g/¼ cup Ginger paste
30 g/5 Tsp Garlic paste
160 g/1 cup Onions
5 g/1 Tsp Red Chilli powder
3 g/½ Tsp Turmeric
25 g/⅓ cup Coconut
75 g/4 Tbs Cashewnut paste
10 g/4 Tbs Sesame seeds
2 g/⅓ Tsp Nutmeg powder
Salt
120 g/⅔ cup Ghee
Whole Garam Masala
- 10 Green Cardamom
- 2 Black Cardamom
- 10 Cloves
- 2 sticks Cinnamon (l-inch)
- 1 Bay Leaf
- 1 g/¼ Tsp Mace

250 g/1⅔ cups Potatoes (medium size)
30 ml/2 Tbs Lemon juice
20 g/⅓ cup Coriander

Serves 4

Preparation time: 40 minutes
Cooking time: 20 minutes

A cashewnut-based chicken curry, flavoured with nutmeg.

Preparation

Chicken: Clean, remove the skin and cut into 8 pieces.

Yoghurt: Whisk in a large bowl.

Vegetables: Peel, wash and slice onions. Peel, wash, cut potatoes into quarters and immerse in water. Clean, wash and chop coriander.

Coconut: Remove the brown skin and grate.

Marination: Mix ginger paste, garlic paste, onions, red chillies, turmeric, coconut, cashewnut paste, sesame seeds, nutmeg and salt with yoghurt and leave the chicken in this marinade for at least 30 minutes.

Cooking

Heat ghee in a *handi,* add whole garam masala and saute over medium heat until it begins to crackle. Add the chicken, alongwith the marinade, bring to a boil and simmer for 5 minutes. Add water (approx 400 ml/1⅔ cups) and boil for 2–3 minutes. Add potatoes (drained) and lemon juice, simmer until chicken is tender and potatoes are cooked. Adjust the seasoning.

To Serve

Remove to a dish, garnish with coriander and serve with rice or an Indian bread of your choice.

Murgh Nizami

A semi-dry chicken 'masala' cooked with nuts (cashewnuts, peanuts and coconut) and seeds (sunflower and sesame).

INGREDIENTS
800 g/1¾ lb Chicken (1 bird)
120 g/⅔ cup Ghee
100 g/⅔ cup Onions
50 g/3 Tbs Ginger paste
50 g/3 Tbs Garlic paste
8 Green Chillies
5 g/1 Tsp Turmeric
30 g/¼ cup Peanuts
10 g/1 Tbs Sesame seeds
10 g/1 Tbs Sunflower seeds
50 g/⅔ cup Coconut
150 g/⅔ cup Yoghurt
Salt
10 g/2 Tsp Garam Masala
30 ml/2 Tbs Lemon juice
20 g/⅓ cup Coriander
20 g/⅓ cup Mint
50 g/⅓ cup Cashewnuts
Groundnut Oil to deep fry

Serves 4

Preparation time: 45 minutes

Cooking time: 25 minutes

Preparation

Chicken: Clean, remove the skin and cut into 8 pieces.

Vegetables: Peel, wash and chop onions. Remove stems, wash, slit, deseed and chop green chillies. Clean, wash and chop coriander and mint.

Nuts and Seeds: Pound peanuts, sesame seeds and sunflower seeds with a pestle. Remove the brown skin and grate coconut. Heat oil in a *kadhai* and deep fry cashewnuts until golden brown.

Yoghurt: Whisk in a bowl.

Cooking

Heat ghee in a *handi,* add onions and saute over medium heat until golden brown. Add ginger and garlic pastes, stir for a minute, add green chillies and turmeric, stir. Then add the pounded nuts and seeds, and grated coconut, stir for a minute, add yoghurt and *bhunno* until fat leaves the masala. Now add chicken, stir, add water (approx 400 ml/1⅔ cups), bring to a boil, simmer until tender. Adjust the seasoning. Sprinkle garam masala, lemon juice, coriander, mint and cashewnuts, stir.

To Serve

Remove to a dish and serve with an Indian bread of your choice.

Murg Do-Piaza Hyderabadi

INGREDIENTS

800 g/1¾ lb Chicken (1 bird)
150 g/¾ cup Ghee
400 g/2⅓ cups Onions
30 g/5 Tsp Ginger paste
30 g/5 Tsp Garlic paste
5 g/1 Tsp Red Chilli powder
5 g/1 Tsp Turmeric
Salt
10 g/2 Tsp Garam Masala
20 g/⅓ cup Coriander
20 g/⅓ cup Mint
20 g/2 Tbs Sunflower seeds
50 g/⅓ cup Cashewnuts
Groundnut Oil to deep fry

Serves 4

Preparation time: 30 minutes
Cooking time: 25 minutes

A mild chicken curry cooked with an abundance of onions and garnished with cashewnuts and sunflower seeds.

Preparation

Chicken: Clean, remove the skin and cut into 8 pieces.

Vegetables: Peel, wash and chop onions. Clean, wash and chop coriander and mint.

Seeds and Nuts: Heat oil in a *kadhai* and deep fry sunflower seeds and cashewnuts until light brown.

Cooking

Heat ghee in a *handi,* add onions and saute over medium heat until golden brown. Add ginger and garlic pastes, red chillies and turmeric—all dissolved in 60 ml/¼ cup of water—and stir for a minute. Then add chicken, stir, add water (approx 600 ml/2½ cups), bring to a boil and simmer until tender. Adjust the seasoning. Sprinkle garam masala, coriander and mint, stir, add sunflower seeds and cashewnuts, bring to a boil.

To Serve

Remove to a dish and serve with rice or an Indian bread of your choice.

Sofyani Biryani

A saffron-flavoured rice delicacy, mild and easy to digest.

INGREDIENTS

800 g/1¾ lb Chicken (1 bird)
450 g/2¼ cups Basmati Rice
150 g/¾ cup Ghee
Salt
Whole Garam Masala
- 6 Green Cardamom
- 2 Black Cardamom
- 6 Cloves
- 2 sticks Cinnamon (1-inch)
- 2 Bay leaves
- A pinch Mace

6 g/2 Tsp Black Cumin seeds
100 g/⅔ cup Onions
25 g/4 Tsp Ginger paste
25 g/4 Tsp Garlic paste
10 g/2 Tsp Red Chilli powder
500 g/2¼ cups Yoghurt
30 ml/2 Tbs Lemon juice
½ g/1 Tsp Saffron
30 ml/2 Tbs Milk
20 g/⅓ cup Mint
20 g/⅓ cup Coriander

Serves 4

Preparation time: 30 minutes
Cooking time: 35 minutes

Preparation

Chicken: Clean, remove the skin and cut into 8 pieces.
Rice: Pick, wash in running water and soak in a *handi* for 30 minutes. Drain, replenish with fresh water, add salt and half each of the whole garam masala and black cumin, bring to a boil and cook until rice is almost done. Drain.
Vegetables: Peel, wash and slice onions. Clean, wash and chop mint and coriander.
Yoghurt: Whisk in a bowl and divide into two equal portions.
Saffron: Dissolve in warm milk. Add one portion of the yoghurt and mix well.
Oven: Pre-heat to 375°F.

Cooking

Heat ghee in a *handi,* add the remaining whole garam masala and black cumin, saute over medium heat until cumin begins to crackle. Add onions and saute until golden brown. Then add ginger paste, garlic paste and red chillies, stir for 15 seconds, add chicken and *bhunno* for 2 minutes. Add the portion of the plain yoghurt, stir, add water (approx 200 ml/¾ cup + 4 Tsp), bring to a boil, then simmer until chicken is three-fourths cooked. Sprinkle lemon juice. Adjust the seasoning.

Assembling

In the *handi* with the semi-cooked chicken, sprinkle half each of the saffron-yoghurt, mint and coriander. Then spread half the rice over the chicken. Sprinkle the remaining saffron-yoghurt, mint and coriander, spread the remaining rice. Place a moist cloth on top, cover with a lid and seal with *atta*-dough.

Finishing

Put the sealed *handi* on *dum* in the pre-heated oven for 15–20 minutes.

To Serve

Break the seal, shift the rice from one side (just enough to remove the chicken), make a bed of chicken in a rice dish, spread the rice on top and serve.

Dalcha Gosht

INGREDIENTS

600 g/1⅓ lb Leg of Spring Lamb
200 g/1 cup Channa Dal
Salt
120 g/⅔ cup Ghee
Whole Garam Masala
 5 Green Cardamom
 1 Black Cardamom
 5 Cloves
 1 stick Cinnamon (1-inch)
 1 Bay Leaf
 A pinch Mace
100 g/⅔ cup Onions
25 g/4 Tsp Ginger paste
25 g/4 Tsp Garlic paste
3 Green Chillies
10 g/2 Tsp Red Chilli powder
3 g/½ Tsp Turmeric
5 g/1 Tsp Coriander powder
400 g/1¾ cups Yoghurt
20 g/3 Tbs Coriander seeds
20 Curry leaves
60 ml/¼ cup Lemon juice

Tempering
30 ml/7½ Tsp Ghee
5 cloves Garlic
4 whole Red Chillies

Serves 4

Preparation time: 40 minutes

Cooking time: 1:05 hours

A sour lamb stew, simmered in a lentil puree.

Preparation

Lamb: Clean and cut into 1½-inch chunks.

Lentil: Pick, wash in running water and soak for 30 minutes in a *handi.* Drain, replenish with freshwater (approx 800 ml/ 3⅓ cups), add salt and boil until cooked. Remove, cool, transfer to a blender and make a puree.

Vegetables: Peel, wash and slice onions. Remove stems, wash, slit, deseed and chop green chillies. Wash curry leaves. Peel and crush garlic.

***Bouquet Garni*:** Tie coriander seeds and curry leaves in muslin.

Yoghurt: Whisk in a bowl.

Cooking

Heat ghee in a *handi,* add whole garam masala and saute over medium heat until it begins to crackle. Add onions and saute until golden brown. Then add ginger paste, garlic paste and green chillies, stir for 15 seconds, add lamb, *bhunno* for 3–4 minutes, add red chilli powder, turmeric and coriander powder, stir. Now add water (approx 1.4 litres/5¾ cups), bring to a boil, remove *handi,* add yoghurt, return to heat, bring to a boil again, suspend the *bouquet garni,* cover and simmer until lamb is tender. Add the lentil puree, bring to a boil, simmer for 15 minutes. Remove the *bouquet garni,* sprinkle lemon juice and stir. Adjust the seasoning.

To prepare the tempering, heat ghee in a pan, add garlic and saute over medium heat until golden brown. Add red chillies and stir. Remove and pour over the lamb stew, stir.

To Serve

Remove to a dish and serve with steamed rice or cumin-tempered *Pulao.*

Dosai
Utthappam
Egg Dosai
Sambhar
Idli
Vengayam Thoviyal
(Onion Chutney)
Thengai Thoviyal
Takkali Thoviyal
(Tomato Chutney)

Shahi Tukrha

Kulfi
Gajjar ka Halwa
Kalajam
Zauq-e-Shahi
Phirni

Jhinga Til Tinka
Samosa
Chaurasia Kathi
Goolar Kebab

Nawabi Tarkari Biryani

Veg

A favourite with the 'Nawabs' of Hyderabad—whenever they wanted to forego meat and yet wanted something delicious. Like the *Sofyani,* the *Nawabi* too is mild and 'light'.

INGREDIENTS

350 g/1¾ cups Basmati Rice
200 g/7 oz Potatoes
200 g/7 oz Carrots
50 g/⅓ cup Cashewnuts
50 g/⅓ cup Almonds
25 g/3 Tbs Sultanas
25 g/1 oz Glazed Cherries
120 g/⅔ cup Ghee
Whole Garam Masala
- 6 Green Cardamom
- 2 Black Cardamom
- 6 Cloves
- 2 sticks Cinnamon (1-inch)
- 2 Bay leaves
- A pinch Mace

Salt
100 g/⅔ cup Onions
4 Green Chillies
30 g/3 Tbs Ginger
20 g/2 Tbs Garlic
3 g/½ Tsp Turmeric
5 g/1 Tsp Red Chilli powder
220 g/1 cup Yoghurt
½ g/1 Tsp Saffron
30 ml/2 Tbs Milk
20 g/⅓ cup Mint
20 g/⅓ cup Coriander
Rosewater to sprinkle (optional)

Serves 4
Preparation time: 35 minutes
Cooking time: 35 minutes

Preparation

Rice: Pick, wash in running water and soak in a *handi* for 30 minutes. Drain, replenish with fresh water, add half whole garam masala and salt, bring to a boil and cook until rice is almost done. Drain.

Vegetables: Peel, wash and dice potatoes and carrots, immerse potatoes in water. Peel, wash and slice onions. Remove stems, wash, slit and deseed green chillies. Scrape, wash and, cut ginger into juliennes. Peel and chop garlic. Clean, wash and chop mint and coriander.

Almonds: Blanch, cool and peel.

Yoghurt: Whisk in a bowl and divide into two equal portions.

Saffron: Dissolve in warm milk. Add one portion of the yoghurt and mix well.

Oven: Pre-heat to 375°F.

Cooking

Heat ghee in a *handi,* add the remaining whole garam masala and saute over medium heat until it begins to crackle. Add onions, saute until golden brown, add green chillies, ginger and garlic, saute for a minute. Then add turmeric and red chillies, stir, add the diced vegetables and stir for a minute. Add the portion of plain yoghurt, stir, add water (approx 150 ml/⅔ cup), bring to a boil, then simmer until vegetables are cooked. Now add dry fruits and nuts. Adjust the seasoning.

Assembling

In the *handi* with the cooked vegetables, sprinkle half each of saffron-yoghurt, mint and coriander. Then spread half the rice over the vegetables. Sprinkle the remaining saffron-yoghurt, mint and coriander, spread the remaining rice. Sprinkle rosewater (optional). Place a moist cloth on top, cover with a lid and seal with *atta*-dough.

Finishing

Put the sealed *handi* on *dum* in the pre-heated oven for 15–20 minutes.

To Serve

Break the seal, shift the rice from one side (just enough to remove the vegetables), make a bed of vegetables in a rice dish, spread the rice on top and serve.

Subz Khada Masala

INGREDIENTS

- 100 g/3½ oz Beans
- 100 g/3½ oz Peas
- 100 g/3½ oz Carrots
- 150 g/5 oz Potatoes
- 250 g/9 oz Cauliflower
- 150 ml/⅔ cup Groundnut Oil
- 25 g/7 Tsp Ginger
- 25 g/7 Tsp Garlic
- 160 g/1 Clip Spring Onions
- 3 g/½ Tsp Turmeric
- 5 g/1 Tsp Red Chilli powder
- 80 g/⅓ cup Tomatoes
- 4 Green Chillies
- 4 Whole Red Chillies
- 20 g/⅓ cup Coriander
- 225 g/1 cup Yoghurt
- 60 g/1 cup Fenugreek
- Salt

Serves 4

Preparation time: 30 minutes

Cooking time: 20 minutes

A chilli 'hot' mixed-vegetable dish with a predominant flavour of fenugreek.

Preparation

Vegetables: Wash, string and dice beans. Peel, wash and dice carrots and potatoes, immerse the potatoes in water. Wash and cut cauliflower into florets. Scrape, wash and roughly chop ginger. Peel and roughly chop garlic. Wash and slice the bulbs of spring onions, discard the greens. Wash and chop tomatoes. Remove stems and wash green chillies. Clean, wash and chop coriander and fenugreek, immerse fenugreek in salted water for 15 minutes and drain.

Yoghurt: Whisk in a bowl.

Cooking

Heat oil in a *kadhai,* add ginger and garlic, saute over medium heat for 30 seconds, add spring onions and saute for 30 seconds. Add beans, peas, carrots, potatoes and cauliflower, stir for a minute, add turmeric and red chilli powder, stir. Then add tomatoes, green chillies, whole red chillies and coriander, stir for a minute, add yoghurt and fenugreek, stir. Now add water (approx 300 ml/1¼ cups), bring to a boil, simmer until vegetables are cooked and the liquid has evaporated. Adjust the seasoning.

To Serve

Remove to a dish and serve with an Indian bread of your choice.

Mitha
(Desserts)

With Manjit S. Gill and Chandra B. Tewari

Hindus believe the only way to *nirvana* is through *puja,* the act of daily worship. This spirituality is the basis for Indian sweets or *mithai,* for it is the *mithai* which is offered by a devotee to please the chosen God or Goddess. In the *Bhagvata Purana,* Lord Krishna describes *mithai* as the Food of Gods. To the Hindus, the centre of the Sea of Nectar is the most sacred abode. It is where they crave to reside. This nectar or *amrit* is prepared from five ingredients: honey, milk, *desi ghee* (clarified butter), sugar and water. With the addition of *tulsi* it is used to bathe the idol or object of worship during *puja.* These five ingredients are intrinsic to all Indian sweets and there is a specific reason for using each one of them. However, for reasons of space, it is impossible to go into specifics. Suffice it to say that blended with fruits, vegetables, aromatic spices, dry fruits, nuts and essences, they help create an astounding variety of exotic sweet dishes.

What distinguishes Indian desserts from the sweets of other lands is that they are not prepared to satisfy a sweet-tooth alone. They are, in fact, intended to provide nourishment. Besides, in this land of rich traditions, to offer sweets is the ultimate act of friendship—a sign of love and affection.

There is a mistaken belief that, like the traditional vegetarian snacks, *mithai* too can only be made by the *halwais* (the word, in all probability, derives from *halwa,* the dessert made by reducing vegetables or fruits with sugar) or professional confectioner. Nothing could be farther from the truth. Indian desserts are as simple—or difficult—to make as

Chandra Bhan Tewari: After initial training in Calcutta—home of the finest Indian sweetmeats—and a two-year apprenticeship with the doyen of Lucknow *halwais,* K.L. Roy, Tewari today heads the *mithai* kitchen at the Welcomgroup *Maurya Sheraton**.

*Designation subject to change.

any other dessert. In fact, like Western confections, exact quantities of ingredients are an imperative for *mithai* making.

A salient feature of preparing Indian sweets is the use of reduced milk. Each dessert requires a level of reduction on which there can be no compromise.

Just as North Indian vegetarian snacks are inconceivable without *ajwain, mithai* shares a unique relationship with green cardamom powder. The other essential is *kewra,* vetivier, which is sprinkled on the dessert at the time of service.

This chapter includes two extraordinary sweets: *Mushq-e-Tanjan* and *Murgh-ki-Burfi*—made from lamb and chicken mince, respectively. Extraordinary because they are, perhaps, the only non-vegetarian desserts in the world!

Assisted by Mohammed Naseem

Rabarhi

The *mithai* that explains the girth of the Northerners and satiates their sweet tooth. Despite the constant attention and time required, *Rabarhi* is a surprisingly simple dessert to make.

INGREDIENTS

3 litres/12½ cups Milk
350 g/1¾ cups Sugar
5 drops Vetivier
20 g/3 Tbs Pistachio
Chandi-ka-Varq (silver leaves)

Yield: 1 kg/2¼ lb
Preparation time: 5 minutes
Cooking time: 2 hours

Preparation

Pistachio: Blanch, cool, remove the skin and cut into slivers.

Cooking

Put milk in a *kadhai,* bring to a boil, reduce to low heat and stir constantly for 20 minutes. Thence stir after every 5 minutes until milk is reduced to 900 ml/3¾ cups and acquires a granular consistency. Remove, add sugar and stir until dissolved. Then add vetivier and stir. Cool, remove to a silver bowl, garnish with pistachio and refrigerate.

To Serve

Remove from the refrigerator, cover with *varq* and serve chilled. (*Rabarhi* is best served in individual *shikoras*—earthenware bowls—and should be portioned out, garnished with pistachio and then refrigerated. It should be covered with *varq* only at the time of service.)

Note:

(i) For *Kulfi, Shahi Tukrha* and *Zauq-e-Shahi,* reduce milk to 1.05 litres/4¼ cups. For *Kulfi,* add 400 g/2 cups of sugar. For the other two, add 300 g/1½ cups of sugar. Do not look for a granular consistency.

(ii) For *Rasmalai,* reduce the milk to 1.2 litres/5⅓ cups, add 350 g/1½ cups of sugar and, again, there will be no granular consistency.

Shahi Tukrha

INGREDIENTS

350 g/¾ lb Rabarhi* (Unsweetened)

600 g/3 cups Sugar

1 drop Vetivier

3 g/½ Tsp Green Cardamom powder

12 slices Milk Bread

Groundnut Oil to deep fry

2 litres/8⅓ cups Milk

10 g/4 Tsp Almonds

5 g/2 Tsp Pistachio

1 g/2 Tsp Saffron

Chandi-ka-Varq (silver leaves)

*See recipe for Rabarhi in this section.

Yield: 12

Preparation time: 1:15 hours (Plus time taken for Rabarhi)

This dessert of the *Nawabs* is without the semblance of a doubt India's most exotic—and famous—sweet dish. Garnished with dry fruits and covered with sheets of *pure* silver leaves, *Shahi Tukrha* is sterling stuff.

Preparation

Rabarhi: Add 100 g/½ cup of sugar while it is still warm and stir until dissolved. Add vetivier and stir.

Syrup: Boil the remaining sugar with water (approx 300 ml/1¼ cups) to make a syrup of one-string consistency. Add cardamom powder and stir.

Bread: Slice off the crust and trim the edges to make discs. Heat oil in a *kadhai* and deep fry over low heat until golden brown and crisp.

Milk: Bring to a boil in a large, flat, thick-bottomed *handi,* remove and reserve 15 ml/1 Tbs to dissolve saffron.

Tukrha: Immerse the fried bread in the remaining milk, the slices at least an inch apart. Return the *handi* to heat and simmer until the milk is absorbed, turning once in between with a spatula without breaking the bread. Remove from heat and pour on the warm syrup.

Nuts: Blanch almonds and pistachio, cool, remove the skin and cut-into slivers.

Saffron: Dissolve in the reserved milk while it is still warm.

Assembling

Arrange the soaked *Tukrha* on a silver platter, spread *Rabarhi* on top, garnish with nuts and sprinkle saffron.

To Serve

Cover the *Shahi Tukrha* with *Varq* and serve warm.

Note: The alternative and just as tasty method is to serve the *Shahi Tukrha* cold. Do not soak in milk, pour on the warm sugar syrup on the crisp bread discs, spread *Rabarhi* on top, garnish with nuts sprinkle saffron and refrigerate. Remove at the time of service, cover with *Varq* and serve.

Kulfi

The creamy and rich ice-cream, made predominantly in saffron, pistachio, saffron-pistachio, and mango flavours—flavours from the real thing, not essence. The recipe below is for saffron-pistachio—*Kesar-Pista.*

INGREDIENTS

1 kg/2¼ lb Rabarhi* (unsweetened)

400 g/2 cups Sugar

30 g/4 Tbs Pistachio

2 g/4 Tsp Saffron

30 ml/2 Tbs Milk

2 g/⅓ Tsp Green Cardamom powder

Falooda for Garnish*

Rose Syrup for topping

*See recipes for **Rabarhi** and **Falooda** in this section.

Yield: 8–10

Preparation time: 10 minutes (Plus time taken for Rabarhi and Falooda)

Freezing time: 6 hours

Preparation

Pistachio: Blanch, cool, remove the skin and cut into slivers.

Saffron: Dissolve in warm milk.

Rabarhi: Add sugar, pistachio, saffron and cardamom while it is still warm and stir until sugar is dissolved. Cool.

Assembling

Put *Rabarhi* in *Kulfi* moulds or an ice-cream mould and freeze.

To Serve

Demould, slice into half vertically (if an ice-cream mould has been used, cut into 1-inch thick slices), garnish with *Falooda,* top with rose syrup and serve.

Note: For Aam-ki-Kulfi, use 200 g/7 oz of mango dices or mango puree instead of saffron and pistachio. Add the puree when the *Rabarhi* has cooled down. The rest of the procedure is same.

Rasmalai

INGREDIENTS

250 g/9 oz Chhenna*

15 g/2 Tbs Flour

1 g/¼ Tsp Baking powder

750 g/3¾ cups Sugar

500 g/18 oz Rabarhi** (unsweetened)

5 g/2 Tsp Pistachio

* See section on Milk.

** See recipe for Rabarhi in this section.

Serves 4

Preparation time: 30 minutes (Plus time taken for Rabarhi)

Cooking time: 30 minutes

Chhenna is synonymous with Bengal. It is used to make the Eastern State's sweetmeats—easily the best in the Subcontinent—including the famous *Rasgoolah. Rasmalai* is a *Rasgoolah* in *Rabarhi.*

Preparation

Chhenna: Knead gently to mash any granules. Sieve 10 g/4 Tsp of flour and baking powder together, mix with *chhenna* and knead to make a dough. Divide into 12 equal portions, make balls and gently squeeze between the palms and flatten to make 'patties' (approx 1½-inch diameter), ensuring that the surface is smooth.

Remaining Flour: Dissolve in 30 ml/2 Tbs of water.

Rabarhi: Add 150 g/¾ cup of sugar while it is still warm and stir until dissolved. Cool and refrigerate in the serving bowl.

Pistachio: Blanch, cool, remove the skin and cut into slivers.

Cooking

Dissolve the remaining sugar in water (approx 400 ml/1⅔ cups) and bring to a boil, add the dissolved flour and, when the syrup rises, add the 'patties' and poach over high heat for 10 minutes. This is a tricky operation because under no circumstances should the syrup be allowed to settle down. To maintain the consistency, add water (approx 180 ml/¾ cup) in a steady trickle. To ascertain whether the *Rasmalai* is cooked, remove one in a spoon and look closely for perforations, akin to those in a sponge, which will appear on the surface for only a second.

Fill water (approx 800 ml/3⅓ cups) in a separate *handi,* transfer *Rasmalai,* alongwith the syrup, and cool.

Assembling

Remove *Rabarhi* from the refrigerator. Gently squeeze out the syrup from the *Rasmalai* and transfer to the bowl of *Rabarhi.* Refrigerate.

To Serve

Remove from the refrigerator, garnish with pistachio and serve cold.

Gulab Jamun

A great favourite with expatriate Indians, *Gulab Jamun* is a *Khoya* delicacy stuffed with pistachio and green cardamom seeds.

INGREDIENTS

300 g/11 oz Khoya*
50 g/2 oz Chhenna*
900 g/4½ cups Sugar
40 g/5 Tbs + 1 Tsp Flour
A pinch Soda bi-carb
10 Green Cardamom
10 g/4 Tsp Pistachio
1 g/2 Tsp Saffron
2 drops Rosewater concentrate
Ghee to deep fry

*See section on Milk.

Yield: 20–24
Preparation time: 40 minutes
Cooking time: 10–12 minutes for each set

Preparation

Khoya: Knead *gently***, to mash any granules.

Chhenna: Crumble and knead *gently***, to mash any granules.

Syrup: Boil sugar with water (540 ml/2¼ cups) to make a syrup of one-string consistency. Keep warm.

Soda bi-Carb: Dissolve in a tablespoon of water.

Gulab Jamun Mixture: Mix *Chhenna* with *Khoya,* add flour and the dissolved soda bi-carb, knead *gently.* Reserve 50 g/2 oz for the filling and make 20–24 balls of 1-inch diameter with the remaining mixture.

Filling: Peel cardamom and discard the skin. Blanch pistachio, cool, remove the skin and cut into slivers. Pound saffron with a pestle to break the flakes. Add cardamom seeds, pistachio slivers, saffron flakes and rosewater concentrate to the reserved mixture and mix well.

Stuffing: Flatten the balls, place a portion of the filling in the middle, seal and make smooth balls.

Cooking

Heat ghee in *kadhai,* add the balls and deep fry over medium heat until golden brown. Swirl ghee with a *pooni* (perforated spoon) constantly and without touching the *Gulab Jamun* until they come to the surface. (This prevents sticking.) Remove and immerse immediately in the syrup.

To Serve

Remove to a glass-bowl, alongwith the syrup, put 2 or 3 *Gulab Jamun* in individual bowls, pour a tablespoon of syrup on top and serve hot.

Note: Kalajam is an overfried version of Gulab Jamun. The balls are deep fried until dark brown, immersed in syrup and removed. Kalajam and vanilla ice-cream make a tasty combination.

**Caution is emphasized because if treated roughly the fat will separate from Khoya.

Zauq-e-Shahi

INGREDIENTS

500 g/18 oz Rabarhi* (unsweetened)

600 g/3 cups Sugar

1 g/2 Tsp Saffron

5 g/1 Tsp Green Cardamom powder

200 g/7 oz Gulab Jamun* mixture

6 g/2 Tsp Poppy seeds

Ghee to deep fry

10 g/4 Tsp Pistachio

20 g/3 Tbs Almonds

*See recipes for Rabarhi and Gulab Jamun in this section.

Serves 4

Preparation time: 1 hour (Plus time taken for Rabarhi and Gulab Jamun mixture)

Marble-size *Gulab Jamun* combine with a creamy *Rabarhi* to make this a classic dessert—a fine example of the innovative spirit of the Indian Chef.

Preparation

Rabarhi: Add 100 g/½ cup of sugar while it is still warm and stir until dissolved. Add saffron and stir.

Syrup: Boil the remaining sugar with water (300 ml/ 1¼ cups) to make a syrup of one-string consistency. Add cardamom and stir. Keep warm.

***Gulab Jamun* Mixture:** Add poppy seeds, knead gently and make 35–40 balls of 1/3-inch diameter. Heat ghee in a *kadhai* and deep fry the marbles over medium heat until golden brown. Swirl ghee with a *pooni,* without touching the marbles, until they come to the surface. (This prevents sticking.) Remove and immerse immediately in the syrup.

Nuts: Blanch pistachio and almonds, cool, remove the skin and cut into slivers.

Assembling

Transfer the soaked marbles to a shallow silver dish, pour on the *Rabarhi,* garnish with nuts and serve warm.

Phirni

A popular dessert, set in *shikoras* (earthenware bowls) and flavoured with cardamom and saffron.

INGREDIENTS

1 litre/4 cups Milk

50 g/¼ cup Basmati Rice

250 g/1¼ cups Sugar

1 g/2 Tsp Saffron

5 g/1 Tsp Green Cardamom powder

2 drops Rosewater concentrate

5 g/2 Tsp Pistachio

10 g/4 Tsp Almonds

Serves 4

Preparation time: 40 minutes

Cooking time: 15 minutes

Preparation

Rice: Pick, wash in running water and soak for 30 minutes. Drain, put in a blender, add water (approx 30 ml/2 Tbs) and make a fine paste.

Saffron: Dissolve in 15 ml/1 Tbs of warm milk.

Nuts: Blanch pistachio and almonds, cool, remove the skin and cut into slivers.

Shikoras: Rinse in running water and then immerse in a *handi* full of water for 25 minutes. Remove and pat dry.

Cooking

Boil remaining milk in a *handi,* add rice paste and sugar whilst stirring with a whisk. Reduce to low heat and cook, stirring constantly (to ensure no lumps are formed), until the mixture becomes thick and is reduced to a custard consistency. Add saffron, cardamom and rosewater concentrate, stir and remove.

Assembling

Pour equal quantities of *Phirni* in the *shikoras* (or glass bowls), garnish with pistachio and almond slivers, cool and refrigerate until set.

To Serve

Remove *shikoras* from refrigerator and serve cold.

Kesari Kheer

INGREDIENTS

- 1.5 litres/6¼ cups Milk
- 75 g/3 oz Basmati Rice
- 15 g/4 Tsp Ghee
- 125 g/2⅔ cup Sugar
- 5 g/1 Tsp Green Cardamom powder
- 20 g/3 Tbs Almonds
- 15 g/5 Tsp Raisins
- 1 g/2 Tsp Saffron
- 30 ml/2 Tbs Milk to dissolve Saffron

Yield: 1 kg/2¼ lb

Preparation time: 1:20 hours

Cooking time: 45 minutes

The traditional rice pudding, consumed on all occasions—is served by rich and poor alike, the garnish reflecting the wealth of the host.

Preparation

Rice: Pick, wash in running water, soak for an hour and drain.

Almonds: Blanch, cool, remove the skin and split.

Saffron: Dissolve in warm milk.

Cooking

Boil milk in a *handi* and remove. Heat ghee in a separate *handi,* add rice and *bhunno* until it begins to colour (approx 4–5 minutes). Transfer the milk and bring to a boil, stirring constantly (to ensure that rice does not stick). Reduce to low heat and simmer until rice is cooked. Then add sugar and continue to cook until reduced to a custard consistency. Now add the remaining ingredients, and stir for a minute.

To Serve

Remove to a silver bowl and serve hot.

Note:

(i) *Kheer* can also be served cold. Use an additional 25 g/2 Tbs of sugar. Then pour equal quantities of *Kheer* in *shikoras* after cooling it and refrigerate. Garnish with *varq*.

(ii) Saffron is optional.

Sevian

It is not unusual even today to see a Punjabi grandmother twirling dough for hours to make *sevian*—vermicelli. This dessert is particularly popular in winter.

INGREDIENTS

1.2 litres/5 cups Milk
60 g/2 oz Sevian
120 g/⅔ cup Ghee
20 g/3 Tbs Almonds
150 g/¾ cup Sugar
15 g/5 Tsp Raisins
6 Green Cardamom
2 drops Vetivier

Serves 4

Preparation time: 10 minutes

Cooking time: 45 minutes

Preparation

Sevian: Heat ghee in a *kadhai,* add vermicelli and saute over medium heat, stirring constantly but gently, lest it crumbles—until golden brown. Drain the fat.

Almonds: Blanch, cool and remove the skin.

Cardamom: Peel, discard the skin and pound the seeds with a pestle.

Cooking

Boil milk in a *handi,* add fried *sevian,* stir carefully and simmer until milk is reduced by half. Add almonds and simmer for 5 minutes. Then add sugar and stir until dissolved. Now add raisins, stir, add the pounded cardamom seeds and vetivier, stir.

To Serve

Remove to a bowl and serve hot.

Shrikhand

Western India's favourite dessert—akin to a souffle—flavoured with saffron and cardamom.

INGREDIENTS

1.5 kg/3 lb Yoghurt
150/1¼ cups Castor Sugar
1 g/2 Tsp Saffron
15 ml/1 Tbs Milk
5 g/1 Tsp Green Cardamom powder
5 g/2 Tsp Pistachio
5 g/1½ Tsp Sunflower seeds

Yield: 1 kg/2¼ lb

Preparation time: 8:30 hours

Preparation

Yoghurt: Hang in muslin in a cool place until completely drained of whey (approx 6–8 hours).

Saffron: Dissolve in warm milk. Cool.

Pistachio: Blanch, cool, remove the skin and cut into slivers.

Shrikhand: Transfer the hung yoghurt to a bowl, add sugar and whisk until fluffy. Add saffron and cardamom, mix well. Remove to a glass bowl and gently thump the bowl to level the *Shrikhand.* (Do not level with a spoon—the dessert is not meant to look like a well-set souffle.) Garnish with pistachio and sunflower seeds. Refrigerate for 2 hours.

To Serve

Remove from the refrigerator and serve cold.

Saeb ki Kheer

INGREDIENTS

1 kg/2¼ lb Apples
1.5 litres/6¼ cups Milk
200 g/1 cup Sugar
1 g/2 Tsp Saffron
30 ml/2 Tbs Milk to dissolve Saffron
3 g/½ Tsp Green Cardamom powder
5 drops Rosewater
Cherries for Garnish
Chandi-ka-Varq (Silver leaves)

Yield: 1 kg/2¼ lb

Preparation time: 35 minutes

Cooking time: 1 hour

A creamy and aromatic—saffron and cardamom—apple dessert.

Preparation

Apples: Peel, core and dice. Put in a *kadhai,* add sugar and stew over medium heat, stirring constantly—but gently (to prevent apples from getting mashed)—until sugar has dissolved and the liquid has evaporated. Remove and cool.

Saffron: Dissolve in warm milk.

Cooking

Boil milk in a *kadhai,* reduce to low heat and simmer until reduced to 600 ml/2½ cups. Add saffron, cardamom and rosewater, stir. Remove when warm, add the stewed apples and stir. Transfer to a silver bowl and refrigerate.

To Serve

Remove from the refrigerator, garnish with cherries, cover with *varq* and serve cold.

Falooda

INGREDIENTS

200 g/7 oz Cornflour
½ Tsp Yellow Colour (optional)

Yield: Approx 800 g/1¾ lb

Preparation time: 45 minutes

Falooda is a noodle-like garnish which not only complements *Kulfi,* but makes it easy to bite into the frozen dessert.

Preparation

Cornflour: Put in a *kadhai,* add colour and water (approx 750 ml/3 cups + 2 Tbs) and stir until dissolved. Then boil over medium heat, stirring constantly, until reduced to a gelatinous—consistency with a sheen on the surface.

Falooda: Force the cooked cornflour immediately through a noodle press, using the 1/16-inch mesh and collect the *Falooda* in a *handi* full of chilled water. (Store in a refrigerator and consume within 48 hours.).

Gajjar ka Halwa

A carrot and *Khoya* dessert, garnished with nuts and raisins.

INGREDIENTS

1 kg/2¼ lb Carrots
1 litre/4 cups Milk
200 g/1 cup Sugar
100 g/7 Tbs Ghee
5 g/1 Tsp Green Cardamom powder
60 g/2 oz Khoya*
20 g/3 Tbs Almonds
10 g/4 Tsp Pistachio
15 g/5 Tsp Raisins

*See section on Milk.

Yield: 1 kg/2¼ lb

Serves 4

Preparation time: 30 minutes (Plus time taken for Khoya)

Cooking time: 45 minutes

Preparation

Carrots: Peel, wash and grate.

Khoya: Grate.

Nuts: Blanch almonds and pistachio, cool and remove the skin. Split almonds, cut pistachio into slivers.

Raisins: Soak in water.

Cooking

Boil milk in a *kadhai,* add the grated carrots, reduce to medium heat and cook, stirring constantly, until carrots are tender and most of the liquid has evaporated. Add sugar and stir until dissolved and the liquid has evaporated. Then add ghee and *bhunno* for 3–4 minutes. Remove, add cardamom and stir.

To Serve

Remove to a silver bowl, garnish with *Khoya,* almonds, pistachio and raisins. Serve hot.

Ananas ka Muzaafar

INGREDIENTS

250 g/1 cups Basmati Rice
500 g/2½ cups Sugar
A pinch Nutmeg
20 ml/4 Tsp Lemon juice
1 g/2 Tsp Saffron
2 drops Vetivier
3 drops Pineapple essence
5 Green Cardamom
5 Cloves
5 drops Yellow Colour
2 Pineapple rings
75 g/⅓ cup Desi Ghee (Clarified Butter only)

Serves 4

Preparation time: 2:15 hours

Cooking time: 1:15 hours

A dessert for all festive occasions in Avadh, *Muzaafar* is made in two popular flavours: mango and pineapple.

Preparation

Rice: Pick, wash in running water and soak for 2 hours. Drain.

Saffron: Pound with a pestle to break the flakes.

Syrup: Boil sugar with water (150 ml/⅔ cup), add nutmeg and lemon juice, stir until the syrup becomes thick. Stir-in saffron, vetivier and pineapple essence.

Cardamom: Peel, discard the skin and pound the seeds with a pestle.

Pineapple Rings: Cut into ½-inch pieces.

Oven: Pre-heat to 250°F.

Cooking

Heat water (approx 1.2 1itres/5 cups) in a *handi,* add drained rice, cardamom, cloves and yellow colour, boil until the rice is *just* cooked. Drain.

Heat the syrup over low heat, add cooked rice, mix well and remove when the syrup starts boiling. Add pineapple pieces, mix well.

Finishing

Transfer the rice and syrup mixture to an earthenware *handi* (or a shallow casserole), cover with a lid, seal with *atta-dough* (or silver foil) and put on *dum* on a *tawa* over low heat (or in the pre-heated oven) for an hour.

To Serve

Break the seal (or tear off the foil) pour *ghee* evenly over the rice in a steady stream and serve from the *handi* (or casserole). If rice is not fully cooked, put on the *tawa* (or in the oven) for a few minutes more.

Non-Veg

Mushq-e-Tanjan

Mushq (Aroma of the Heavens) *tanjan* (treasure)—is a sweet lamb-rice—a dessert of classic proportions. A delicacy cooked in varying quantities of sugar: equal, double, treble, quadruple and the halves in between. The calibre of a chef is discerned by his ability to get the rice to absorb as much of the sweet stuff as is possible—without sticking. For you, we have taken the easiest quantity—equal—and do not fret if a thin layer does stick. It does not detract from the taste.

INGREDIENTS

Rice

500 g/2½ cups Basmati Rice
4 Green Cardamom
4 Cloves
2 sticks Cinnamon (1-inch)
Salt
½ g/1 Tsp Saffron
15 ml/1 Tbs Milk

Lamb

750 g/1⅔ lb Spring Lamb (assorted cuts)
120 g/½ Cup Desi Ghee (Clarified Butter only)
15 g/5 Tsp Garlic
Salt
100 ml/7 Tbs Milk
4 Green Cardamom
4 Cloves
4 sticks Cinnamon (1-inch)
100 g/½ cup Yoghurt
3 drops Vetivier
3 g/½ Tsp Mace powder
3 g/½ Tsp Green Cardamom powder
½ g/1 Tsp Saffron
10 ml/2 Tsp Lemon juice

Syrup

500 g/2½ cups Sugar

Garnish

Chandi-ka-Varq (silver leaves)

Serves 4

Preparation time: 1:15 hours

Cooking time: 2:30 hours

Preparation

Rice: Pick, wash in running water, soak for 1 hour and drain. Dissolve saffron in warm milk.

Lamb: Clean and cut breast, leg and shins into 1½-inch chunks. Peel garlic and cut into juliennes. Whisk yoghurt in a bowl. Dissolve saffron in 15 ml/l Tbs of warm milk.

Syrup: Boil sugar with water (approx 250 ml/1 cup) over medium heat for 7–8 minutes, stirring constantly, to make a thick syrup.

Cooking

Heat ghee in a *handi,* add garlic and saute over medium-heat until light brown. Add meat, salt, the remaining milk and water (approx 240 ml/1 cup), bring to a boil, add green cardamom, cloves and cinnamon, cover and simmer for 20 minutes. Then add yoghurt, stir, cover and simmer, stirring occasionally, until the liquid is reduced to one-third, add water (approx 300 ml/2¼ cups), bring to a boil, cover and simmer, stirring occasionally, until lamb is almost cooked. Remove, add vetivier, mace, cardamom powder, saffron and lemon juice, stir and keep aside.

Boil water (approx 2 litres/8½ cups) in a separate *handi,* add the drained rice, cardamom, cloves, cinnamon and salt, continue to boil until rice is three-fourths cooked. (To test, remove a few grains and squeeze between the thumb and forefinger—the rice will be slightly hard, will get mashed but a few white specks will show. The specks are a sign of uncooked rice.) Drain and spread three-fourths over the cooked meat, sprinkle saffron and cover with the remaining rice. Seal the *handi* with *atta*-dough and cook over low heat for 12–14 minutes. Break the seal, pour on the syrup evenly and seal again with *atta-dough.*

Heat a *tawa,* reduce to medium heat, place the *handi* on the *tawa* and cook for 20 minutes. Reduce to low heat and cook for 25 minutes.

To Serve

Break the seal, stir, remove to a shallow silver dish and garnish with *varq.*

Note: The *Mushq-e-Tanjan* can be put on *dum* in a pre-heated (250°F) oven, but the results will never be the same.

Paruppu Payasam

INGREDIENTS

1.5 litres/6¼ cups Milk

100 g/½ cup Moong Dal

150 g/¾ cup Sugar

5 g/1 Tsp Green Cardamom powder

200 g/2½ cups Coconut

Garnish

20 g/3 Tbs Cashewnuts

Groundnut Oil to deep fry

Yield: 1 kg/2¼ lb

Preparation time: 20 minutes

Cooking time: 1 hour

What *Kheer* is to the North Indians, *Paruppu Payasam* is to the denizens of the South. It is a must for *Onam* (the harvest festival) and *Vishu* (the New Year).

Preparation

Lentil: Pick, wash in running water and pat dry. Broil over medium heat in a *kadhai* until light golden.

Coconut: Remove the brown skin, reserve 20 g/¼ cup for garnish and grate the rest.

Garnish: Split cashewnuts and cut the reserved coconut into fine slices. Heat oil in a *kadhai* and deep fry both until golden brown.

Cooking

Put the broiled lentil in a *handi,* add water (approx 440 ml/ 1⅔ cups) and cook over low heat until *dal* is tender and the liquid almost absorbed. Add milk, bring to a boil and then simmer until reduced by half. Then add sugar and cardamom, stir and simmer for 5 minutes. Now add the grated coconut and stir.

To Serve

Remove to a bowl, garnish and serve hot.

Non-Veg Murgh-ki-Burfi

This is an incredible dessert—a chicken sweetmeat, which can also be made from lamb mince.

INGREDIENTS

100 g/⅔ lb Breasts of Chicken
800 g/1¾ lb Khoya*
200 g/1 cup Sugar
1 g/2 Tsp Saffron
10 ml/2 Tsp Milk
10 g/2 Tsp Green Cardamom powder
2 drops Vetivier

Garnish

20 g/3 Tbs Almonds
20 g/3 Tbs Pistachio
Chandi-ka-Varq (silver leaves)

*See section on Milk.

Yield: 1 kg 2¼ lb
Preparation time: 1:15 hours
Cooking time: 25 minutes

Preparation

Chicken: Clean, remove the skin, debone, mince and refrigerate for 15 minutes. Mince again, refrigerate for 15 minutes and mince a third time. Put the mince in a *handi,* add water (approx 1 litre/4 cups) and whisk until homogenised. Force the homogenised liquid through fine muslin into a *kadhai,* and reduce over medium heat, stirring constantly, until devoid of moisture and mince starts leaving the sides (Ensure that the mince does *not* stick, *nor* gets coloured.).

Khoya: Knead gently to mash any granules.

Saffron: Dissolve in warm milk.

Garnish: Blanch, cool, remove the skin and cut almonds and pistachio into slivers.

Cooking

Heat *khoya* and sugar in a *kadhai* over medium heat and stir constantly until sugar is dissolved and *khoya* starts boiling. Add the cooked chicken mince and stir vigorously until fully incorporated and the mixture starts boiling. Then add saffron, cardamom and vetivier, stir for a minute and transfer the mixture immediately to a shallow tray. Level with a spatula, sprinkle almonds and pistachio, thump the tray on a table or on the floor. Keep aside to set in a cool place.

To Serve

With the tip of a knife and a scale to guide, cut the set *Burfi* into 1½ inch squares (or diamonds). Remove carefully (with a flexible spatula) to a silver platter, cover with *varq* and serve.

Paal Poli

INGREDIENTS

1 litre/4 cups Milk

200 g/1 cup Sugar

½ g/1 Tsp Saffron

5 g/1 Tsp Green Cardamom powder

200 g/7 oz Flour

50 ml/3 Tbs Groundnut Oil

Groundnut Oil to deep fry puffs

Serves 4

Preparation time: 40 minutes

Cooking time: 1:10 hours

Flour puffs soaked in cardamom-flavoured milk—a favourite with Tamilians.

Preparation

Dough: Add groundnut oil to the flour and rub against the palms. Then add water (approx 90 ml/6 Tbs) and knead to make a soft dough. Cover with a moist cloth and keep aside for 30 minutes. Divide into 12 equal portions, make balls and flatten with a rolling pin into 4-inch discs.

Cooking

Boil milk in a *kadhai,* reduce to low heat, stir constantly for 20 minutes. Thence stir after every 5 minutes until milk is reduced to one-third. Remove, add sugar, saffron and cardamom, stir until sugar is dissolved.

Heat oil in a separate *kadhai* and fry the discs, one-at-a-time, over medium heat until they puff up and become light golden. Soak puffs in the reduced milk for *not* more than 5 minutes (or else they will disintegrate).

To Serve

Arrange 3 *Poli* on 4 individual plates, pour on the remaining reduced milk and serve warm.

Snacks

With Michael Graham

Indians are compulsive nibblers. They constantly need a 'fix' of snacks to satisfy their 'urge'. It is not unusual to eat one full meal and gobble snacks for the rest of the day. Until a few years ago, it was considered 'unhealthy' to eat out. An exception was made in the case of snacks. Little wonder, then, that this nation boasts of an astonishing range of minor delicacies.

Unlike in the West, where it is customary to offer tea, coffee or a drink when a guest drops in, Indians look for an excuse to offer you a snack with a *cuppa*—it's a part of our hospitable tradition. Almost the entire range of Indian snacks were—and still are—vegetarian. Perhaps this, too, had something to do with a mistrust of the kind of meat used in the market. Not any more. *Murgh Pakora, Kheema Samosa,* etc., are recent innovations. There is even *Kheema Dosai!* The number of non-vegetarian snacks, however, still remains small. Regionwise, they find greater favour in the more 'carnivorous' North. The *Kheema Dosai* is surely the 'creation' of some up-country chef.

Ajwain is the pre-eminent spice in North Indian vegetarian snacks. It lends its unique flavour and aroma to any number of them. The only other constant is a spicy and piquant chutney—fresh mint or *Saunth,* occasionally both—which accompany all snacks—vegetarian and non-vegetarian—of the region.

Southern snacks owe their popularity to the vast number of Uddippi restaurants around the country. Actually, Uddippi is a province in the State of Karnataka. Intrepid Uddippis established snack bars at every street corner making these eateries the mainstay of almost every metropolitan city. They provided excellent value for money with their

Michael Graham: Having the brilliant Richard Graham for a brother might have been a handicap for a lesser chef. Not for this Executive Chef at the *Holiday Inn**, Bombay, who has emerged as a culinary virtuoso in his own right.

*Designation subject to change.

cheap snacks. So successful were they that other Indians came to believe that *Dosai, Vadai, Idli, Uppamma* and *Bonda* was all there was to South Indian cuisine.

An amazing aspect of the Southern snacks is the variety one can make with rice flour as a base. These snacks owe their popularity to the fact that besides being tasty and wholesome, the use of spices and fat is restricted to the minimum. The lack of both is, however, made up by their abundance in the accompaniments—*Sambhar,* chutneys and *Mulagapodi.*

Surprisingly, almost all Indian snacks are either shallow fried or deep fried. The steamed *Idli* is a notable exception. The other surprising aspect of Indian snacks is that except for the odd *Aloo Tikki* or *Pakora,* most snacks are still consumed in the bazaar because they are thought difficult to make. They are not. In fact, they are quite simple—as you will see when you try out the recipes in this chapter.

Reduced in size, these mini delights make excellent cocktail snacks.

Assisted by Nilesh Nadkami

Jhinga Til Tinka

Ajwain-flavoured prawns, coated with sesame seeds and spiced with mace and cardamom.

Preparation

Prawns: Shell, devein, wash and pat dry.

First Marination: Mix all the ingredients and rub prawns with this mixture. Keep aside for 30 minutes. Squeeze the prawns gently to remove excess moisture.

Second Marination: Hang yoghurt in fine muslin for 4 hours to remove whey and then whisk in a bowl. Grate cheese and mix with yoghurt. Add the remaining ingredients and mix well. Rub the marinated prawns with this mixture and keep aside for 30 minutes.

Skewering: Skewer an equal number of prawns, without a gap, on 8 wooden sticks (6-inch long).

Coating: Mix breadcrumbs with sesame seeds, roll the skewered prawns in the mixture and refrigerate for 15 minutes.

Cooking

Heat oil in a *kadhai* and deep fry the skewered prawns over medium heat for 4–5 minutes. Remove and keep aside for 4–5 minutes. Return to *kadhai* and deep fry for 2–3 minutes.

To Serve

Place a paper doiley on a silver platter, arrange the skewers on top and serve with *Mint Chutney* and lemon wedges.

Note:

(i) The prawns can be kept aside after first frying until ready to serve.

(ii) *Murgh Til Tinka* is prepared from 12 chicken breasts (deboned and each cut into 6 *tikka*) and cumin seeds are used instead of *ajwain.* The rest of the procedure is the same.

INGREDIENTS

1 kg/2¼ lb Prawns (medium size)

Groundnut Oil to deep fry

First Marination

30 g/5 Tsp Garlic paste

25 g/4 Tsp Ginger paste

3 g/½ Tsp White Pepper powder

3 g/½ Tsp Yellow Chilli powder

Salt

60 ml/4 Tbs Lemon juice

Second Marination

120 g/½ cup Yoghurt

60 g/½ cup Cheddar Cheese (semi-hard)

8 g/1 Tbs Ajwain

60 ml/¼ cup Cream

3 g/½ Tsp Mace and Green Cardamom powder

30 g/3 Tbs Flour of Roasted Channa Dal

Coating

50 g/⅓ cup Sesame seeds

100 g/1 cup Breadcrumbs

Serves 4

Preparation time: 5:45 hours

Cooking time: 10–12 minutes

Jaan-e-Man

INGREDIENTS

1 kg/2¼ lb Chicken breasts
1 litre/4 cups Milk
½ g/1 Tsp Saffron
10 g/4 Tsp Fennel
10 Green Cardamom
4 Cloves
2 sticks Cinnamon (1-inch)
2 Bay Leaves
Seasoning
Groundnut Oil to deep fry

Batter

50 g/¼ cup Basmati Rice
3 g/½ Tsp Fennel powder
3 g/½ Tsp Yellow Chilli powder
Salt
50 g/10½ Tsp Yoghurt

Serves 4

Preparation time: 1:45 hours
Cooking time: 10–12 minutes

Tender chicken pieces, simmered in saffron and fennel-flavoured milk, skewered, dipped in rice batter and deep fried to make an extraordinary snack.

Preparation

Chicken: Clean, remove the skin, debone and cut into 1-inch *tikka.* Boil milk in a *handi,* add *tikka* and the remaining ingredients, except groundnut oil, and simmer over medium heat until tender. Remove *tikka* (but leave the coating on), strain and reserve the cooking liquor. Refrigerate the *tikka.*

Batter: Pick rice, wash in running water and soak for an hour. Drain, put in a blender, add fennel powder, yellow chillies, salt and the reserved liquor (approx 100 ml/7 Tbs) and make a fine, but thick, paste. Remove. Whisk yoghurt in a bowl, add the rice paste and mix well.

Skewering: Skewer 4 chicken pieces, without a gap, on 4-inch wooden sticks.

Cooking

Heat oil in a *kadhai,* dip skewers in the batter and deep fry over medium heat until lightly coloured. Remove and cool. Reheat oil and deep fry over medium heat until light golden and crisp.

To Serve

Place a paper doiley on a platter, arrange the skewers in a pattern of your choice and serve hot.

Chaurasia Kathi

An 'herbal' lamb masala rolled in a square *Paratha*—a meal-size snack.

INGREDIENTS

800 g/1¾ lb Spring Lamb undercut

100 g/7 Tbs Ghee

60 g/3 Tbs Fried Onion paste*

5 g/1 Tsp Garam Masala

30 g/3 Tbs Flour of Roasted Channa Dal

10 g/2 Tbs Mint

10 g/2 Tbs Coriander

30 ml/2 Tbs Lemon jurce

8 Varqi Paratha (6″ × 6″)**

Marination

60 g/2 oz Raw Papaya

30 g/5 Tsp Ginger paste

30 g/5 Tsp Garlic paste

15 g/1 Tbs Coriander powder

5 g/1 Tsp Red-Chilli powder

Salt

30 ml/2 Tbs Lemon juice

*See section on Pastes.
**See section on Breads.

Serves 4

Preparation time: 2:45 hours
Cooking time: 35 minutes

Preparation

Lamb: Clean and cut into ½-inch cubes.

Vegetables: Clean, wash and finely chop mint and coriander.

Marination: Peel papaya, deseed, put in a blender and make a fine paste. Remove, add the remaining ingredients and mix well. Rub lamb cubes with the mixture and keep aside for 2 hours.

Paratha: Keep warm.

Cooking

Heat ghee in a *handi,* add lamb cubes, alongwith marinade, and *bhunno* over low heat until tender. Add fried onion paste, stir for 2 minutes, add garam masala and the flour of roasted gram, stir. Remove, sprinkle mint, coriander and lemon juice, mix well. Divide into 8 equal portions.

Assembling

Place a portion of the cooked lamb along one edge of each *Paratha* and roll. Secure with tooth-picks or cocktail sticks.

To Serve

Place a paper doiley on a flat dish, arrange the rolls in a neat row and garnish with *Kachchumbar****. Serve with *Mint Chutney.*

***See section on Salads.

Goolar Kebab

INGREDIENTS

600 g/1⅓ lb Lamb Mince
75 g/⅓ Cup Channa Dal
4 Green Cardamom
4 Black Cardamom
6 Cloves
2 sticks Cinnamon (1-inch)
2 Bay leaves
Salt
2 Eggs
Groundnut Oil to deep fry

Chutney

40 g/⅔ cup Mint
40 g/⅔ cup Coriander
4 Green Chillies
10 g/4 Tsp Orange rind
50 g/⅓ cup Raisins
Salt
5 g/1 Tsp Mango powder
15 g/1½ Tsp Sugar

Serves 4

Preparation time: 1:35 hours

Cooking time: 4–5 minutes for each set

A Kashmiri snack of meatballs stuffed with a tangy chutney of raisins and mint 'n' coriander.

Preparation

Lentil: Pick and wash in running water.

Mince: Put mince and *dal* in a *handi,* add the whole spices, salt and water (approx 720 ml/3 cups), bring to a boil, cover and simmer until the lentil is just cooked. Increase to high heat and *bhunno* until the liquid has *completely* evaporated and the mixture has become dry. Remove, cool, discard whole spices and make a mince. Whisk eggs and knead into the mince. Divide into 24 equal portions, make balls and keep aside.

Chutney: Clean and wash mint and coriander. Remove stems, wash, slit and deseed green chillies. Remove the white coating on the inside and finely chop orange rind. Put mint, coriander and green chillies in a blender, add raisins and salt, make a paste. Remove, add mango powder, orange rind and sugar, mix well. Divide into 24 equal portions.

Stuffing: Flatten the mince balls between the palms, place a portion of the chutney in the middle of each and make balls again. Refrigerate for 15 minutes.

Cooking

Heat oil in a *kadhai* and deep fry the stuffed balls over medium heat until golden brown.

To Serve

Place a paper doiley on a silver platter, arrange *Kebab* on top and serve with lemon wedges.

Note: To make cocktail snack-size *Goolar,* make 48 mince balls and divide the filling into 48 equal portions. Rest of the procedure is same.

Aloo Tikki

Veg

A Potato patty stuffed with a variety—mince, lentils, white gram or green peas of fillings and then either shallow fried or deep fried.

INGREDIENTS

1 kg/2¼ lb Potatoes
50 g/2 oz Cornflour
Salt
Ghee to shallow fry

Filling

150 g/1 cup Green Peas
30 g/2 Tbs Ghee
3 g/1 Tsp Cumin seeds
20 g/4 Tsp Coriander powder
5 g/1 Tsp Red Chilli powder

Yield: 12

Preparation time: 1:30 hours
Cooking time: 10 minutes

Preparation

Potatoes: Boil, cool, peel and grate. Add cornflour and salt, mix well. Divide into 12 equal portions and make balls.

Filling: Boil peas until cooked, drain. Heat ghee in a *kadhai,* add cumin and saute over medium heat until it begins to crackle. Add peas and stir for a minute. Then add the remaining ingredients and stir for a minute. Cool and mash the peas. Divide into 12 equal portions.

Stuffing: Flatten each ball between palms, place a portion of the filling in the middle, make balls again and flatten into 3/4-inch thick patties.

Cooking

Heat ghee on a *tawa,* and shallow fry the *Tikki* over medium heat until golden brown and crisp on both sides. Press with a spatula and remove.

To Serve

Place a paper doiley on a silver platter. Arrange *Tikki* on top and serve with *Mint Chutney* and *Saunth**.

*See section on Chutneys.

Veg

Pakora

INGREDIENTS

150 g/5 oz Cauliflower

150 g/5 oz Potatoes (medium size)

100 g/3½ oz Onions (medium size)

75 g/3 oz Brinjals (medium size)

75 g/3 oz Spinach

4 Green Chillies

Mustard Oil to deep fry

Batter

250 g/1⅔ cups Gramflour

2 g/⅓ Tsp Soda bi-carb

Salt

5 g/2 Tsp Ajwain

5 g/1 Tsp Red Chilli powder

5 g/1¾ Tsp Pomegranate seed powder

Serves 4

Preparation time: 30 minutes

Cooking time: 20 minutes

A snack of vegetable fritters, *Pakora* is made in some shape or size across the length and breadth of the Sub-continent. It is generally believed that the Multanis are the best purveyors of the art of making *Pakora.* They owe this reputation, we suspect, to the use of mustard oil. That it is not uncommon to make a meal of it (with *Phulka* or bread) merely underlines its popularity. So versatile is its batter that you can make/ fritters of almost anything. Other than vegetables, *Paneer* is a popular *Pakora* ingredient. The compulsive non-vegetarian has confounded the predominantly vegetarian Indian by 'creating' chicken and egg *Pakora.* The recipe below is for assorted vegetable *Pakora.*

Preparation

Vegetables: Wash and cut cauliflower into large florets (approx 2½-inch). Peel, wash and cut potatoes and onions into roundels (approx ⅙-inch thick). Wash and cut brinjals into roundels, discard the ends. Remove stems and wash spinach leaves in running water. Wash, slit on one side and deseed green chillies. Immerse potatoes and brinjals in water.

Batter: Sieve gramflour, soda bi-carb and salt together, add *ajwain,* red chillies, pomegranate seed powder and enough water (approx 200 ml/3/4 cup) to make a batter of fritter consistency.

Cooking

Heat mustard oil in a *kadhai* to smoking point, reduce to medium heat, dip vegetable florets, roundels, leaves and chillies in the batter and deep fry until light golden. Remove and cool. Reheat oil and deep fry over moderately high heat until golden brown and crisp.

To Serve

Place a paper doiley on a platter, arrange *Pakora* on top and serve with *Mint Chutney.*

Note: The second frying is imperative. The best time to fry again is when ready to serve. This enables the housewife to half-cook *Pakora* well in advance and produce the fritters at very short notice.

Samosa

Veg

The Nation's favourite tea-time snack, *Samosa,* like *Aloo Tikki,* can be stuffed with a variety of fillings—mince, mixed vegetables, lentils or spiced peas and potatoes.

INGREDIENTS

300 g/⅔ lb Flour
Salt
60 ml/4 Tbs Groundnut Oil
Flour to dust
Groundnut Oil to deep fry

Filling

750 g/5 cups Potatoes
250 g/1⅔ cups Green Peas
50 g/3 Tbs Ghee
5 g/1¾ Tsp Cumin seeds
30 g/3 Tbs Cups Ginger
5 g/1 Tsp Red Chilli powder
Salt
10 Green Chillies
15 g/5 Tsp Pomegranate seed powder
20 g/⅓ cup Coriander

Yield: 12

Preparation time: 1 hour

Cooking time: 7–8 minutes for each set

Preparation

Dough: Sieve flour and salt together, make a bay, pour oil in it and start mixing gradually. When oil is fully mixed, add water (approx 90 ml/6 Tbs), knead gently to make a semi-hard dough, cover with a moist cloth and keep aside for 15 minutes. Divide into 6 equal portions and make balls. Cover with a moist cloth.

Filling: Peel, wash, cut potatoes into ¼-inch cubes and immerse in water. Boil peas until cooked, drain. Scrape, wash and finely chop ginger. Remove stems, wash, slit, deseed and finely chop green chillies. Clean, wash and finely chop coriander.

Heat ghee in a *kadhai,* add cumin and saute over medium heat until it begins to crackle. Add ginger and saute for a minute. Then add potatoes, red chillies and salt, *bhunno* for 5 minutes. Reduce to low heat, cover and cook, stirring occasionally, until potatoes are tender—not mashed. Now add boiled peas and green chillies, stir until liquid has evaporated and the mixture is completely dry. Sprinkle

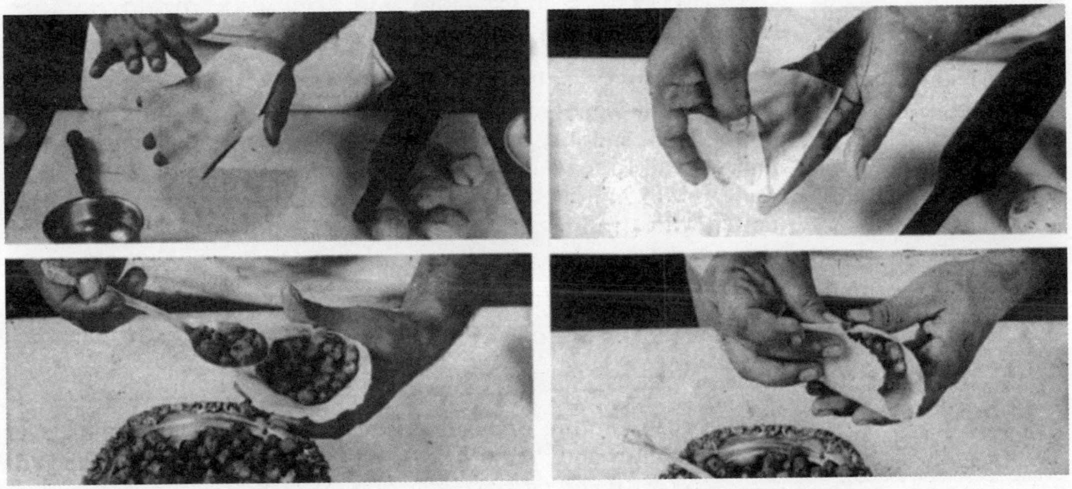

pomegranate seed powder and coriander, stir. Remove, cool and divide into 12 equal portions.

Stuffing: Place the balls on a lightly flouted surface, flatten each ball with a rolling pin into a round disc (approx 8-inch diameter) and cut into half. Stuff as follows: place a half flat on the palm with the straight edge along the forefinger *(see photographs),* dip the other forefinger in water, line the edges, make a cone, stuff a portion of the filling in it and seal the open end by pressing firmly. Sprinkle flour on a tray, arrange the stuffed *Samosa* on it and keep aside until ready to fry.

Cooking

Heat oil in a *kadhai* and deep fry *Samosa* over medium heat until golden brown and crisp.

To Serve

Place a paper doiley on a silver platter, arrange *Samosa* on top and serve with *Mint Chutney* and *Saunth**.

*See section on Chutneys.

Veg

Mathi

INGREDIENTS

600 g/1⅓ lb Flour
Salt
5 g/2 Tsp Ajwain
60 ml/4 Tbs Groundnut Oil
240 ml/1 cup Milk
10 g/1 Tbs Black Peppercorns
Groundnut Oil to deep fry

Yield: 40

Preparation time: 30 minutes

Cooking time: 15–18 minutes for each set

Ajwain shares a unique 'relationship' with Indian vegetarian snack—they are practically inseparable and very, very compatible. This exotic spice is responsible for the fine aroma in *Mathi*—a crisp savoury laced with pepper.

Preparation

Dough: Sieve flour and salt together, add *ajwain,* mix, make a bay, *pour* oil in it and start mixing gradually. When the oil is fully mixed, add milk, knead to make a hard dough, cover with a moist cloth and keep aside for 15 minutes. Divide into 40 equal portions, make balls and flatten with a rolling pin into round discs (approx 3-inch diameter and 1/8-inch thick). Embed each disc with a peppercorn or two and prick the entire surface with a fork.

Cooking

Heat ghee in a *kadhai* and deep fry over high heat for 90 seconds, reduce to between low and medium heat and fry until golden brown and crisp.

To Serve

Place a paper doiley on a platter, arrange *Mathi* on top and serve with *Aam ka Achaar* (Mango Pickle)*.

*See section on Pickles.

Kachori

Veg

Not only is this crisp, stuffed delicacy Madhya Bharat's (Central India's) favourite snack, it is also a must at every wedding in the region.

INGREDIENTS

250 g/2 cups Flour
1 g/¼ Tsp Soda bi-carb
A pinch Salt
75 ml/5 Tbs Groundnut Oil
Ghee to deep fry

Peethi

60 g/⅓ Cup Urad Dal (washed)
10 g/2 Tsp Coriander powder
Salt
3 g/½ Tsp Red Chilli powder
A pinch Asafoetida
A pinch Soda bi-carb
10 g/4 Tsp Atta (if necessary)

Yield: 12

Preparation time: 1:30 hours

Cooking time: 10 minutes for each set

Preparation

Dough: Sieve flour, soda bi-carb and salt together, make a bay, pour oil in it and start mixing gradually. When oil is fully mixed, add water (approx 100 ml/7 Tbs) and knead to make a soft dough. Cover with a moist cloth and keep aside for 15 minutes. Divide into 12 equal portions, make balls and cover with a moist cloth.

Peethi: Pick, wash *dal* in running water and soak for 30 minutes. Drain, put in a blender and coarsely grind. Remove, add coriander, red chillies, salt, asafoetida and soda bi-carb, mix well (add *atta* if the *peethi* is soft). Divide into 12 equal portions.

Stuffing: Flatten each ball between palms, ensuring it is thinner around the edges, place a portion of *peethi* in the middle, enfold the *peethi* and pinch off excess dough to seal the edges *(see photographs)*. Then flatten between palms into discs (approx 2½-inch diameter).

Cooking

Heat ghee in a *kadhai* and deep fry *Kachori* over medium heat until golden brown and crisp.

To Serve

Place a paper doiley on a silver platter, arrange *Kachori* on top and serve with *Saunth.*

South Indian Snacks

Veg Dosai

INGREDIENTS

225 g/8 oz Parboiled Rice
75 g/3 oz Basmati Rice
150 g/¾ cup Urad Dal
2 g/½ Tsp Fenugreek seeds
Salt
80 ml/⅓ cup Groundnut Oil

Yield: 8

Preparation time: 5:30 hours

Cooking time: 3–4 minutes for each Dosai

The rice pancake that is synonymous with South Indian food. If one dish has dominated the cuisine of the Southern half of the Sub-continent it is the *Dosai.* So overpowering has been its influence that very often even people in the rest of India believe that the Southerner's staple is *Dosai-Sambhar.*

Preparation

Rice & Lentil: Pick, wash in running water and soak alongwith fenugreek seeds overnight.

Baitter: Put the soaked ingredients in a blender, add salt and water (approx 50 ml/3 Tbs + 1 Tsp) and make a fine paste. Remove to a large bowl and keep aside for at least 5 hours.

***Tawa*:** Peel an onion, cut into half, tie one half in muslin, dip in oil and rub the surface of a pre-heated *tawa* with the flat side.

Cooking

Warm *tawa* over low heat, spread a portion of the batter over almost the entire surface by moving a ladle in concentric circles from the centre going outwards (12-inch diameter). When the batter rises and little perforations appear on the rapidly cooking pancake (approx 2 minutes) sprinkle a little oil (approx 10 ml/1 Tbs) along the periphery and cook until golden (lift on one side to see if the pancake is golden). Fold.

To Serve

Remove to individual plates and serve with *Sambhar** and *Thengai Thovial***.

*See section on South India.
**See section on Chutneys.

Masala Dosai

Veg

The *Dosai* can be stuffed with a variety of fillings—potatoes and lamb mince being the most popular.

INGREDIENTS

350 g/12 oz Dosai Batter*

45 ml/3 Tbs Groundnut Oil

Filling

300 g/2 cups Potatoes

60 ml/4 Tbs Groundnut Oil

4 g/1 Tsp Mustard seeds

10 g/1 Tbs Channa Dal

100 g/⅔ cup Onions

4 Green Chillies

1 g/¼ Tsp Turmeric

Salt

15 ml/1 Tbs Lemon juice

12 Cashewnuts

Groundnut Oil to deep fry Cashewnuts

10 Curry leaves

20 g/⅓ cup Coriander

30 g/2 Tbs Butter

*See recipe for Dosai in this section.

Serves: 4

Preparation time: 25 minutes (Plus time taken to prepare batter)

Cooking time: 25 minutes

Preparation

Vegetables: Boil potatoes, cool, peel and mash. Peel, wash and slice onions. Remove stems, wash, slit, deseed and finely chop green chillies. Wash curry leaves. Clean, wash and chop coriander.

Lentil: Pick, wash in running water and pat dry.

Cashewnuts: Split. Heat oil in a *kadhai* and deep fry over medium heat until golden brown. Remove.

Filling: Heat oil in a *kadhai,* add mustard seeds and stir over medium heat until they begin to crackle. Add *dal,* stir until light brown, add-onions and saute until transparent. Then add green chillies, stir for a minute, add turmeric and salt, stir. Sprinkle lemon juice, stir, add potatoes and *bhunno* for 4–5 minutes. Now add cashewnuts, curry leaves and coriander, stir. Adjust the seasoning. Divide into 4 equal portions.

Tawa: Peel an onion, cut into half, tie one half in muslin, dip in oil and rub the surface of a pre-heated *tawa* with the flat side.

Cooking

Warm the *tawa* over low heat, spread a portion of the batter over the surface by moving a ladle in concentric circles from the middle going outwards (12-inch diameter). When the batter rises and little perforations appear on the rapidly cooking pancake, sprinkle a little oil along the periphery and cook until golden brown (lift on one side to see if the pancake is golden). Place a portion of the filling in one half, top with a knob of butter and fold the other half over.

To Serve

Remove to individual plates and serve with *Sambhar* and *Thengai Thovial.*

Note:

(i) **For *Kheema* Filling**

600 g/1⅓ lb Lamb mince
100 ml/7 Tbs Groundnut oil
400 g/2⅓ cups Onions (chopped)
10 g/1 Tbs Ginger paste
10 g/1 Tbs Garlic paste
5 g/1 Tsp Red Chilli powder
3 g/½ Tsp Turmeric
Salt
220 g/1 cup Tomatoes (chopped)
2 g/½ Tsp Clove powder
10 Curry leaves
10 g/1 Tbs Coriander (chopped).

To cook, heat oil in *kadhai,* add onions and saute over medium heat until transparent. Add ginger and garlic pastes, saute until onions are light brown. Then add red chillies, turmeric and salt, stir for a minute, add tomatoes and *bhunno* until fat leaves the masala. Now add mince, *bhunno* for 4–5 minutes, add clove powder, stir and *bhunno* until the mince is cooked and the liquid, if any, has evaporated. Add curry leaves and coriander, stir.

(ii) **For Egg *Dosai***: Break 2 or 3 eggs over the batter immediately after spreading it on the *tawa.* The eggs will be ready about the same time as the *Dosai.*

Urla Kazhangu Bonda

Veg

Spicy potato-balls, dipped in a gramflour batter and deep fried—a perfect snack.

Preparation

Potatoes: Boil, cool, peel and mash.

Lentils: Pick, wash in running water and pat dry.

Vegetables: Peel, wash and finely chop onions. Boil peas until cooked, drain. Remove stems, wash, slit, deseed and finely chop green chillies. Scrape, wash and finely chop ginger. Wash curry leaves. Clean, wash and chop coriander.

Cashewnuts: Split.

Mixture: Heat ghee in a *kadhai,* add mustard seeds and lentils, saute over medium heat until lentils are light golden. Add onions, saute until transparent, add turmeric and salt, stir. Then add peas and potatoes, *bhunno* for 4–5 minutes. Now add green chillies, ginger, curry leaves and coriander, stir for 3–4 minutes. Sprinkle lemon juice and stir cool, divide into 8 equal portions, flatten between palms, randomly place 2 cashewnut halves in each, make balls and refrigerate for 15 minutes.

Batter: Sieve gramflour and soda bi-carb together, add salt and water (approx 200 ml/3/4 cup) to make a batter of fritter consistency.

Cooking

Heat oil in a *kadhai,* dip potato balls in the batter and deep fry over medium heat until golden brown.

To Serve

Place a paper doiley on a platter, arrange *Bonda* on top and serve with a chutney of your choice.

INGREDIENTS

600 g/4 cups Potatoes
50 g/¼ cup Ghee
3 g/¾ Tsp Mustard seeds
15 g/1 Tbs Urad Dal
15 g/1 Tbs Channa Dal
50 g/⅓ cup Onions
3 g/½ Tsp Turmeric
Salt
100 g/½ cup Green Peas
8 Green Chillies
20 g/2 Tbs Ginger
10 Curry leaves
20 g/⅓ cup Coriander
45 ml/3 Tbs Lemon juice
8 Cashewnuts
Groundnut Oil to deep fry

Batter

200 g/1⅓ cups Gramflour
A pinch Soda bi-carb
Salt

Yield: 8

Preparation time: 45 minutes

Cooking time: 8–10 minutes for each set

Veg

Idli

INGREDIENTS

350 g/1¾ cups Parboiled Rice

150 g/¾ cup Urad Dal

Salt

Groundnut Oil to grease moulds

Yield: 16

Preparation time: 8:15 hours

Cooking time: 8–10 minutes for each set

A steamed rice-cake, usually eaten for breakfast with *Sambhar* and chutney or a knob of white butter.

Preparation

Rice: Put in a grinder and make a coarse powder. Wash carefully in running water (ensure that the powder is not drained away) and soak for 10 minutes.

Lentil: Pick, wash and soak for 1 hour. Drain, put in a blender and make a fluffy (sponge-like) paste.

Idli Mixture: Put the soaked rice flour in muslin, squeeze out the excess moisture, mix with the lentil paste, add salt and keep in a warm place for 6 hours.

Cooking

Grease the *Idli* moulds, pour equal quantities of the mixture in each and steam in a steamer or pressure cooker for 8–10 minutes. (To make sure the *Idli* is cooked, poke the mixture with a needle; if the mixture sticks, steam for a few minutes more. The needle must eventually come out clean.)

To Serve

Demould, place *Idli* in 4 individual plates and serve with, *Sambhar**, *Thengai Thovial*** and *Mulagapodi****.

Note:

(i) It is always better to place a moist cloth on the moulds and then pour the mixture—it facilitates demoulding.

(ii) *Idli* moulds are easily available. If you cannot find a set, use darioles or *katoris* and steam in a double boiler. The ideal alternative is an egg poacher.

*See section on South India.
**See section on Chutneys.
***See section on Masalas.

Kanjeevaram Idli

Veg

Kanjeevaram, famed for the finest silk sarees, 'drapes' its steamed rice-cakes with the same finesse as its weavers have draped generations of Indian women.

INGREDIENTS

160 g/6 oz Parboiled Rice
40 g/1½ oz Basmati Rice
80 g/3 oz Toor Dal
80 g/3 oz Urad Dal
80 g/3 oz Channa D0al
5 g/1½ Tsp Black Peppercorns
3 g/1 Tsp Cumin seeds
5 g/1 Tsp Ginger powder
100 g/1½ cup Ghee
Salt
10 Curry leaves
Groundnut Oil to grease moulds

Yield: 16

Preparation time: 7:20 hours

Cooking time: 8–10 minutes for each set

Preparation

Rice and Lentils: Pick, wash in running water and soak parboiled rice, rice and the three *dals* together for an hour. Drain, put in a blender and make a rough paste.

Curry Leaves: Wash.

***Idli* Mixture:** Mix all the ingredients with the rice and lentil paste and keep aside for 6 hours.

Cooking

Grease the *Idli* moulds, pour equal quantities of the mixture in each and steam in a steamer or pressure cooker for 8–10 minutes. (To make sure the *Idli* is cooked, poke the mixture with a needle; if the mixture sticks, steam for a few minutes more. The needle must eventually come out clean.)

To Serve

Demould, place *Idli* in 4 individual plates and serve with *Sambhar**, *Thengai Thovial*** and *Mulagapodi***.

* See section on South India.
** See section on Chutneys.
*** See section on Masalas.

Veg

Medu Vadai

INGREDIENTS

300 g/1½ cups Urad Dal
5 g/1½ Tsp Black Peppercorns
A pinch Asafoetida
Salt
5 Curry leaves
Groundnut Oil to deep fry

Yield: 16
Preparation time: 1:15 hours
Cooking time: 30 minutes

A doughnut-shaped savoury spiced with black peppercorns—a popular tea-time snack.

Preparation

Lentil: Pick, wash in running water and soak for an hour. Drain.

Pepper: Pound with a pestle.

Asafoetida: Dissolve in 5 ml/1 Tsp of water.

Curry Leaves: Wash.

Batter: Put lentil in the blender and make a fluffy batter, adding a little water at a time (80 ml/⅓ cup in all). Transfer to a large bowl, add pepper, asafoetida, salt and curry leaves, mix well.

Cooking

Heat oil in a *kadhai,* moisten a spatula or steak-turner, place 2 portions of the batter at a time on it, flatten into a round shape (approx 2-inch diameter) with a moist hand, make a doughnut-like hole with the index finger and invert the spatula deftly over the *kadhai.* Deep fry over medium heat until light golden. Remove, keep aside for 2 minutes, return to the *kadhai* and deep fry until crisp and golden brown.

To Serve

Remove to a flat dish and serve with *Sambhar**.

*See section on South India.

Pickles, Chutneys and Murabba

With NIPENDAR P. SINGH

My fondest childhood memories are of dining at my Grandmother's—she is still the best cook in the family—eating *Paratha* with *Aam-ka-Achaar* (Mango Pickle). These simple meals were culinary events for me for two reasons: one, the quality of the pickle, and the peppercorn and *ajwain* laced *Paratha.* Two, I wasn't allowed to eat pickles at home because of my tonsils, which weren't removed until much later. Once, my mother walked into the kitchen store just as I had 'stolen' some mango pickle. I quickly hid the piece in my pocket. She suspected what I had been up to but when she questioned me, I denied eating any pickle. There was no way I could escape my punishment though. A tell-tale smudge of mustard colour—thanks to the oil—began to spread on my knickers. The thrashing that followed didn't hurt as much as the giant padlock that was posted on the store's door!

There is nothing unusual about the popular *Achaar-Paratha* combination. In fact, in a land where refrigerator was a luxury until a decade ago, pickles, carefully matured in earthenware jars, were a 'multi-purpose' food—relish, accompaniment and entree. The quickest meal a housewife could 'whip up' for unexpected visitors was—you have probably guessed it—pickle served with *Paratha, Roti,* even a slice of conventional bread. Pickles are, therefore, never dismissed as mere accompaniments. They require all the cooking skills that go into the making of exotic delicacies.

N.P. Singh: Another leading light among the present crop of bright young chefs, Singh is the Chef of *Taj Group's Ile de Kashmir*,* Paris—surely the most coveted assignment his company has on offer for the cooks of his generation.

*Designation subject to change.

In any event, pickles, chutneys and *murabba* (sweet preserves) are an intrinsic part of our daily diet and play an important role in our cuisine. Eaten at the right time of the day and during the appropriate season, they tickle the palate, revive a sagging appetite and even cure stomach and digestive ailments. Some, especially the *murabba,* are veritable tonics.

This may surprise many, but in most households, not everyone is allowed to make pickles and *murabba.* In an entire family, just a handful of women are believed to possess a 'hand' capable of pickling. An antiseptically clean pair of hands is not enough. It is believed that most hands set off a chemical reaction, which encourages fungal growth ruining the preserves almost immediately. Such people are not even allowed to remove the preserves from the jars. After the initial maturing (in the sun), the jars are kept in a dark place as light 'affects' the preserves. Pickles and *murabba* are never, never removed from the jar after sundown—in 'unnatural' light. I, for one, wouldn't dare dismiss this as superstition or hocus-pocus. I have seen strange things happen to preserves touched by 'unworthy hands'.

It is best to mature pickles in glazed earthenware jars. The inert porcelain prevents any chemical reaction. For maturing it is important to secure the opening of the jar with muslin—this allows the pickle to 'breathe' and excess moisture to evaporate.

Pickling is generally done in mustard oil, vinegar or lemon juice. *Murabba* are preserved in sugar syrup. Pickles matured in vinegar and lemon juice have a short shelf life—usually a fortnight. Those preserved in mustard oil, with the notable exception of meat pickles, and *murabba,* can last for years. In fact, like good wines, they mature and become better with the years—up to a point, of course. Then their quality starts deteriorating before eventually becoming unfit for consumption.

Chutneys are of two types—those that are preserved, like pickles and *murabba,* and those that are freshly prepared everyday. The Southern chutneys in this chapter are all of the latter variety.

The pickle and *murabba* recipes here have, as is the tradition, been handed down to my Mother by my Grandmother. They have been tried, tested and standardised by my 'co-authors', who join me in dedicating this chapter to my only living grandparent. The North Indian chutneys are exclusively from my Mother's collection.

Assisted by Sujata Kanianthra

Jhinga Achaar

A prawn pickle that is tempting enough to be consumed as an entree. Resist or the stomach will go for a six. It is only a relish.

INGREDIENTS
1 kg/2¼ lb Prawns (medium size)
50 g/3 Tbs Ginger paste
50 g/3 Tbs Garlic paste
10 g/2 Tsp Red Chilli powder
3 g/½ Tsp Turmeric
Salt
800 ml/3⅔ cups Mustard Oil
5 Black Cardamom
10 Green Cardamom
2 Bay leaves
5 g/1 Tsp Asafoetida
5 g/1¾ Tsp Kalonji
5 g/1¼ Tsp Fenugreek seeds
200 g/1¼ cups Onions
5 g/1 Tsp Black Cardamom powder
10 g/2 Tsp Green Cardamom powder
10 g/2 Tsp Fennel powder
5 g/1 Tsp Cumin powder
350 ml/1½ cups Malt Vinegar
150 g/5 oz Jaggery

Preparation time: 1 hour
Cooking time: 20 minutes
Maturing time: 2 days

Preparation

Prawns: Clean, devein, wash and pat dry.

Marination: Mix red chillies, turmeric and salt with half each of the ginger and garlic pastes, rub prawns with this marinade. Keep aside for 30 minutes.

Onions: Peel, wash and grate.

Preserve: In a stainless steel *handi,* dissolve jaggery in vinegar.

Cooking

Heat oil in a *kadhai* to a smoking point, reduce to medium heat and deep fry the marinated prawns for 2 minutes. Remove prawns and strain the oil. Heat the strained oil in a separate *kadhai,* add black cardamom, green cardamom, bay leaves, asafoetida, *kalonji* and fenugreek seeds, saute over medium heat for 30 seconds, add onions and fry until golden brown. Then add the remaining ginger and garlic pastes, stir for 2 minutes, add the remaining spices, stir for a minute, add the preserve, bring to a boil, then cook over high heat for 2–3 minutes. Now add fried prawns and cook for 2–3 minutes. Remove and cool.

Maturing

Transfer the contents of the *kadhai* to a sterilised earthenware or glass jar. Secure muslin around the opening of the jar and keep in the sun or a warm place for 2 days. Remove the muslin and cover with a lid. Consume within 60 days.

Murgh Achaar

INGREDIENTS

1 kg/2¼ lb Chicken
50 g/3 Tbs Ginger paste
50 g/3 Tbs Garlic paste
10 g/2 Tsp Red Chilli powder
5 g/1 Tsp Turmeric
Salt
800 ml/3⅔ cups Mustard Oil
5 g/1 Tsp Asafoetida
200 g/1¼ cups Onions
5 g/1 Tsp Black Cardamom powder
5 g/1 Tsp Green Cardamom powder
20 g/4 Tsp Fennel powder
10 g/1 Tbs Black Cumin seeds
5 g/1 Tsp Fenugreek seeds
10 g/2½ Tsp Mustard seeds
3 Bay leaves
400 ml/1⅔ cups Malt Vinegar

Preparation time: 1 hour
Cooking time: 15 minutes
Maturing time: 2 days

A sharp chicken pickle, its taste is enhanced by pounded mustard and fenugreek seeds.

Preparation

Chicken: Remove the skin, debone and cut into 1½-inch *tikka.* (Chicken legs are preferable because the meat from legs will became more succulent as the pickle matures.)

Marination: Mix red chillies, turmeric and salt with half each of ginger and garlic pastes, rub *tikka* with this marinade. Keep aside for 30 minutes.

Onions: Peel, wash and finely chop.

Cooking

Heat oil in a *kadhai* to a smoking point, reduce to medium heat and deep fry the marinated *tikka* for 2–3 minutes. Remove chicken and strain the oil. Heat the strained oil in a separate *kadhai,* add asafoetida, stir for 15 seconds, add onions and deep fry until golden brown. Then add the remaining ginger and garlic pastes, stir for 2 minutes, add the remaining spices and stir for a minute. Now add vinegar, bring to a boil, add fried chicken and cook over high heat for 3–4 minutes. Remove and cool.

Maturing

Transfer contents of the *kadhai* to a sterilised earthenware or glass jar, secure muslin around opening of the jar and leave it in the sun or in a warm place for 2 days. Remove the muslin and cover with a lid. Consume within 60 days.

Note:

(i) Ensure all moisture is removed from *tikka* before pickling. The presence of moisture induces fungal growth and reduces shelf life.

(ii) For *Chaamp* (lamb chops) *Achaar,* follow the recipe above, except use 100 g/3½ oz each of ginger and garlic pastes and 1 litre/4 cups of malt vinegar. Also, the lamb must be boiled, until tender, before marination.

(iii) For Pork, Wild Boar and Venison pickles, meat has to be boiled over an extended period—until tender. Rest of the recipe is same as above.

Aam Ka Achaar

Veg

It is a common sight to see pickle jars in the sun outside every Indian home in summer—the housewives are making mango pickle. Every home has its own recipe, the one below is the most popular.

INGREDIENTS

1 kg/2¼ lb Raw Mangoes
400 ml/1⅔ cups Mustard Oil
60 g/½ cup Fennel seeds
40 g/3 Tbs Fenugreek seeds
Salt
10 g/2 Tsp Turmeric
20 g/4 Tsp Red Chilli powder

Preparation time: 30 minutes
Maturing time: 4 days

Preparation

Mangoes: Wash, pat dry, cut into 1-inch long pieces and remove the kernel.

Mustard Oil: Heat in a *kadhai* to a smoking point, remove and cool.

Masala: Pound fennel and fenugreek with a pestle, add salt, turmeric, red chillies and half the mustard oil to make a coarse paste.

Assembling

Put mango pieces in a large bowl, pour masala and mix thoroughly.

Maturing

Transfer contents of the bowl to a sterilised earthenware or glass jar, pour the remaining oil, secure muslin around opening of the jar and leave it in the sun for 4 days. Remove the muslin and cover with a lid.

Veg

Bharvan Lal Mirch

INGREDIENTS

1 kg/2¼ lb Whole Red Chillies (fresh)

300 ml/¼ cup Mustard Oil

60 g/½ cup Fennel seeds

40 g/3 Tbs Fenugreek seeds

Salt

Preparation time: 30 minutes

Maturing time: 4 days

A pickle of stuffed red chillies.

Preparation

Chillies: Wash, pat dry and slit on one side.

Mustard Oil: Heat in a *kadhai* to a smoking point, remove and cool.

Filling: Pound fennel and fenugreek with a pestle. Add salt and half mustard oil to make a coarse paste.

Stuffing: Stuff chillies with the filling.

Maturing

Transfer the chillies to a sterilised earthenware or glass jar, pour the remaining oil, secure muslin around opening of the jar and leave it in the sun for 4 days. Remove the muslin and cover with a lid.

Veg

Nimbu Achaar

INGREDIENTS

1 kg/2¼ lb Lemons

45 g/3 Tbs Cumin powder

Salt

2 g/4 Tsp Red Chilli powder

250 g/1¼ cups Sugar

Preparation time: 30 minutes

Maturing time: 10 days

Stuffed lemon pickle—the perfect digestive.

Preparation

Lemons: Wash, pat dry and make deep cross-cuts (for stuffing masala) on each.

Masala: Mix cumin powder, salt and red chillies in a bowl.

Stuffing: Fill the cross-cut incisions in the lemons with the masala and transfer to a sterilised earthenware or glass jar. Pour the remaining masala on top and secure muslin around the opening of the jar.

Maturing

Keep the jar in the sun or in a warm place for 5 days. On the sixth day, uncover the jar and sprinkle the pickle with sugar, shake the jar well, secure it again and keep in the sun or in a warm place for another 5 days. Remove muslin and cover with a lid.

Khatta-Meetha Achaar

Veg

A mixed-vegetable relish, spiced with cumin and garam masala and sweetened with jaggery or sugar.

INGREDIENTS

400 g/14 oz Cauliflower
300 g/11 oz Turnips
300 g/11 oz Carrots
325 ml/1¼ cups Mustard Oil
60 g/⅓ cup Onions
15 g/2½ Tsp Ginger paste
10 g/1¾ Tsp Garlic paste
25 g/5 Tsp Garam Masala
20 g/4 Tsp Red Chilli powder
25 g/8 Tsp Cumin seeds
30 g/7½ Tsp Mustard seeds
Salt
200 g/1 cup Sugar or Jaggery
200 ml/¾ cup White Vinegar
5 g/1 Tsp Acetic Acid

Preparation time: 20 minutes
Cooking time: 10 minutes
Maturing time: 3 days

Preparation

Vegetables: Wash and cut cauliflower into florets. Peel, wash, cut turnips into halves and then make medium thick slices (⅛-inch). Peel, wash and cut carrots into batons. Peel, wash and finely chop onions. Spread cauliflower, turnips and carrots on a tray and keep in the sun or in a warm place for drying (2–3 days).

Cumin: Pound with a pestle.
Preserve: Dissolve sugar or jaggery in vinegar.

Cooking

Heat oil in a *kadhai* to a smoking point, reduce to medium heat, add onions, saute until light golden, add ginger paste and garlic paste, stir until onions are golden brown. Add dry spices and salt, stir, add dried vegetables and stir. Then add the preserve and cook vegetables for 5 minutes. Remove and cool. Sprinkle acetic acid and stir.

Maturing

Transfer contents of the *kadhai* to a sterilised earthenware or glass jar, secure muslin around opening of the jar and keep in the sun or in a warm place for 3 days. Remove muslin and cover with a lid.

Veg

Aam ki Chutney

INGREDIENTS

1 kg/2¼ lb Raw Mangoes
1 kg/5 cups Sugar
100 g/⅔ cup Onions
50 g/3 Tbs Ginger paste
20 g/3½ Tsp Garlic paste
5 g/1 Tsp Garam Masala
10 g/2 Tsp Red Chilli powder
15 Green Cardamom
3 g/½ Tsp Cinnamon powder
200 ml/¾ Cup White Vinegar
Salt
20 Almonds
100 g/⅔ cup Raisins

Preparation time: 30 minutes
Cooking time: 30 minutes
Maturing time: 2 days

A delectable mango relish—the favourite chutney of millions of Indians.

Preparation

Mangoes: Peel and grate.

Vegetables: Peel, wash and grate onions. Mix with ginger and garlic pastes, put in muslin and squeeze out the juice. Discard the residue.

Almonds: Blanch and peel.

Cardamom: Peel and discard the skins.

Cooking

Mix sugar with mangoes in a *kadhai* and cook over medium heat for 10 minutes. Add the onion-ginger-garlic juice, stir, add garam masala, red chillies, cardamom seeds and cinnamon powder, stir and continue to cook until the mixture attains consistency of a jam. Then add vinegar and salt, cook for 2–3 minutes and remove. Add almonds and raisins, stir and cool.

Maturing

Transfer the contents of the *kadhai* to a sterilised jar, cover with a lid and leave it to mature for 2 days.

Gajjar ki Chutney

Veg

A sweet 'n' sour carrot chutney with raisins—makes an excellent sandwich spread.

INGREDIENTS

1 kg/2¼ lb Carrots
700 g/3½ cups Sugar
250 ml/1 cup White Vinegar
10 g/1¾ Tsp Ginger paste
10 g/1¾ Tsp Garlic paste
20 g/4 Tsp Red Chilli powder
Salt
10 g/2 Tsp Cumin powder
20 g/4 Tsp Garam Masala
200 g/1⅓ cups Raisins

Preparation time: 40 minutes
Cooking time: 25 minutes
Maturing time: 2 days

Preparation

Carrots: Peel, wash and grate. Keep in the sun for 30 minutes to draw out the moisture.

Pastes: Put ginger and garlic pastes in muslin and squeeze out the juice. Discard the residue.

Cooking

Mix sugar with vinegar in a *kadhai* and boil until it dissolves. Add carrots, the ginger-garlic juice and the remaining ingredients, except raisins, and simmer until the liquid has evaporated. Then add raisins and simmer until the carrots are absolutely dry. Remove and cool.

Maturing

Transfer the contents of the *kadhai* to a sterilised jar, cover with a lid and leave it to mature for 2 days.

Veg

Sookhe Kale Angur ka Murabba

INGREDIENTS

1 kg/2¼ lb Sultanas
1 litre/4 cups White Vinegar
100 g/½ cup Sugar
20 g/4 Tsp Red Chilli powder
10 g/2 Tsp Fennel powder
10 g/2 Tsp Ginger powder
5 g/1 Tsp Black Cardamom powder
10 g/2 Tsp Cumin powder
Salt

Preparation time: 15 minutes
Cooking time: 18 minutes
Maturing time: 1 day

A tangy tribute to Nature's Candy—easy to make, easy on the palate and yet unique in every way.

Preparation

Sultanas: Remove the stems, wash and pat dry.

Preserve: In a stainless steel *handi,* dissolve sugar in vinegar. Add the remaining ingredients and stir.

Cooking

Simmer the preserve in stainless steel *handi* for 2–3 minutes, add sultanas and bring to a boil. Then simmer, stirring constantly to prevent sticking, until the liquid has evaporated (approx 15 minutes). Remove and cool.

Maturing

Transfer contents of the *handi* to a sterilised earthenware or glass jar, secure muslin around the opening of the jar and leave it to mature for 1 day. Remove muslin and cover with a lid. Consume within 15 days.

Lassi
Makki ki Roti
Sarson ka Saag

Paratha
Pedha
Bhatura
Phulka

Jalebi Paratha
Varqui Paratha
Sheermal

Murgh Achaar   Chaamp Achaar

Aamle ka Murabba

Veg

Rich in Vitamin 'C', this *murabba* not only keeps the winter blues at bay but also provides 'cool' in the summer. An invaluable preserve.

INGREDIENTS

1 kg/2¼ lb Aamla (large size)

Salt

1.5 kg/7½ cups Sugar

1 Lemon

Preparation time: 30 minutes
Cooking time: 3 minutes
Maturing time: 2 days

Preparation

Aamla: Wash and soak in salted water for 2 days to make the skin firm or else the skin would rupture when boiled. Drain, prick with a fork, add water (enough to cover) and boil for 3–4 minutes. Drain.

Lemon: Wash and cut into quarters.

Syrup: Boil water (approx 500 ml/2 cups) in a *handi,* add sugar and lemon, bring to a boil and remove the scum.

Cooking

Bring the syrup to a boil and continue to cook until it is of a two-string consistency. Add the boiled *aamla* and cook for 2–3 minutes. Remove and cool.

Maturing

Transfer the contents of the *handi* to a sterilised earthenware or glass jar, secure muslin around opening of the jar and leave it to mature for 2 days. Remove the muslin and cover with a lid.

Veg Gajjar ka Murabba

INGREDIENTS

1 kg/2¼ lb Red Carrots (medium size)

1 kg/5 cups Sugar

3 g/½ Tsp Acetic Acid

Preparation time: 35 minutes

Cooking time: 45 minutes (15 minutes a day over 3 days)

Maturing time: 2 days

It is India's belief—strongly supported by our age-old schools of medicine, *Ayurvedic* and *Unani*—that this *murabba* can help 'preserve' eye-sight, and very often improve it if it has deteriorated.

Preparation

Carrots: Peel, wash and cut into 1½-inch pieces. Prick the pieces with a fork.

Syrup: Boil water (approx 1 litre/4 cups) in a *handi,* add sugar and acetic acid, bring to a boil and remove the scum.

Cooking

Bring the syrup to a boil, add carrots, bring to boil again and cook for 15 minutes. Remove, cool, cover and store overnight. The following day, boil the *murabba* for 15 minutes, remove, cool, cover and store overnight. Repeat the procedure on the third day—boil until the syrup is of a one-string consistency.

Maturing

Transfer the contents of the *handi* to a sterilised earthenware or glass jar, secure muslin around the opening of the jar and leave it to mature for at least 2 days. Remove the muslin and cover with a lid.

Note: Blanched and peeled almonds and green cardamom are optional. They may be added before transferring to the jar.

Adrak ka Murabba

Veg

A ginger preserve that always soothes the stomach, especially after a 'spicy' and 'heavy' Indian meal. Consume in very small quantity—just a few pieces.

INGREDIENTS

1 kg/2¼ lb Ginger
1.5 kg/7¼ cups Sugar
1 Lemon
8 g/2 Tsp Acetic Acid

Preparation time: 35 minutes
Cooking time: 1 hour
Maturing time: 2 days

Preparation

Ginger: Scrape, wash and make 1/8-inch thick slices.

Lemon: Wash and cut into quarters.

Syrup: Boil water (approx 500 ml/2 cups) in a *handi,* add sugar, lemon and half the acetic acid, bring to a boil and remove the scum.

Cooking

Put ginger in a *handi,* add water, bring to a boil, add the remaining acetic acid and continue to boil for 30 minutes. Drain. Add the syrup, bring to a boil and cook until the syrup is of a one-string consistency (approx 30 minutes). Cool and store overnight. The following day, boil the *murabba* for 15 minutes.

Maturing

Transfer the contents of the *handi* to a sterilised earthenware or glass jar, secure muslin around the opening of the jar and leave it to mature for 2 days. Remove muslin and cover with a lid.

Keri ki Launjee

Veg

A piquant raw-mango delicacy, spiced with fennel and *kalonji,* cooked in mustard oil.

INGREDIENTS

900 g/2 lb Raw Mangoes
225 ml/1 cup Mustard Oil
3 g/¾ Tsp Fenugreek seeds
10 g/4 Tsp Fennel seeds
2 g/½ Tsp Kalonji
5 g/1 Tsp Coriander powder
5 g/1 Tsp Red Chilli powder
3 g/½ Tsp Turmeric
Salt
250 g/1¼ cups Jaggery

Preparation time: 35 minutes
Cooking time: 20 minutes

Preparation

Mangoes: Peel, cut lengthwise into quarters and remove the kernel.

Jaggery: Pound with a pestle.

Cooking

Heat oil in a *kadhai* to a smoking point, reduce to medium heat, add fenugreek and saute until it begins to change colour (approx 15 seconds). Add fennel, *kalonji,* coriander, red chillies, turmeric and salt, stir, add mangoes and stir for 5 minutes. Then add jaggery and water (approx 120 ml/½ cup), bring to a boil, cover and simmer, stirring occasionally, for 7–8 minutes. Remove and cool.

To Serve

Remove to a dish and serve as an accompaniment.

Veg Saunth (Sweet Chutney)

INGREDIENTS

- 50 g/10 Tsp Mango powder
- 250 g/1¼ cups Sugar or Jaggery
- 15 g/5 Tsp Cumin seeds
- 5 g/1 Tsp Black Salt
- 6 g/2 Tsp Black Peppercorns
- 8 g/2 Tsp Black Cardamom seeds
- 10 g/2 Tsp Red Chilli powder
- Salt
- 1 drop Red colour
- 1 Mango (medium size)

Yield: 400 g/14 oz

Preparation time: 15 minutes

Cooking time: 15 minutes

A chutney that is made from mango powder, it is usually served with snacks.

Preparation

Mango Powder: Sieve to break up the lumps.

Remaining Spices: Broil cumin seeds on a *tawa,* remove and cool. Pound black salt with a pestle. Put both in a blender, add peppercorns and cardamom seeds, make a fine powder. Remove to a clean, dry bowl, add red chillies and salt, mix well.

Mango: Peel, halve, stone and dice.

Cooking

Put water (approx 240 ml/l cup) in a *handi,* add mango powder and whisk to prevent lumps from forming. Then cook over medium heat, stirring constantly, until it acquires a sauce-like consistency. Add the remaining ingredients, except mango, and stir until the sugar dissolves. Now simmer for 5–6 minutes. Remove, force through a soup strainer into a separate *handi* and cool. Add the mango dices, stir and refrigerate.

Note:

(i) *Saunth* can be garnished with grapes, bananas and/or dry fruits instead of mangoes.

(ii) It has a shelf life of 4–5 days in the refrigerator—in a sterilised container—but without the mangoes or any other fresh fruit.

South Indian Chutneys

Thengai Thoviyal (Coconut Chutney)

Preparation

Coconut: Remove the brown skin and grate.

Vegetables: Remove stems, wash, slit and deseed green chillies. Scrape and Wash Ginger. Wash curry leaves.

Lentil: Pick, wash in running water and pat dry. Heat oil in a *kadhai* and fry over medium heat until light golden. Drain.

Paste: Mix green chillies, ginger, fried *dal* and salt with grated coconut, put in a blender, add coconut water (approx 100 ml/7 Tbs) and make a fine paste.

Cooking

Tempering: Heat oil in a *kadhai,* add red chillies and stir over medium heat for a few seconds. Add mustard seeds and stir until they begin to crackle.

Chutney: Transfer the paste to a glass bowl, add curry leaves, pour on the tempering and mix well. Refrigerate.

Note: Coconut Chutney can also be made with roasted gram instead of fried *channa dal.*

INGREDIENTS

200 g/2½ cups Coconut
3 Green Chillies
5 g/1½ Tsp Ginger
20 g/2 Tbs Channa Dal
Groundnut Oil to fry
Salt
5 Curry leaves

Tempering

10 ml/2 Tsp Groundnut Oil
2 whole Red Chillies
3 g/¾ Tsp Mustard seeds

Yield: Approx 350 g/¾ lb

Preparation time: 30 minutes

Takkali Thoviyal (Tomato Chutney)

INGREDIENTS

200 g/1 cup Tomatoes
30 ml/2 Tbs Groundnut Oil
20 g/2 Tbs Channa Dal
120 g/⅔ cup Onions
3 Whole Red Chillies
3 g/½ Tsp Turmeric
A pinch Asafoetida
Salt
5 Curry leaves

Tempering

10 ml/2 Tsp Groundnut Oil
2 Whole Red Chillies
3 g/¾ Tsp Mustard seeds

Yield: Approx 350 g/¾ lb

Preparation time: 15 minutes
Cooking time: 20 minutes

Preparation

Tomatoes: Wash and roughly chop.
Lentil: Pick, wash in running water and pat dry.
Remaining Vegetables: Peel, wash and chop onions. Wash curry leaves.

Cooking

Heat oil in a *kadhai,* add *channa dal,* saute over medium heat until light golden, add onions and saute until transparent. Add red chillies, turmeric, asafoetida and salt, stir, add tomatoes and *bhunno* until mashed. Remove, cool, put in a blender, add water (90 ml/6 Tbs) and make a coarse paste. Transfer to a glass bowl and add curry leaves.

To prepare the tempering, heat oil in a frying pan, add red chillies and stir over medium heat for a few seconds. Add mustard seeds and stir until they begin to crackle. Pour the tempering over the chutney and mix well. Serve at room temperature.

Vengayam Thoviayal (Onion Chutney)

INGREDIENTS

225 g/1⅓ cups Onions
75 ml/5 Tbs Groundnut Oil
100 g/½ cup Urad Dal
A pinch Asafoetida
20 g/3½ Tsp Tamarind pulp*
3 whole Red Chillies
Salt

Tempering

10 ml/2 Tsp Groundnut Oil
2 Whole Red Chillies
3 g/¾ Tsp Mustard seeds

*See section on Tamarind.

Yield: Approx 350 g/¾ lb

Preparation time: 10 minutes
Cooking time: 20 minutes

Preparation

Onions: Peel, wash and chop.
Lentil: Pick, wash in running water and pat dry.
Tamarind: Dissolve in 20 ml/4 Tsp of water.

Cooking

Heat oil in a *kadhai,* add *dal* and saute over medium heat until light golden. Add asafoetida, stir, add onions and saute until transparent. Reduce to low heat, add tamarind, red chillies and salt, stir for 5 minutes. Remove and cool. Transfer to a blender, add water (approx 75 ml/⅓ cup) and make a rough paste. (The chutney should be crunchy and so the lentil should not be mashed in the blender). Remove to a glass bowl.

To prepare the tempering, heat oil in a frying pan, add red chillies and stir over medium heat for a few seconds. Add mustard seeds and stir until they begin to crackle. Pour the tempering over the chutney and mix well. Serve at room temperature.

Roti
(Breads)

With Mohammed Rahees and Shishir Sharma

*R*oti or Bread may be the most basic of all foods, but more has been written about the making of breads than any other aspect of cooking. If one wants to simplify things, *roti* is nothing more than grain, water and salt, kneaded and baked. Yet there is a lot to the art of baking breads. The variety is infinite and each bread has its own individuality. And none more than the Indian breads, which are mostly unleavened and can be baked, shallow fried or deep fried. Again each variety may be eaten plain or stuffed.

In Northern and Central India, wheat is the more popular grain and consequently people eat *roti*—in its myriad forms—in preference to rice. To be sure, it is easier and much quicker to make *roti* than it is to make the Western-style breads. Though maize *(makki),* millet *(jowar),* milo *(bajra),* lentils *(dals)* and even rice are used to make some form of *roti,* it is *atta* (whole-wheat flour) which is the basic ingredient for making Indian

Mohammad Rahees: He probably took his first steps on the road to becoming a chef at about the same time that he began toddling around the floor in the courtyard of his family home in Lucknow! At a very tender age he was inducted into the innermost secrets of bread-making by his uncle, Mohammad Imtiaz, whose laudable influence in Rahees' work is dearly discernible.

Shishir Sharma: The other man on our *Roti* team, this young man's star is obviously on the ascendant. From one of the many junior chefs at a coffee shop to the prized position of *Chef of Haveli at the Taj Mahal Hotel, New Delhi* in three short years sums up Sharma's success story. Today, he is Indian Chef at the *Taj Samudra, Colombo**.

*Designation subject to change.

breads. And, as Indian breads are usually made from *atta,* grain, they are nutritionally superior to their cousins elsewhere.

The methods of making Indian breads are as varied as there are varieties. Any of the following may be used to make them:

Tandoor: The breads—*Naan, Paratha, Khameeri Roti*—made in this clay oven are the most popular.

Concave Tawa: Commonly used in the household to make *Phulka, Paratha, Makki-ki-Roti, Bajre-ki-Roti* etc.

Kadhai: Used to fry *Poori, Bhatura, Kachori,* etc.

Conventional Oven: Used only by professional bakers—usually Muslims—to bake *Bakarkhani, Sheermal,* etc.

Tandoori Roti

The common unleavened whole-wheat flour bread, consumed by millions of North Indians at every meal.

INGREDIENTS

550 g/4½ cups Atta

Salt

Atta to dust

Ghee to grease baking tray

Yield: 8

Preparation time: 40 minutes

Cooking time:

In Tandoor: 2 minutes

In Oven: 5–6 minutes

Preparation

Atta: Sieve with salt into a *paraat.*

Dough: Make a bay in the sieved *atta,* pour water (approx 350 ml/1½ cups) in it and start mixing gradually. When fully mixed, knead to make a soft dough, cover with a moist cloth and keep aside for 30 minutes. Divide into 8 equal portions, make balls, dust with *atta,* cover and keep aside for 5 minutes.

Oven: Pre-heat to 375°F.

Cooking

Flatten each ball between palms to make a round disc (approx 6-inch diameter), place the *Roti* on a *gaddi* (cushioned pad), stick inside a moderately hot *tandoor* and bake for 2 minutes. In a pre-heated oven, place on a greased baking tray and bake for 5–6 minutes.

To Serve

Serve as soon as it is removed from the *tandoor* or oven.

Note: To make *Phulka* and *Chappati* flatten the balls with a rolling pin into round discs (4-inch and 8-inch diameter, respectively). Both are cooked on a heated *tawa.* The *Phulka* is puffed over an open fire (it *cannot* be done on an electric range). The *Chappati,* by pressing the edge of the disc. However, it will not puff as much as the *Phulka.*

Aloo Paratha

INGREDIENTS

400 g/14 oz Atta-dough*
120 g/½ cup Butter
Atta to dust

Filling

175 g/6 oz Potatoes
20 g/2 Tbs Ginger
4 Green Chillies
10 g/2 Tbs Coriander
3 g/1 Tsp Pomegranate seeds
5 g/1 Tsp Red Chilli powder
Salt

*See recipe for Tandoori Roti.

Yield: 4

Preparation time: 20 minutes

Cooking time: 15 minutes

A shallow-fried *atta* bread with a filling of spiced potatoes.

Preparation

Potatoes: Boil, cool, peel and grate.

Remaining Vegetables: Scrape, wash and chop ginger. Remove stems, wash slit, deseed and chop green chillies. Clean, wash and chop coriander.

Filling: Mix all the ingredients in a bowl. Divide into 4 equal portions.

Paratha: Divide the dough into 4 equal portions, make balls, cover with a moist cloth and keep aside for 5 minutes. Place the balls on a lightly floured surface and flatten each with a rolling pin into round discs (approx 4-inch diameter). Place a portion of the filling in the middle, enfold the filling and pinch off the excess dough to seal the edges. Then flatten again with a rolling pin (approx 8-inch diameter).

Cooking

Place *Paratha* on a heated *tawa* and half-bake, turning over once. Melt 30 g/2 Tbs of butter all around and shallow fry both sides over low heat until golden brown.

To Serve

Remove and serve immediately with yoghurt and pickle.

Note: To make *Kheema Paratha* follow the above recipe, using 175 g/6 oz lamb mince, 50 g/¼ cup ghee, 15 g/2½ Tsp ginger paste, 15 g/2½ Tsp garlic paste, 5 g/1 Tsp red chilli powder, 4 green chillies (chopped), 100 g/½ cup tomatoes (chopped), 10 g/2 Tbs coriander (chopped) and salt.

To prepare the filling, heat ghee in a *kadhai,* add ginger paste, garlic paste and red chillies, saute over medium heat for 30 seconds, add green chillies and tomatoes, *bhunno* until fat leaves the masala. Add the mince and *bhunno* over low heat until cooked and dry. Sprinkle coriander and stir. Adjust the seasoning, cool and divide into 4 equal portions.

Batti

Batti was the desert—Thar—warrior's staff of life. Legend says that the bread was semi-prepared, buried in the sand and the location carefully marked. If supply lines were cut off during war, *Batti*—by now fully baked in the heat of the sand—were dug out and depressed on one side to crack open the crust. Clarified butter—*desi ghee*—was then poured in copious quantities. In crises, it provided more than the requisite nourishment. Times have changed. Chefs have devised easier—perhaps even better—ways of making this unleavened whole-wheat bread. For example, they now make use of baking powder to make it lighter. Also, they have started using ovens to bake *Batti.*

INGREDIENTS

500 g/4 cups Atta

5 g/1 Tsp Baking powder

Salt

380 g/1⅔ cups Desi Ghee (Clarified Butter only)

Desi Ghee (Clarified Butter only) to grease baking tray

Yield: 16

Preparation time: 40 minutes

Cooking time: 16–18 minutes

Preparation

Atta: Sieve with baking powder and salt into a *paraat.*

Dough: Make a bay in the sieved *atta,* pour water (approx 330 ml/1⅓ cups) in it and start mixing gradually. When fully mixed, knead to make a dough, cover with a moist cloth and keep aside for 10 minutes. Add 80 g/⅓ cup of *ghee* and incorporate gradually. When fully mixed, knead to make a soft dough, cover and keep aside for 10 minutes. Divide into 16 equal portions, make balls, cover and keep aside for 10 minutes. Flatten the balls slightly to make *pedha* (approx 2½-inch diameter), cover and keep aside until ready to bake.

Oven: Pre-heat to 350°F.

Cooking

Grease a baking tray with *ghee,* arrange the *pedha* on it and bake in the pre-heated oven for 16–18 minutes.

To Serve

Remove, depress on one side to crack open the crust, pour on melted *ghee* with a spoon and serve immediately.

Note: Ideally, *Batti* is baked in hot charcoal ash. The ash is dusted off before serving.

Khameeri Roti

INGREDIENTS

500 g/4 cups Atta

Salt

8 g/½ small block Yeast (fresh)

Atta to dust

Ghee to grease baking tray

Yield: 8

Preparation time: 1:20 hours

Cooking time:

In Tandoor: 2–3 minutes

In Oven: 4–5 minutes

Khameeri means leavened, which makes this a rare whole-wheat bread. Indians still prefer to use a combination of yoghurt, *atta* and sugar (2 : 1 : 1)* to make the flour rise—it provides a distinct flavour. The recipe below uses yeast.

Preparation

***Atta*:** Sieve with salt into a *paraat.*

Yeast: Dissolve in 100 ml/7 Tbs of warm water.

Dough: Make a bay in the sieved *atta,* pour water (approx 300 ml/1¼ cups) in it and start mixing gradually. When fully mixed, knead to make a hard dough, cover with a moist cloth and keep aside for 15 minutes. Add the dissolved yeast and incorporate gradually. When fully mixed, knead until the dough is *not* sticky. Cover and keep in a warm place for 30 minutes to allow the dough to rise. Divide into 8 portions, make balls, dust with *atta,* cover and keep aside for 5 minutes.

Oven: Pre-heat to 475°F.

Cooking

Flatten each ball between palms to make a round disc (approx 9-inch diameter), place the *Roti* on a *gaddi* (cushioned pad), stick inside a moderately hot *tandoor* and bake for 2–3 minutes. In the pre-heated oven, place on a greased baking tray and bake for 4–5 minutes.

To Serve

Serve as soon as it is removed from the tandoor or oven.

*The mixture is kept overnight to make *khameer,* which is then used instead of yeast. Use 50 g/2 oz.

Poori

What *Roti* is to the North, *Poori* is to the people of Central India—it is unleavened puffed bread, deep-fried in a *kadhai.*

INGREDIENTS

500 g/4 cups Atta

Salt

Groundnut Oil to apply on pedha and to deep fry

Yield: 20

Preparation time: 40 minutes

Cooking time: 1 minute for each set

Preparation

Atta: Sieve with salt into a *paraat.*

Dough: Make a bay in the sieved *atta,* pour water (approx 250 ml/1 cup) in it and start mixing gradually. When fully mixed, knead to make a dough, cover with a moist cloth and keep aside for 30 minutes. Divide into 20 equal portions, make *pedha,* apply a little oil on both sides of the *pedha* and flatten each with a rolling pin into round discs (approx 4-inch diameter).

Cooking

Heat oil in a *kadhai* and deep fry the *Poori* until golden brown, turning once to ensure it puffs up.

To Serve

Serve as they are removed from the *kadhai.*

Naan

INGREDIENTS

500 g/4 cups Flour
Salt
1 g/¼ Tsp Soda bi-carb
5 g/1 Tsp Baking powder
1 Egg
10 g/2½ Tsp Sugar
25 g/2 Tbs Yoghurt
50 ml/3 Tbs Milk
25 ml/5 Tsp Groundnut Oil
Atta to dust
Ghee to grease baking tray
3 g/1 Tsp Kalonji
5 g/1¾ Tsp Melon seeds
30 g/2 Tbs Butter

Yield: 6

Preparation time: 2:30 hours
Cooking time:
In Tandoor: 3 minutes
In Oven: 10 minutes

A simple—but delicious—unleavened flour bread, garnished with *kalonji* and melon seeds.

Preparation

Flour: Sieve with salt, soda bi-carb and baking powder into a *paraat.*

Egg Mixture: Break egg in a bowl, add sugar, yoghurt and milk, whisk.

Dough: Make a bay in the sieved flour, pour water (approx 200 ml/¾ cup + 4 Tsp) in it and start mixing gradually. When fully mixed, knead to make a dough. Add the egg mixture and incorporate gradually. When fully mixed, knead to make a soft—but smooth—dough (it should not stick to the fingers), cover with a moist cloth and keep aside for 10 minutes. Then add oil, knead and punch the dough, cover with a moist cloth and keep aside for 2 hours to allow the dough to rise.

Divide into 6 equal portions, make balls and place on a lightly floured surface. Sprinkle *kalonji* and melon seeds, flatten the balls slightly to make *pedha,* cover and keep aside for 5 minutes. Flatten each *pedha* between the palms to make a round disc and then stretch on one side in the shape of an elongated oval.

Oven: Pre-heat to 375°F.

Cooking

Place the *Naan* on a *gaddi* (cushioned pad), stick inside a moderately hot *tandoor* and bake for 3 minutes. In the pre-heated oven, place on a greased baking tray and bake for 10 minutes.

To Serve

Apply butter on *Naan* as soon as it is removed from the *tandoor* or oven and serve immediately.

Bhatura

A deep-fried flour and semolina bread, commonly served with *Chholey* (white gram).

INGREDIENTS
400 g/14 oz Flour
100 g/4 oz Semolina
1 g/¼ Tsp Soda bi-carb
3 g/½ Tsp Baking powder
Salt
25 g/2 Tbs Yoghurt
10 g/2½ Tsp Sugar
20 g/5 Tsp Ghee
Groundnut Oil to grease surface and to deep fry

Yield: 15

Preparation time: 1:20 hours

Cooking time: 1 minute for each Bhatura

Preparation

Flour: Sieve with semolina, soda bi-carb, baking powder and salt into a *paraat.*

Yoghurt Mixture: Whisk together with sugar.

Dough: Make a bay in the sieved flour, pour water (approx 240 ml/1 cup) and the yoghurt mixture in it, start mixing gradually. When fully mixed, knead to make a dough, cover with a moist cloth and keep aside for 10 minutes. Add melted ghee and incorporate gradually. When fully mixed, knead to make a soft dough, cover with a moist cloth and keep aside for 50 minutes. Divide the dough into 15 equal portions, make balls and place on a lightly greased surface. Cover and keep aside.

Cooking

Heat oil in a *kadhai* to smoking point, reduce to medium heat, flatten each ball between lightly oiled palms to make a round disc (approx 5-inch diameter) and deep fry until golden brown, turning once to ensure it puffs up.

To Serve

Serve as they are removed from the *kadhai.*

Kerala Paratha

INGREDIENTS

450 g/1 lb Flour
A pinch Soda bi-carb
2 Eggs
150 ml/⅔ cup Milk
10 g/2½ Tsp Sugar
Salt
60 ml/4 Tbs Groundnut Oil
100 g/7 Tbs Butter
Flour to dust
Ghee to shallow fry

Yield: 6

Preparation time: 50 minutes

Cooking time: 4–5 minutes for each Paratha

A flaky *paratha* from the Malabar coast—a delightful contribution to the expansive world of Breads.

Preparation

Flour: Sieve with soda bi-carb into a *paraat.*

Egg & Milk Mixture: Break the eggs in a bowl, add milk, sugar, salt and oil, whisk.

Dough: Make a bay in the sieved flour, pour the egg and milk mixture in it and start mixing gradually. When fully mixed, knead to make a soft dough, cover with a moist cloth and keep aside for 30 minutes.

Divide the dough into 6 equal portions and make balls. Flatten each with a rolling pin into a round disc. Grease the rolling surface with oil, place the flattened dough and stretch evenly on all sides until it is very thin (approx 15-inch diameter). Apply melted butter over the entire surface, dust with flour, hold from two ends and gather ensuring there are many folds. Place the dough on the table and roll to make a *pedha (see photographs)* and then flatten slightly. Keep aside for 5 minutes. Flatten each *pedha* with a rolling pin into a round disc (approx 9-inch diameter), dusting with flour while rolling.

Cooking

Place *Paratha* on a heated *tawa* and half-bake, turning over once. Pour melted ghee all round and shallow fry both sides over low heat until golden brown.

To Serve

Remove and serve immediately.

Bakarkhani

A rare leavened Indian bread, *Bakarkhani* is popular with the Muslims of the Deccan.

INGREDIENTS

500 g/4 cups Flour
5 g/1 Tsp Baking powder
Salt
250 ml/1 cup Milk
20 g/5 Tsp Sugar
2 drops Vetivier
8 g/½ small block Yeast (fresh)
150 g/⅔ cup Desi Ghee (Clarified Butter only) or White Butter
20 g/3 Tbs Almonds
15 g/5 Tsp Raisins
10 g/1 Tbs Sunflower seeds
Flour to dust
Desi Ghee (Clarified Butter only) or White Butter to grease tray and brush the bread

Yield: 12

Preparation time: 1:35 hours

Cooking time: 7–8 minutes for each set

Preparation

Flour: Sieve with baking powder and salt into a *paraat.*

Milk: Dissolve sugar in warm milk, add vetivier and stir.

Yeast: Dissolve in warm water (approx 120 ml/½ cup).

Almonds: Blanch, cool, remove the skin and cut into slivers. Soak in water along with raisins and sunflower seeds. Drain.

Dough: Make a bay in the sieved flour, pour the milk and the dissolved yeast in it, start mixing gradually. When fully mixed, knead to make a dough. Cover with a moist cloth and keep aside for 10 minutes. Add the melted *ghee* and incorporate gradually. When fully mixed, knead to make a soft dough. Then add almonds, raisins and sunflower seeds, knead, cover and keep in a warm place for 30 minutes to allow the dough to rise. Divide into 12 equal portions, make balls, dust with flour, cover and keep aside for 10 minutes. Place the balls on a lightly floured surface and flatten each with a rolling pin into round discs (approx 6-inch diameter). Prick the entire surface with a fork.

Oven: Pre-heat to 350°F.

Cooking

Grease a baking tray with *ghee* (or butter), arrange the discs on it and bake in the pre-heated oven for 7–8 minutes.

To Serve

Brush *Bakarkhani* with *ghee* (or butter) as soon as it is removed from the oven and serve immediately.

Sheermal

INGREDIENTS

500 g/4 cups Flour

Salt

430 ml/1¾ cups Milk

10 g/2½ Tsp Sugar

2 drops Vetivier

225 g/1 cup Desi Ghee (Clarified Butter only) or White Butter

Flour to dust

1 g/2 Tsp Saffron

Desi Ghee (Clarified Butter only) or White Butter to grease tray and brush the bread

Yield: 12

Preparation time: 1:30 hours

Cooking time: 8–9 minutes for each set

Mehmoodabad's answer to the Hyderabadi *Bakarkhani, Sheermal* is a rich bread, its quality judged by the amount of ghee incorporated in the dough. The Master Chefs can knead equal quantities of flour, milk and ghee.

Preparation

Flour: Sieve with salt into a *paraat.*

Milk: Dissolve the sugar in 400 ml/1⅔ cups of warm milk, reserve the rest to dissolve saffron. Add vetivier and stir.

Dough: Make a bay in the sieved flour, pour milk in it and start mixing gradually. When fully mixed, knead to make a dough, cover with a moist cloth and keep aside for 10 minutes. Add the melted *ghee* (or butter) and incorporate gradually. When fully mixed, knead to make a soft dough, cover and keep aside for 10 minutes. Divide into 12 equal portions, make balls, dust with flour, cover and keep aside for 10 minutes. Place the balls on a lightly floured surface and flatten each with a rolling pin into round discs (approx 7-inch diameter). Prick the entire surface with a fork.

Saffron: Dissolve in the reserved milk, which must be warm.

Oven: Pre-heat to 350°F.

Cooking

Grease a baking tray with *ghee* (or butter), arrange the discs on it and bake in the pre-heated oven for 4 minutes. Remove, brush immediately with saffron, return to the oven and bake for 3–4 minutes.

To Serve

Brush *Sheermal* with *ghee* (or butter) as soon as it is removed from the oven and serve immediately.

Varqi Paratha

This flaky, fried bread of the Nawabs of Avadh is much more than a mere accompaniment—it is a meal in itself.

INGREDIENTS

500 g/4 cups Flour

Salt

250 ml/1 cup Milk

10 g/2½ Tsp Sugar

2 drops Vetivier

180 g/6½ oz Desi Ghee (Clarified Butter only) or White Butter

Flour to dust

Desi Ghee (Clarified Butter only) to shallow fry

Yield: 12

Preparation time: 2:15 hours

Cooking time: 8–10 minutes for each Paratha

Preparation

Flour: Sieve with salt into a *paraat.*

Milk: Dissolve the sugar in warm milk, add vetivier and stir.

Dough: Make a bay in the sieved flour, pour milk and water (approx 120 ml/½ cup) into it, start mixing gradually. When fully mixed, knead to make a dough, cover with a moist cloth and keep aside for 10 minutes. Add two-thirds of the melted *ghee* (or butter) and incorporate gradually. When fully mixed, knead to make a soft dough, cover and keep aside for 15 minutes. Place the dough on a lightly floured surface and flatten with a rolling pin into a rectangular shape. Apply one-fourth of the remaining *ghee* (or butter) evenly over the rolled-out dough, dust with flour, fold one end and then the other to make 3 folds. Cover and refrigerate for 10 minutes. Repeat the process—rolling, applying fat, dusting, folding and refrigerating—thrice. Remove from the refrigerator, place on the floured surface, flatten into a rectangle (approx ⅛-inch thick) and make discs (5-inch diameter) with a round cutter. Then make 3 criss-cross incisions (approx ½-inch) evenly spaced on the surface of each disc. Place the discs on individual sheets of butter paper and refrigerate until ready to serve. (The longer you refrigerate it—not more than 8–10 hours, though—the more distinct will become the *varq* or flakes.)

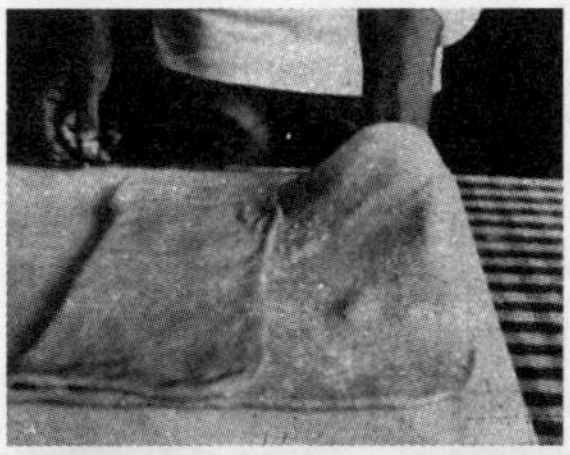

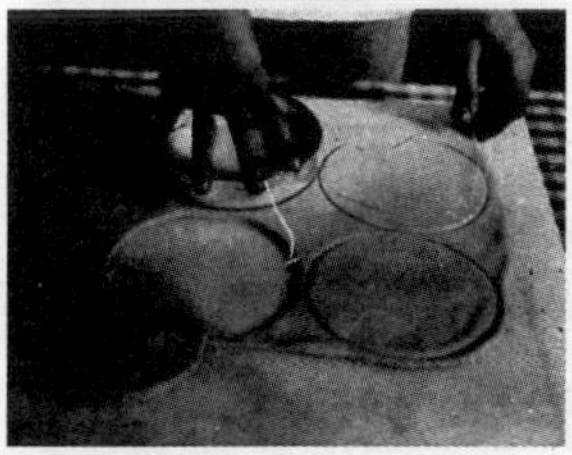

Cooking

Melt *ghee—not* butter—on a heated *tawa* and shallow fry both sides over low heat until light golden.

To Serve

Remove and serve immediately.

Note: To avoid wastage, cut the *Varqi* into squares or triangles.

Jalebi Paratha

INGREDIENTS

500 g/4 cups Flour

Salt

250 ml/1 cup Milk

180 g/6½ oz Desi Ghee (Clarified Butter only) or White Butter

10 g/3 Tsp Fennel

Flour to dust

Desi Ghee (Clarified Butter only) to shallow fry

Yield: 12

Preparation time: 5 hours

Cooking time: 8–10 minutes for each Paratha

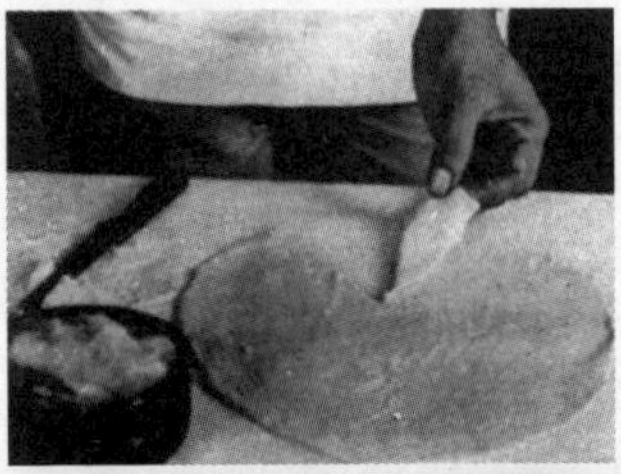

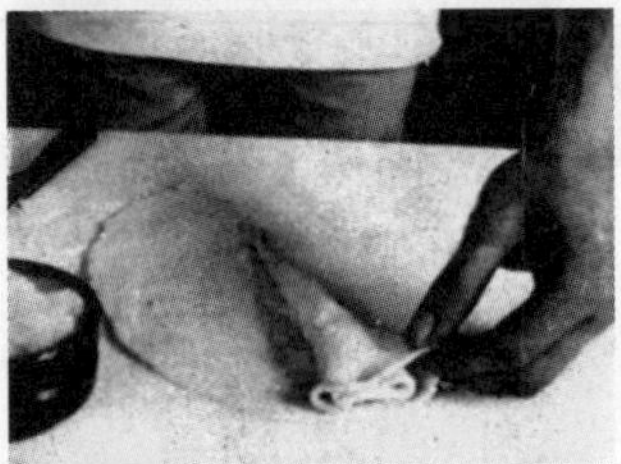

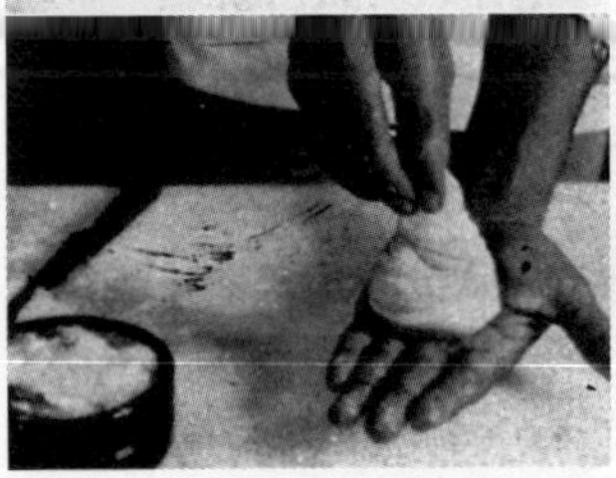

This exotic fennel-flavoured multi-layered bread has its origins in rural Avadh. It was accorded its rightful place in the 'Pantheon' of classic Indian Breads by the Chefs of Nawab Dara. The Nawab was Prime Minister in the Court of that supreme gourmet, Wajid Ali Shah.

Preparation

Flour: Sieve with salt into a *paraat.*

Fennel: Pound with a pestle.

Dough: Make a bay in the sieved flour, pour milk and water (approx 120 ml/½ cup) into it, start mixing gradually. When fully mixed, knead to make a dough, cover with a moist cloth and keep aside for 10 minutes. Add two-thirds of the melted *ghee* (or butter) and incorporate gradually. When fully mixed, knead to make a soft dough. Then add the pounded fennel, knead, cover and keep aside for 10 minutes. Divide into 12 equal portions, make balls, dust with flour, cover and keep aside for 10 minutes. Place the balls on a lightly floured surface and flatten each with a rolling pin into round discs (approx 8-inch diameter). Apply 5 g/1 Tsp of melted *ghee* (or butter) evenly over the discs and dust with flour.

Make a radial cut with a knife and starting with one end of the cut, roll the discs firmly into conical shapes *(see photographs).* Hold each cone between thumb and forefinger, half an inch above the base, and make spiral movements to compress the rest of the cone to make a *pedha.* (Do *not* press to flatten the *pedha.*) Refrigerate for 4 hours. Remove, press the *pedha,* place on a lightly floured surface and flatten with a rolling pin into discs (approx 8-inch diameter). Place the discs on individual sheets of butter paper and refrigerate.

To Serve

Remove and serve immediately.

Cooking

Melt *ghee* on a heated *tawa* and shallow fry both sides over low heat until light golden.

Appendices

Masalas

Garam Masala

If spices are the basis of Indian cooking, the blending of these spices to make a garam masala or 'hot spices' is the essence of it. The use of a solitary spice or herb is all the rest of the world, particularly the West, can 'cope' with. There seems to be a fear of using more than one spice. Which is why Westerners find the use of a melange of spices in Indian cookery incomprehensible. To us, each spice in the melange has a specific purpose to perform. To go into the details of each spice is beyond the scope of this book, leave alone this chapter. Suffice it to say that it is important to be a good *masalchi* before one can become a good chef. It is advisable to tryout various combinations of spices fearlessly. Before that, however, a clear understanding of each and every spice is imperative. Accordingly, the proportions of spices can be changed as the seasons change. For example, in the hot summer months, reduce the quantity of mace and nutmeg—they can give a nosebleed.

There are as many versions of garam masala as there are chefs. However, in general, some garam masala are chilli hot (those with cloves and pepper), while others use only aromatic spices (cinnamon, mace, nutmeg, cardamom, etc.). Garam masala is used sparingly or it will put the 'body on fire'. It is almost always introduced toward the end of cooking a delicacy. Often it is used as a garnish—sprinkled over cooked food to provide aromatic flavouring at the time of service.

The art of blending garam masala involves grinding or pounding a combination of dried spices. All the spices are roasted in the oven (or under the salamander) before they are ground into a fine powder. It is important that the spices be blended freshly.

If you are using a grinder, it is better to sun-dry the spices instead of roasting them. The reason is very simple. When pounded with a pestle, the heat dissipates. In the grinder, on the other hand, there is no 'outlet' for the heat emitted by the grinding. If the spices are broiled, it is likely that the garam masala will be 'over-done' and darker. The same holds true for the other masala.

Garam Masala I

INGREDIENTS

- 200 g/7 oz Cumin seeds
- 60 g/2 oz Coriander seeds
- 45 g/1½ oz Black Cardamom
- 35 g/1¼ oz Black Peppercorns
- 30 g/1 oz Green Cardamom
- 30 g/1 oz Ginger powder
- 20 sticks Cinnamon (1-inch)
- 20 g/¾ oz Cloves
- 20 g/¾ oz Mace
- 15 g/½ oz Bay leaves
- 2 Nutmeg

Yield: Approx 450 g/1 lb

This blend is ideally suited for meat preparations.

Preparation

Put all the ingredients in a mortar and pound with a pestle to make a fine powder. Sieve and store in a sterilised, dry and airtight container.

Garam Masala II

INGREDIENTS

- 90 g/3 oz Cumin seeds
- 75 g/2½ oz Black Cardamom seeds
- 75 g/2½ oz Black Peppercorn
- 45 g/1½ oz Green Cardamom
- 30 g/1 oz Coriander seeds
- 30 g/1 oz Fennel seeds
- 20 g/¾ oz Cloves
- 20 sticks Cinnamon (1-inch)
- 20 g/¾ oz Mace
- 20 g/¾ oz Black Cumin seeds
- 15 g/½ oz Bay leaves
- 15 g/½ oz Dry Rose petals
- 15 g/½ oz Ginger powder
- 3 Nutmeg

Yield: Approx 450 g/1 lb

This masala is for Dum Pukht, Avadh, Punjabi and Rajasthani cuisines.

Preparation

Put all the ingredients, except ginger powder, in a mortar and pound with a pestle to make a fine powder. Transfer to a clean, dry bowl, add ginger powder and mix well. Sieve and store in a sterilised, dry and airtight container.

Aromatic Garam Masala

This blend is used in mildly-spiced gravies.

INGREDIENTS

175 g/6 oz Green Cardamom
125 g/4½ oz Cumin seeds
125 g/4½ oz Black Peppercorn
20 sticks Cinnamon (1-inch)
20 g/¾ oz Cloves
2 Nutmeg

Yield: Approx 450 g/1 lb

Preparation

Put all the ingredients in a mortar and pound with a pestle to make a fine powder. Sieve and store in a sterilised, dry and airtight container.

Chaat Masala

The use of this masala requires caution. Excess will certainly ruin the dish. Used in small quantities, it can add immeasurably to the flavour.

INGREDIENTS

65 g/2¼ oz Cumin seeds
65 g/2¼ oz Black Peppercorn
60 g/2 oz Black Salt (pound, if using a grinder)
30 g/1 oz Dry Mint leaves
5 g/2 Tsp Ajwain
5 g/1 Tsp Asafoetida (pound, if using a grinder)
4 g/¾ Tsp Tartric (pound, if using a grinder)
150 g/5¼ oz Mango powder
60 g/2 oz Salt
20 g/¾ oz Ginger powder
20 g/¾ oz Yellow Chilli powder

Yield: Approx 450 g/1 lb

Preparation

Put all the ingredients, except mango powder, salt, ginger powder and yellow chilli powder, in a mortar and pound with a pestle to make a fine powder. Transfer to a clean, dry bowl, add the remaining ingredients and mix well. Sieve and store in a sterilised, dry and airtight container.

Tandoori Chaat Masala

INGREDIENTS

- 50 g/1¾ oz Cumin seeds
- 50 g/1¾ oz Black Peppercorn
- 50 g/1¾ oz Black Salt (pound if using a grinder)
- 30 g/1 oz Dry Mint leaves
- 20 g/¾ oz Fenugreek (Kasoori Methi)
- 30 Green Cardamom
- 15 Cloves
- 5 sticks Cinnamon (1-inch)
- 5 g/2 Tsp Ajwain
- 5 g/1 Tsp Asafoetida (pound, if using a grinder)
- 4 g/¾ Tsp Tartric (pound, if using a grinder)
- 2 g/½ Tsp Mace
- 125 g/4½ oz Mango powder
- 50 g/1¾ oz Salt
- 20 g/¾ oz Ginger powder
- 20 g/¾ oz Yellow Chilli powder

Yield: Approx 450 g/1 lb

Like *Chaat Masala,* the *Tandoori Chaat Masala* must be used in small quantities and not indiscriminately.

Preparation

Put all the ingredients, except mango powder, salt, ginger powder and yellow chilli powder, in a mortar and pound with a pestle to make a fine powder. Transfer to a clean, dry bowl, add the remaining ingredients and mix well. Sieve and store in a sterilised, dry and airtight container.

Dum ka Masala

INGREDIENTS

- 45 g/1½ oz Fennel seeds
- 45 g/1½ oz Ginger powder
- 20 g/¾ oz Green Cardamom
- 20 g/¾ oz Black Cardamom

Yield: Approx 125 g/¼ lb

This masala is used in very small quantities—usually a pinch—after the dish has been cooked and before it is put on *dum.* That is, before you seal the *handi* with a lid. It adds to the aroma.

Preparation

Put all the ingredients in a mortar and pound with a pestle to make a fine powder. Sieve and store in a sterilised, dry and airtight container.

Dhansak Masala

Preparation

Put all the ingredients in a mortar and pound with a pestle to make a fine powder. Sieve and store in a sterilised, dry and airtight container.

INGREDIENTS

45 g/1½ oz Fenugreek (Kasoori Methi)

45 g/1½ oz Cloves

45 g/1½ oz Black Cardamom

Yield: Approx 125 g/¼ lb

Sambhar Masala

Preparation

Lentils: Pick, wash the *dals* together in running water and pat dry. Heat oil in a *kadhai* and fry the lentils over medium heat until light golden. Transfer the *dals* to an absorbent paper napkin to remove excess fat. Cool.

Asafoetida: Reheat the oil in which the lentils were fried and fry asafoetida over medium heat until it swells up. Transfer to an absorbent paper napkin to remove excess fat. Cool and then break it up into little pieces.

Masala: Put all the ingredients, except turmeric and garlic powder, in a mortar and pound with a pestle to make a fine powder. Transfer to a clean, dry bowl, add the remaining ingredients and mix well. Sieve and store in a sterilised, dry and airtight container.

INGREDIENTS

120 g/4¼ oz Coriander seeds

80 g/2¾ oz Cumin seeds

30 g/1 oz Black Peppercorn

30 g/1 oz Mustard seeds

30 g/1 oz Fenugreek seeds

20 whole Red Chillies

30 g/1 oz Turmeric powder

10 g/2 Tsp Garlic powder

60 g/2 oz Channa Dal

60 g/2 oz Urad Dal

10 g/2 Tsp Asafoetida

Groundnut Oil to fry

Yield: Approx 450 g/1 lb

Mulagapodi

INGREDIENTS

20 whole Red Chillies
5 g/1 Tsp Asafoetida
100 g/½ cup Channa Dal
100 g/½ cup Urad Dal
10 g/2 Tsp Sesame seeds
Sesame seed oil to fry
Salt

Yield: Approx 250 g/9 oz

Preparation

Lentils: Pick, wash in running water and pat dry.

Cooking

Heat oil in a *kadhai,* add asafoetida and stir over low heat until it swells. Remove the asafoetida, add the *dals* and stir until golden brown. Remove the *dals,* add red chillies and stir until crisp, remove. Broil the sesame seeds on a *tawa* until they stop popping.

Put the fried lentils in a grinder and make a coarse powder, remove. Put the fried red chillies, asafoetida and salt in the grinder and make a coarse powder, remove. Put the broiled sesame seeds in the grinder and make a coarse powder. Mix all the powders. Store in a sterilised, dry and airtight container.

Note: Add a spoon of clarified butter or sesame seed oil with every spoon of *Mulagapodi* to reduce its pungency.

Gravies

The success of an Indian banquet lies in the extensive variety of gravies served. Only a hack would allow the dishes—vegetarian and non-vegetarian—to taste the same. It reflects a lack of interest and imagination. Even simple fare can be made tasty and interesting with a slight variation of spices and herbs in the gravies. The hallmark of a good chef is his ability to create different aromas, hues and flavours.

The purpose of this chapter is not to make you reliant on these basic gravies. It is to enable you to first strengthen the base and then let your artistic talent come to the fore. Let your imagination run riot and create gravies that will make the epicure want to chew his fingers. I repeat: *Do Not* follow the recipes blindly and cook *everything* in these basic gravies.

Basic Gravy I

This is a yoghurt-based gravy, used mainly for kofta, korma and pasanda delicacies.

INGREDIENTS

150 g/¾ cup Ghee
Whole Garam masala
- 5 Green Cardamom
- 1 Black Cardamom
- 5 Cloves
- 1 Stick Cinnamon (1-inch)
- 1 Bay Leaf
- A pinch Mace

250 g/1 cup Boiled Onion paste*
30 g/5 Tsp Ginger paste
30 g/5 Tsp Garlic paste
10 g/2 Tsp Red Chilli powder
5 g/1 Tsp Coriander powder
3 g/½ Tsp Turmeric
Salt
225 g/1 cup Yoghurt
50 g/3 Tbs Fried Onion paste*
30 g/5 Tsp Cashewnut paste
100 ml/7 Tbs Cream
5 g/1 Tsp Garam Masala
3 g/½ Tsp Green Cardamom and Mace powder

*See section on Onions.

Preparation

Yoghurt: Whisk in a bowl.

Cooking

Heat ghee in a *handi,* add whole garam masala and saute over medium heat until it begins to crackle. Add boiled onion paste and saute for 2 minutes. Then add ginger and garlic pastes, saute for 30 seconds, add red chillies, coriander powder, turmeric and salt. Remove the *handi,* add yoghurt (this is done to prevent curdling), return to heat, add water (approx 200 ml/3/4 cup + 4 Tsp), bring to a boil and then simmer until fat comes to the surface.

Add fried onion paste, cashewnut paste and cream, bring to a boil, reduce to medium heat, add garam masala, cardamom and mace, powder, stir.

Yield: Approx 700 ml/1½ lb

Preparation time: 5 minutes

Cooking time: 15–18 minutes

Basic Gravy II

INGREDIENTS

150 g/¾ cup Ghee
Whole Garam masala
- 5 Green Cardamom
- 1 Black Cardamom
- 5 Cloves
- 1 Stick Cinnamon (1-inch)
- 1 Bay Leaf
- A pinch Mace

125 g/½ cup Boiled Onion paste*
10 g/1¾ Tsp Ginger paste
10 g/1¾ Tsp Garlic paste
10 g/2 Tsp Red Chilli powder
5 g/1 Tsp Coriander powder
3 g/½ Tsp Turmeric
Salt
1 kg/2¼ lb Tomatoes
30 g/5 Tsp Fried Onion paste*
30 g/5 Tsp Cashewnut paste
100 ml/7 Tbs Cream
5 g/1 Tsp Garam Masala
2 g/⅓ Tsp Green Cardamom and Mace powder

*See section on Onions.

Yield: Approx 800 ml/1¾ lb
Preparation time: 10 minutes
Cooking time: 35 minutes

This is a tomato-based gravy, used for basic lamb and chicken curries.

Preparation

Tomatoes: Wash and chop.

Cooking

Heat ghee in a *handi,* add whole garam masala and saute over medium heat until it begins to crackle. Add boiled onion paste, saute for 2 minutes, add ginger and garlic pastes and saute for 30 seconds. Then add red chillies, coriander powder, turmeric and salt, *bhunno* for 2 minutes. Add tomatoes, stir constantly until fat comes to the surface, add water (approx 200 ml/¾ cup + 4 Tsp), bring to a boil and then simmer until once again the fat comes to the surface.

Now add fried onion paste, cashewnut paste and cream, bring to a boil. Correct the consistency by adding water. Add garam masala, cardamom and mace powder, stir.

Makhani Gravy

Preparation

Vegetables: Wash and chop tomatoes. Remove stems, wash, slit, deseed and chop green chillies. Scrape, wash and cut ginger into juliennes.

Cooking

Put tomatoes in a *handi*, add water (approx 1 litre/4 cups), add the ginger and garlic pastes, green chillies, red chillies, cloves, cardamom and salt, reduce to a sauce consistency over low heat. Force through a strainer into a separate *handi,* bring to a boil, add butter and cream, stir. If the gravy is excessively sour, add honey. Then add fenugreek and ginger juliennes, stir.

INGREDIENTS

1 kg/2¼ lb Tomatoes
10 g/1¾ Tsp Ginger paste
10 g/1¾ Tsp Garlic paste
6 Green Chillies
10 g/2 Tsp Red Chilli powder
10 Cloves
8 Green Cardamom
Salt
150 g/⅔ cup Butter
150 ml/⅔ cup Cream
15 ml/4½ Tsp Honey (optional)
10 g/2½ Tsp Fenugreek (Kasoori Methi)
10 g/1 Tbs Ginger

Yield: 550 ml/1¼ lb

Preparation time: 20 minutes

Cooking time: 20–25 minutes

Kadhai Gravy

Preparation

Spices: Pound coriander seeds and whole red chillies with a pestle.

Vegetables: Remove stems, wash, slit, deseed and chop green chillies. Scrape, wash and chop ginger. Wash and chop tomatoes.

Cooking

Heat ghee in a *kadhai,* add garlic paste and saute over medium heat until light brown. Add the pounded spices, saute for 30 seconds, add green chillies and ginger, saute for 30 seconds. Then add tomatoes and *bhunno* until fat comes to the surface. Now add fenugreek and salt, stir. Sprinkle garam masala and stir.

INGREDIENTS

75 g/6 Tbs Ghee
30 g/5 Tsp Garlic paste
15 g/7½ Tsp Coriander seeds
10 Whole Red Chillies
4 Green Chillies
45 g/¼ cup Ginger
675 g/3 cups Tomatoes
5 g/1 Tbs Fenugreek (Kasoori Methi)
Salt
5 g/1 Tsp Garam Masala

Yield: Approx 550 ml/1¼ lb

Preparation time: 25 minutes

Cooking time: 18–20 minutes

Pastes

THE ONION PASTES

In a cuisine renowned for its exotic gravies—each sauce different from the other—one of the most important ingredients is the humble onion. It is chopped, sliced, grated or quartered before being fried or boiled to make a paste, which is the basis of most gravies. Different gravies require onions to be processed differently. The gravy that goes with *kofta* for example, requires a boiled onion paste. A *Rogan Josh* gravy, on the other hand, will require a fried onion paste.

Frying of Onions

When we talk of sauteeing onions in Indian cooking, we are actually describing the process of browning them. Contrary to how easy it sounds, the process requires great skill and concentration. There are many hues and shades of brown and each imparts its colour to the final product.

Boiled Onion Paste

INGREDIENTS

1 kg/2¼ lb Onions
3 Bay Leaves
3 Black Cardamom

Yield: Approx 1 kg/2¼ lb

Preparation

Peel, wash and roughly cut onions. Put in a *handi,* add bay leaves, cardamom and 200 ml/3/4 cup + 4 Tsp of water, bring to a boil, simmer until onions are transparent and the liquid has evaporated. Transfer to a blender and make a fine puree.

Note: The onion-water ratio is crucial to this preparation. Excess water will make a thin puree and if the water is not enough, the onions will remain uncooked and in all likelihood the lower layer will stick. The correct ratio is 5:1.

Fried Onion Paste

Preparation

Peel, wash and slice onions. Heat oil in a *kadhai,* add onions and saute over medium heat until brown. Remove onions, spread over any absorbent material and cool. Transfer to a blender, add yoghurt and make a fine paste.

Note: This paste can be stored in sterilised, airtight containers for up to 15 days in a refrigerator.

INGREDIENTS

1 kg/2¼ lb Onions
Groundnut Oil to fry
100 g/3½ oz Yoghurt

Yield: Approx 300/⅔ lb

OTHER PASTES

Ginger Paste

Preparation

Ginger: Scrape, wash and roughly chop.

Paste: Put the chopped ginger in a blender, add 45 ml/3 Tbs of water and make a fine paste. Remove and refrigerate.

Shelf Life: 72 hours in the refrigerator.

Note: The containers in which these pastes are kept must be covered with foil or plastic wrap before refrigeration. The alternatives are ziplock bags or freezer bags.

INGREDIENTS

170 g/1 cup Ginger

Yield: Approx 210 g/7½ oz

Garlic Paste

Preparation

Garlic: Peel and roughly chop.

Paste: Put the chopped garlic in a blender, add 45 ml/3 Tbs of water and make a fine paste. Remove and refrigerate.

Shelf Life: 72 hours in the refrigerator.

INGREDIENTS

170 g/1 Cup Garlic

Yield: Approx 210 g/7½ oz

Cashewnut Paste

Preparation

INGREDIENTS

160 g/1 cup Cashewnuts (broken)

Yield: Approx 250 g/9 oz

Cashewnuts: Soak in water for 30 minutes and drain.

Paste: Put the drained cashewnuts in a blender, add 100 ml/7 Tbs of water and make a fine paste. Remove and refrigerate.

Shelf Life: 24 hours in the refrigerator.

Coconut Paste

INGREDIENTS

100 g/1¼ cup Coconut

Yield: Approx 160 g/5½ oz

Preparation

Coconut: Remove the brown skin and grate.

Paste: Put the grated coconut in a blender, add 75 ml/5 Tbs of water (preferably coconut water) and make a fine paste. Remove and refrigerate.

Shelf Life: 12 hours in the refrigerator.

Poppy Seed Paste

INGREDIENTS

150 g/1 cup Poppy seeds

Yield: Approx 330 g/11 oz

Preparation

Poppy Seeds: Soak in warm water for 30 minutes and drain.

Paste: Put the drained seeds in a blender, add 100 ml/7 Tbs of water and make a fine paste. Remove and refrigerate.

Shelf Life: 24 hours in the refrigerator.

TAMARIND PULP

Tamarind grows on tropical trees, is shaped like a bean (except that it is longer and wider) and the main 'fruit' is the pulp inside the brittle shell. *Imli* is dried before it is sold and, before use, it is soaked in lukewarm water until soft—usually 25 to 30 minutes. It is squeezed until it dissolves in the water at which stage the seeds and fibres are strained out.

INGREDIENTS

50 g/2 oz Tamarind

Yield: Approx 75 ml/3 oz

Preparation

Soak tamarind in 50 ml/10 Tsp of lukewarm water for 30 minutes and force through a strainer. Discard the residue.

Milk Products

Dahi *(Yoghurt)*

An Indian meal is inconceivable without *dahi* or yoghurt. It is omnipresent, so to speak. Either a part of the food is cooked in it or it is partaken in its natural form—unflavoured. Derivatives are consumed as *raita, lassi,* or *chaas* (buttermilk). Remember, in Indian cooking, yoghurt is always unflavoured.

Setting yoghurt is not as easy as it looks. It requires an understanding of the role enzymes play in the process. This is how it is done.

Boil the milk and allow it to cool. The temperature of milk at which the ferment is to be added has a direct co-relation with the atmospheric temperature. If the weather is cold, the milk should be warm and, after introducing the ferment, the vessel in use must be placed in warm surroundings (well-wrapped in a blanket at home and in the warmest place, not the oven, in a commercial kitchen). In summer months, the milk should be allowed to cool to room temperature and the vessel must be kept in a cool place.

If the milk is too hot, the *dahi* is likely to become sour. It will leave water and will not set firmly. On the other hand, if the milk is not warm enough (approx 80–90°F) it will not set properly. Once the milk is kept for setting, do not move or shake the container. If you do, the yoghurt will not set.

Traditionally, yoghurt is set in clay bowls. It sets just as well in other vessels.

It takes between four to six hours to set. Once it is set, the utensil *must* be placed in the refrigerator to prevent any further souring.

The most commonly used ferment to set *dahi* is *dahi* itself. Lemon juice and vinegar make excellent substitutes. In ideal conditions, a tablespoon of the ferment is sufficient to make approx 1 kg/4½ cups of yoghurt. One litre/4 cups of milk give you 1 kg/4½ cups of yoghurt.

The recipes below are from my mother's collection.

Amrit Dahi

INGREDIENTS

500 g/2¼ cups Yoghurt (full fat)

20 g/2 Tbs Ginger

10 g/1 Tbs Mango puree

5 g/1 Tsp Green Cardamom powder

250 ml/1 cup Milk

20 g/3 Tbs Castor Sugar

½ g/1 Tsp Saffron

10 g/4 Tsp Pistachio

Serves: 4

Preparation time: 8–10 hours

Amrit is Nectar and this yoghurt delicacy is a divine offering.

Preparation

Yoghurt: Hang in muslin until reduced by half (approx 6–8 hours).

Ginger: Scrape, wash, roughly cut, put in a blender, add water (approx 15 ml/1 Tbs) and make a fine paste. Remove and squeeze the paste through muslin over a cup to collect the juice. Use 10 ml/2 Tsp of juice. Discard the residue.

Milk: Boil (reserve 30 ml/2 Tbs) and keep aside. When it is warm, add sugar and stir until dissolved. Chill.

Saffron: Dissolve in the reserved milk while it is still warm.

Pistachio: Blanch, cool, remove the skin and make slivers.

Assembling

Whisk the reduced yoghurt in a bowl add ginger juice, mango puree and cardamom powder, mix well. Incorporate the sweetened milk. Stir, add saffron and stir. Transfer equal quantities of the mixture to 4 small *shikoras* (earthenware bowls) and refrigerate.

To Serve

Remove *shikoras* from the refrigerator, garnish with pistachio and serve chilled.

Kesari Dahi

There isn't a better way to start a hot summer's day than with a bowl of this saffron-flavoured yoghurt.

INGREDIENTS

1 litre/4 cups Milk (full fat)
80 g/⅔ cup Castor Sugar
1 g/2 Tsp Saffron
1 drop Vetivier
5 g/1 Tsp Yoghurt Ferment
10 g/4 Tsp Almonds

Serves: 4

Preparation time: 8:30 hours

Preparation

Milk: Boil until reduced by half (reserve 30 ml/2 Tbs) and keep aside. When it is warm, add sugar and stir until dissolved.

Saffron: Dissolve in the reserved milk while it is still warm.

Almonds: Blanch, cool, remove the skin and make slivers.

Assembling

When the milk is lukewarm, transfer to an earthenware *handi,* add saffron and vetivier, stir, add the ferment, stir and allow it to set in a warm place (approx 6 hours). Refrigerate.

To Serve

Remove *handi* from the refrigerator, garnish with almonds and serve chilled.

How to Make Desi Ghee from Butter

Heat and fully melt unsalted butter over low heat in a heavy-bottomed *handi* without letting it brown. Now increase the heat and bring the butter to a boil. When the butter starts foaming, stir once and reduce to very low heat. Simmer gently for about 45 minutes until the milk solids settle on the bottom of the pan and the transparent butter is afloat.

Drain the transparent butter, i.e., *desi ghee,* through muslin into another container without disturbing the sediment. Once cold, it will solidify. Store at room temperature.

Paneer

INGREDIENTS

3 litres/12½ cups Milk

90 ml/6 Tbs Lemon juice or White Vinegar

Yield: Approx 600 g/1⅓ lb

Preparation time: 8:30 hours

There is no Western or Oriental equivalent of *Paneer,* which is often called cottage cheese in India. The cottage cheese available on the shelves of supermarkets elsewhere is quite different. Riccotta cheese is the nearest in terms of taste but not in terms of texture. In fact, Riccotta cheese cannot be converted into a block like *Paneer.* Besides, Riccotta cheese becomes sticky and 'leathery' when heated. *Paneer* is an extraordinary source of protein in a largely vegetarian sub-continental diet. It is no exaggeration to say that what meat is to non-vegetarians, *Paneer* is to the vegetarians. The spin-off in terms of the number of delicacies that can be conceived with our *desi* cheese matches that of the meats. Strangely, it is the easiest cheese to make and requires no curing time or expertise.

Preparation

Boil milk in a *handi,* stirring occasionally to ensure that skin does not form on the surface. When the milk begins to rise, add lemon juice or vinegar. The milk will curdle and the whey will separate. Strain the curdled milk through fine muslin allowing the whey to drain out. Hang the muslin for at least an hour to ensure that any remaining moisture is drained out. What is left behind is *Paneer.* It can be used as it is for a number of dishes. Or it can be converted into a block. To convert the *Paneer* into a block, keep it wrapped in the muslin and place a weight on top for 2–3 hours. The block facilitates the cutting of *Paneer* into cubes, slices and batons.

Shelf Life: 48 hours in the refrigerator.

Chhenna

Preparation

Put milk in a *handi,* bring to a boil, remove and cool to 120°F. Add vinegar in a steady stream over the entire surface and stir until the milk curdles (approx 3 minutes). Pour the curdled milk onto muslin spread in a strainer placed over the sink to drain out the whey. Then hold the four corners of the muslin and prod and gently squeeze the residue until a 'milky' whey starts to ooze out. Transfer the residue—*Chhenna*—while it is still warm onto a flat tray and knead firmly with palm to mash the granules. Cool, wrap in silver foil and refrigerate.

Shelf Life: 24 hours in the refrigerator.

INGREDIENTS

2 litres/8⅓ cups Milk (fresh and full fat)

160 ml/⅔ cup White Vinegar

Yield: Approx 400 g/14 oz

Preparation time: 1 hour

Khoya

Preparation

Put milk in a *kadhai,* bring to a boil and reduce to low heat. Thence stir after every 5 minutes until reduced by half. Thereafter, stir constantly and simultaneously scrape the dried layer of milk that sticks to sides into the *kadhai*—this will ensure that the milk does not acquire a 'burnt' flavor—until reduced to a mashed potato consistency. Remove to a bowl, cool and refrigerate.

Shelf Life: 48 hours in the refrigerator.

Note: A teflon-coated *wok* or pan is an ideal alternative to the *kadhai.*

INGREDIENTS

2 litres/8⅓ cups Milk (fresh and full fat)

Yield: Approx 400 g/14 oz

Preparation time: 1:30 hours

Coconut

While coastal cooking is inconceivable without it, the coconut is an important ingredient in the kitchens of the North as well. The only difference is that whereas in the coastal areas, fresh coconut is used, north of the Vindhyas it is the dry coconut that is in greater use.

While fresh, grated coconut is used mainly as a garnish or as an ingredient for wet masala, when it comes to cooking, it is 'coconut milk' that lends its unique flavour. Coconut milk is not to be confused with the liquid inside the coconut—that is just coconut water and is a delicious and cool soft drink sold at street corners and even in restaurants. Coconut milk is extracted by squeezing the freshly ground white meat of a mature coconut. Here is how to do it:

Remove the brown skin, grate 100 g/1¼ cups of the white meat, put in a blender, add lukewarm water (approx 100 ml/7 Tbs) and liquidise. Then force the liquid through a fine strainer. The strained liquid is called the 'First Milk' or 'First Extract'.

To obtain the 'Second Milk' or 'Second Extract', put the residue in the blender, add lukewarm water (approx 100 ml/7 Tbs) and liquidise. Force the liquid through a fine strainer. The 'Second Milk' is thinner and has less flavour.

The "Supporting Cast"

Bijoy K. Joseph: The Zurich-trained Joseph excels in the "cold kitchen". *Garde Manger* Chef at the Welcomgroup *Maurya Sheraton**, he chose to join the author's team for the novel Cold Food experiment because "it offered a unique opportunity to explore an aspect of Indian cuisine ignored until now."

Mohan Lal Thakur: An acknowledged master of his craft, Thakur is *Garde Manger* Chef at *The Oberoi**, New Delhi. That he was invited to prepare and display his creations at the coronation of the King of Bhutan, in 1978, is a tribute to his skill in the cold kitchen and expertise in ice displays and butter sculptures.

E.B. Almeida: His curriculum vitae—trained in Italy and at the Culinary Institute of America—is misleading. For, this native of Goa excels in a variety of Indian cuisines—particularly Goan cooking—and boasts of skills that won him the coveted job of Chef at *Raga*, the popular Indian restaurant in New York. Presently he is Chef at the *Taj Samudra**, Colombo.

Cyrus Todiwala: Acknowledged to be an excellent chef, a reputation earned at the *Taj Mahal Hotel*, Bombay, Todiwala today is Chef at Fort Aguada*, which makes him master of the kitchen of that incomparable beach resort in Goa.

Satinderpal Singh Chaudhury: For a by-the-book man, Chaudhury has a particularly light hand and displays uncommon finesse with gravies—as is evident in the recipes in the Punjab Section. At present, he is Indian Chef at the *Oberoi Babylon**, in Iraq.

*Designation subject to change.

Ponnapatti Papaiah: He wasn't quite 10 when his mother died and Papaiah had to miss classes to cook for the family. An unwanted chore became a hobby, then a vocation and, finally, a passion which has made Papaiah the pride of Welcomgroup *Chola Sheraton**, Madras.

Mohammed Naseem: Like many talented chefs, Naseem is also a fine *halwai*—his creations more exciting than the sweetmeats prepared in most *mithai* shops. The two non-vegetarian delights in the Desserts Section are the work of this man who presides over the banquet kitchen of the Welcomgroup *Maurya Sheraton**.

Sujata Kanianthra: One of less than half-a-dozen women chefs in India, which is surprising when one considers the oft repeated statement that the best cooking is done in homes—by women. Ms Kanianthra's family recipes of South Indian desserts and chutneys helped complete these chapters.

Ghulam Rasool: In a tribute, Corporate Chef Richard Graham described Rasool as a "true artiste"—and asked him to join his team that toured the U.S. during the Festival of India. Rasool is currently Indian Chef at the Welcomgroup *Chola Sheraton**, Madras. He assisted with the *Avadh, Dum Pukht* and *Bread* Sections.

Nilesh P. Nadkarni: The other member of "Team Snack", Nadkarni has been instrumental in providing a selection of savouries with tantalizing tastes and exquisite shapes. He is Sous Chef at the Welcomgroup *Searock**, Bombay.

*Designation subject to change.